With this book, Twiza has succeeded in causing a crack in the fortress built by certain obsolete educational practices that tend, more often than not, to buckle from the inside, a community of practice that is eager and ready to develop collaborative outreach programmes. These extra-curricular activities constitute the soft skills universities continue to ignore. Through constant dialogue across borders of all sorts, Twiza will undoubtedly broaden the crack until all voices are heard to let a genuine civil society emerge, aware of its individual and collective engagement towards human rights. The envisaged result: a society more prone to commitment towards equity and justice. This is not dreamland. It is the sheer volume of the youth potential.

Dr. Mohamed MILIANI Dip. TEFL, M.Ed, PhD
University of Oran-Algeria

An ambitious yet fully realized project that truly embarks on transnational knowledge making, civil engagement, and cross-cultural dialogue through writing. The voices in this book demonstrate that undergraduate students have the ability to creatively enact social justice to develop a better world. They offer a deep hope for an improved global society. This is a must read for composition teachers who seek to engage their students in real-world matters and a must read for students who seek a vision for a different world.

Dr. Rebecca Dingo
University of Massachusetts

Working and Writing for Change
Series Editors: Steve Parks and Jessica Pauszek

The Writing and Working for Change series began during the 100th anniversary celebrations of NCTE. It was designed to recognize the collective work of teachers of English, Writing, Composition, and Rhetoric to work within and across diverse identities to ensure the field recognize and respect language, educational, political, and social rights of all students, teachers, and community members. While initially solely focused on the work of NCTE/CCCC Special Interest Groups and Caucuses, the series now includes texts written by individuals in partnership with other communities struggling for social recognition and justice.

Books in the Series
CCCC/NCTE Caucuses
History of the Black Caucus National Council Teachers of English by Marianna White Davis
Listening to Our Elders: Working and Writing for Social Change by Samantha Blackmon, Cristina Kirklighter, and Steve Parks
Building a Community, Having a Home: A History of the Conference on College Composition and Communication edited by Jennifer Sano-Franchini, Terese Guinsatao Monberg, K. Hyoejin Yoon
Viva Nuestro Caucus: Rewriting the Forgotten Pages of Our Caucus, edited by Romeo García, Iris D. Ruiz, Anita Hernández and María Paz Carvajal Regidor

Community Publications
Other People's English: Code-Meshing, Code-Switching, and African American Literacy by Vershawn Ashanti Young, Rusty Barrett, Y'Shanda Young-Rivera, and Kim Brian Lovejoy
Becoming International: Musings on Studying Abroad in America, edited by Sadie Shorr-Parks
Dreams and Nightmares: I Fled Alone to the United States When I Was Fourteen by Liliana Velásquez. Edited and translated by Mark Lyon
The Weight of My Armor: Creative Nonfiction and Poetry by the Syracuse Veterans' Writing Group, edited by Ivy Kleinbart, Peter McShane, and Eileen Schell
PHD to PhD: How Education Saved My Life by Elaine Richardson

Equality and Justice
An Engaged Generation, A Troubled World

Michael Chehade, Alex Granner, Ahmed Abdelhakim Hachelaf,
Madhu Napa, Samantha Owens, Steve Parks

The Twiza Project
New City Community Press
Working and Writing for Change, Parlor Press

Parlor Press LLC, Anderson, South Carolina, USA
Copyright © 2020 New City Community Press
Printed on acid-free paper
Manufactured in the United States of America

No part of this book may be reproduced or transmitted in any form, by any means electronic or mechanical, including photocopying and recording, or by any information storage or retrieval system, without written permission from the publisher.

Library of Congress Cataloging-in-Publication Data on File

1 2 3 4 5

978-1-64317-137-1 (paperback)
978-1-64317-138-8 (PDF)
978-1-64317-139-5 (ePub)

WORKING AND WRITING FOR CHANGE

An Imprint Series of Parlor Press

Series Editors: Steve Parks and Jessica Pauszek

Cover photograph by Andrew Shurtleff / Daily progress | Mohamed Messara / EPA
Cover Design by Lucia Shuff-Heck
Interior design by Lucia Shuff-Heck, with contributions from Abigail Dougherty

Parlor Press, LLC is an independent publisher of scholarly and trade titles in print and multimedia formats. This book is available in paper and eBook formats from Parlor Press on the World Wide Web at http://www.parlorpress.com or through online and brick-and-mortar bookstores. For submission information or to find out about Parlor Press publications, write to Parlor Press, 3015 Brackenberry Drive, Anderson, South Carolina, 29621, or email editor@parlorpress.com.

The Twiza Project Writing Group

Project Directors

Ahmed Abdelhakim Hachelaf, Ecole Normale Supérieure
Stephen Parks, University of Virginia.

Project Members

Isabelle Alexander
Hind Belakhal
Djoumana Hadil Boughazi
Najwa Harzi
Michael Anthony Chehade
Allaoua Hisham Khallil
Hachemi Chaima
Fouad Cherif Belfard
Boucherit Nadjet
Meredith Diloia
Abigail Dougherty
Jonathan Hart Ellis
Isabelle Ezratty
Meredith Gallagher
Alex Granner
Omari John

Khadidja Khelid
Salima Aya Talbi
Madhumita Napa
Samantha Rose Owens
Kathleen Regalado
Chiraz Retimi
Bouchra Rahmouni
Saqib Rizvi
Aissa Seddik
Lucia Shuff-Heck

Table of Contents

XI   *Acknowledgments*
1   *Introduction*

1   Education and Leadership

Opening Thoughts
19   Aspasia Tsampas

Dialogue: Education and Leadership
21   Chiraz Retimi
      Samantha Owens
      Chiraz Retimi
23   Bouchra Rahmouni
      Meredith Gallagher

Further Engagement
24   Monica Mills
27   Alex Granner
28   Melissa Mercado and Divya Pariti
31   Gabrielle Hersey
33   Djoumana Hadil Boughazi
34   Joshua Farris
40   Claire Song
45   Taylor Blackley
      Jayden Williams
47   Khadidja Khelid
55   Shelby Wayment
      Hachemi Chaima

Concluding Thoughts
56   Bouchra Rahmouni

2 Civil Society and Injustice

Opening Thoughts
59   Mahieddine Ouafi

Dialogue: Civil Society and Injustice
61   Chiama Hachemi
     Samantha Owens
     Nadjet Boucherit
62   Allaoua Hisham Khalil
     Aissa Seddiki
     Najwa Harizi
63   Aissa Seddikki
     Najwa Harizi
     Madhu Napa
64   Aissa Seddikki
65   Meredith Gallagher
     Aissa Seddikki
     Meredith Gallagher
66   Chaima Hachemi

Further Engagement
66   Chiraz Retimi
67   Victoria Hunter
68   Perris Jones
72   Erynn Brantley-Ridgeway
     Kristian Cavander
74   Shelby Host
76   Samantha Owens
80   Meredith Diloia
85   Nour Elhouda Belakhdar
86   Bouchra Rahmouni

Concluding Thoughts
90   Fouad Cherif Belferd
     Allaoua Hisham Khalil
     Fouad Cherif Belferd

3   Social Media and Activism

Opening Thoughts
93   Sophie Beeckman

Dialogue: Social Media and Activism
95   Algerian and United State Activists

Further Engagement
103   Ally Masterson
104   Isabelle Ezratty
109   Michael Chehade
113   Caroline Campos
118   Jonathan Brownlee
120   Friederike Piehler
122   Alex Martinez
125   Amithav Reddy
        Simran Kaur
126   Emma Ashley-Grose
        Talbi Salima Aya
128   Hind Benlakhal
129   Hamdi Soufian Abdelkarim
130   Alex Martinez
        Bouchra Rahmouni
132   Mohand Chibane
135   Chaima Hachemi
138   Devin Willis

Concluding Thoughts
148   Chiraz Retimi
149   Djoumana Hadil Boughazi

x

Photography

Cover	Andrew Shurtleff	Daily progress (Top) Mohamed Messara	EPA (Bottom)
TOC	Becker1999 Flickr "*IMG_1001(3)*" (Top) Lucia Shuff-Heck (Bottom)
20	John Omari "*March for Our Lives, Washington, DC*"
60	Hannah WIlliams "*National Walkout for Gun Control at the University of Virginia*" (Top) Wass07 Wikimedia Commons (Bottom)
73	Anthony Crider Flickr CC by 2.0
134	Cheep "*Anti-Bouteflika Paris 2019*" Wikipedia Commons CC By 4.0
145	Anthony Crider Flickr CC by 2.0
Interior	Becker1999 "*IMG_1000(1)*" (Upper Left) Wikimedia Commons "*Médeá University*" (Lower Left) Bob Mical "*UVA Rotunda*" (Upper Right) Lucia Shuff-Heck (Lower Right)

Photographs and illustrations have been edited to appear in Black & White

Acknowledgments

"You already have everything you need to achieve what you want."
I often use this phrase in community organizing spaces. It's designed as a call to have the community recognize the skills, insights, and resources already existing within a community. Equality and Justice: An Engaged Generation, A Troubled World is a testament to the truth of that statement.

Our collective work in Algeria and the United States began during my first week at the University of Virginia, working with students enrolled in an introductory writing course. Together, we were both still learning to navigate the campus, make new friends/colleagues, understand the new political terrain which now surrounded our lives. For that reason, I want to begin by acknowledging the students who took up the task of creating dialogues with students in Algeria, imagining a possible book, gathering over 200 submissions from across the United States and Algeria, then selecting and editing the writing and, ultimately, designing the publication before you. The special contributions of Alex Granner, Samantha Owens, Madhu Napa, Lucia Shuff-Heck, Michael Chehade, who continued to work on this project over the summer, must also be noted. As a collective, they demonstrated that University of Virginia students already possess what is needed to use their education to make a positive change in the world.

Any teacher who engages their students in a local or international project only succeeds through the support of their university, college, and department. Without the insight and labor of the following individuals, this publication would not have occurred: Kate Stephenson, James Seitz, Keith Driver, Steve Arata, Kevin Smith, Terese Monberg, Mikala Jones, Carolina Campos, Wafa Salah, Victor Luftig, Lori Shorr, Traci Swiecki, Kate Vieira, Patricia Sullivan, Rafaela Evans, Romeo Garcia, Camilo Sanchez, Sarah O'Brien, Cory Shaman, Jon D'Errico, Lindgren Johnson, Kate Kostelnik, and DeVan Ard. Anna Fleming also played a vital key role ensuring this project achieved both its aspirations and its completion. Here I want to be sure to add that Madhu Napa wants to acknowledge the important and continual support from Lavanya, Ramesh, and Monish Napa. And Alex Granner would like to express his gratitude to Mark, Stacy, Katie, Daryl, Nancy Granner, as well as Kay and Keith Tschannen for their consistent and valuable support as well.

I want to specifically thank Sarah Arrington, Stacey Trader, Collette Dabney, and Randy Swift, whose wise counsel enabled me to navigate the myriad of University of Virginia policies and practices. That they did so with such patience and understanding is a kindness I will long remember.

Finally, I want to acknowledge the friendship and insight Ahmed Hachelaf, whose vision and labor enabled the Twiza Project (twizaproject.org), as well as the powerful contributions of his students featured in this publication. That these students continued to focus on their education as well as their work with my students while marching in the streets for changes which would transform Algeria was inspiring. I hope they such values enacted in the pages that follow.

Steve Parks
Writing and Rhetoric Program
Department of English
University of Virginia

To all teachers and students, who far from the limelight, are shaping the face of the future and struggling for justice everywhere in this world. This work would never have been possible without the amazing group of student leaders on both sides of the Atlantic, who reversed the direction of teaching and taught us the meaning of unabated engagement despite the troubling political moment.

I am extremely indebted to Steve Parks, a wonderful human being, who has an amazing ability to bring out the best in people and make things possible through magic. He was able to render topsy-turvy pieces of writing into a coherent book.

I would like also to thank all officials, who despite not giving us the frank authorization to work on the Twiza Project, allowed it to happen.

I would like to thank specifically Amina Boulafaa for her help in the editing process and all educators who gave us needed encouragement.

Ahmed Abdelhakim Hachelaf
Education and Civic Engagement Specialist
Higher Normal/Training School — Laghouat — Algeria

Introduction

Michael Chehade, Alex Granner, Ahmed Abdelhakim Hachelaf, Madhu Napa, Samantha Owens, Steve Parks

Proposing an International Dialogue
The traditional first-year undergraduate college student is approximately nineteen years old.

In this short span of time, their lives have been marked by the following:

The September 11, 2001 World Trade Center Attacks

The Afghanistan War

The Iraq War

The 2008 Global Collapse

The Occupy Wallstreet Movement

The Arab Spring

These global events have crossed international borders in their impact, leaving generational scars on those who have fought in the wars, struggled for peace, and attempted to find justice. There has been a global effort to find the language, the structures, which can implement the lessons learned from these events, to build a civic society which address the needs and aspirations of those who have survived.

One such attempt occurred in the winter of 2019.

Beginning in January and continuing through May, we came together as students and faculty enrolled in courses at the University of Virginia, United States, and the Higher Normal School at Laghouat, Algeria, to consider possible paths forward. Our goal was to engage in dialogues about the meaning of human rights at this current political moment as well as the role of civil engagement pointed toward equity and justice. We hoped that our dialogues might produce a new way of speaking, writing, understanding that would be useful not only to us, but to others outside our classes.

For students in the United States, the goals of the course were potentially a bit of a surprise. Neither we (Chehade, Napu, Owens) nor our classmates were not aware that we would engage in such dialogues. When registering for the course, this project not been featured. Many of us were still attempting to navigate the campus as new freshman. And while we listened excitedly to our professor (Parks, also new to our university), we were also sharing a fair bit of skepticism. What did it mean our course would engage in dialogues with students in Algeria? Would we also invite individuals from our campus and beyond to take part? What would our collective work result in? Were we talking about producing a book?

For those students in Algeria, each came to the project a bit more aware of the work to be done having previously taken part in a similar project with their own Algerian professor (Hachelaf) as well as our professor (Parks). Still, the logistics of the project which relied on steady internet access, consistent dialogue across time zones and national borders, seemed to stretch the limits of possibility. And like their United States counterparts, the idea of producing a book seemed complicated. What would be the focus of the book? Who would choose the content? Would other students in the United States and Algeria be able to take part? After some initial conversations among all the students involved, it seemed none of us had much experience in such work.

Yet as the book in your hands now demonstrates, collectively, we did manage to produce a publication. Our hope is that it speaks to a cross-border understanding of what it means to be civically engaged and how a college education should enable students to become active participants in their communities after graduation. Before reading the published work, however, we want to provide you with the story of how a set of proposed dialogues led to this book, Equality and Justice: An Engaged Generation, A Troubled World.

Establishing Dialogues Across Borders

Our two classes made contact initially through a set of on-line dialogues. It is probably fair to say that these initial conversations were more about sharing personal experiences than providing any profound political insights. Looking back, the importance of establishing trust, demonstrating that all of us share some common experiences in our classrooms and communities, seemed vital. We had all sat in high school courses where lectures and standardized tests shrunk what counted as knowledge. We had all aspired to have an education that would enable us to become active in our communities. We had all worried about how this disconnect between our education and civic goals could make it difficult for our generation to build on the successes of our elders. And as we engaged in dialogues, our specific conversations began to integrate themselves into The Twiza Project, which had provided the support for the initial dialogues and potential future publication.

The Twiza Project emerged as a collaborative effort among faculty in North America, North Africa, and the Middle East. The project attempts to speak back to the sectarian divisions, often coupled with polarized debate, that have radicalized a politics seemingly premised on bigotry and hate. Such politics, the project believes, have led to an increase of hate crimes in local communities and a rise in global intolerance towards political/economic refugees. As such, project's goal was to build platforms to allow young adults to respond to the human rights crises occurring locally, nationally, and internationally.

It was designed to create a space in which to imagine, then build, an alternative future marked by greater cultural, economic, and political freedoms. As such, the project hopes to be part of collective efforts to build a public space in which everyone has the right and ability to participate. Indeed, the term "Twiza" speaks to the communal act of individuals coming together to build a material structure, such as barn or house, to support a neighbor. The term is intended to speak to the collective work of youth who actively work to build their societies and to build the material structures which can support human rights for everyone in their community.

Through The Twiza Project, then, expanded our dialogues. We were asked what makes a leader in civil society? What is the basis for this civil society? Who can be a leader? How has social media affected the way we act as leaders within our societies? Despite growing up in countries separated by many miles, histories, and cultural differences, our classes began to find a shared concept of the ideal civil society. Collectively, our classes were able to agree that many of the values of democracy that were conceptually held to be important were not being fully realized in our respective countries. Then as dialogues progressed, collectively, we began to share possible solutions. To use our experience and education to imagine how our classrooms might be different.

Yet, we did not always agree. Solutions posed for our own context might not work for our colleagues in a different country. Ideas did not always cross national boundaries with ease. Indeed, we often found that the very language used, the terms by which one of us understood the world, also faced "translation" issues. What one of us took to be a neutral term, a term of endearment, of friendship, might be seen as offensive as it crossed borders. And political terminology, always fraught, needed to be discussed, defined, and re-articulated to that a common understanding could be developed. In a course about writing, we soon discovered the difficulties of bending our particular languages and ways of speaking to common purpose.

It was out of this common sense of education needing to support civil society, out of a sense that this common value would have to be implemented different locally, that our sense of possible book project emerged. We began to recognize there might be a need for a publication which supported such conversations. There might be a value to a publication which turned our initial cynicism about the goals of education into a positive vision which spoke to a generation's aspirations. We might have an opportunity to capture how other students, in other universities, in other countries were attempting to build an engaged, publicly-oriented education. And we might learn from their efforts.

Building Our Own Publication

With these new insights, we began to put pieces in place to create our publication.

Our initial step was to create a series of prompts for circulation across our respective campuses and, if possible, across universities in the United States and Algeria. Our goal was to ask a series of short evocative questions, then allow students to respond in whatever genre – academic essay, personal essay, poem, or artwork, - best met their needs. We then developed a list of individuals, courses, faculty, and student organizations to contact and seek their participation. Emerging from our dialogues, the prompts touched on education's effect in creating civil leaders, how we define and address injustice and inequality, as well as who can be an activist and how to define activism. Our goal was to invite respondents to consider the following issues:

The role of education in preparing them to be active in the civil life of their community and country.

The gap between the public rhetoric on education/civil engagement and their actual experience as students.

The gap between a public rhetoric premised on political equality across genders/heritages and their actual experience as community members.

The insights gain from participating in civil engagement projects designed to broaden the practices of civil society.

The meaning of leadership within civil societies committed to equality and equal rights.

With an idea of what we wanted the book to tackle, we divided ourselves into task groups based on our strengths. The content group worked on writing prompts to generate content for the book. The outreach group drafted letters and emails to be sent out to potential authors. The design group illustrated the writing prompts and began working on the book's visual elements. Slowly, things began to fall into place and what once seemed like a lofty, far away creation became increasingly real. Once responses to the prompts began coming in, the in-class evaluation process began to decide upon emergent themes, choose work for inclusion, send back work for further revision. We took on the role of editors crafting a publication which took on our creative vision.

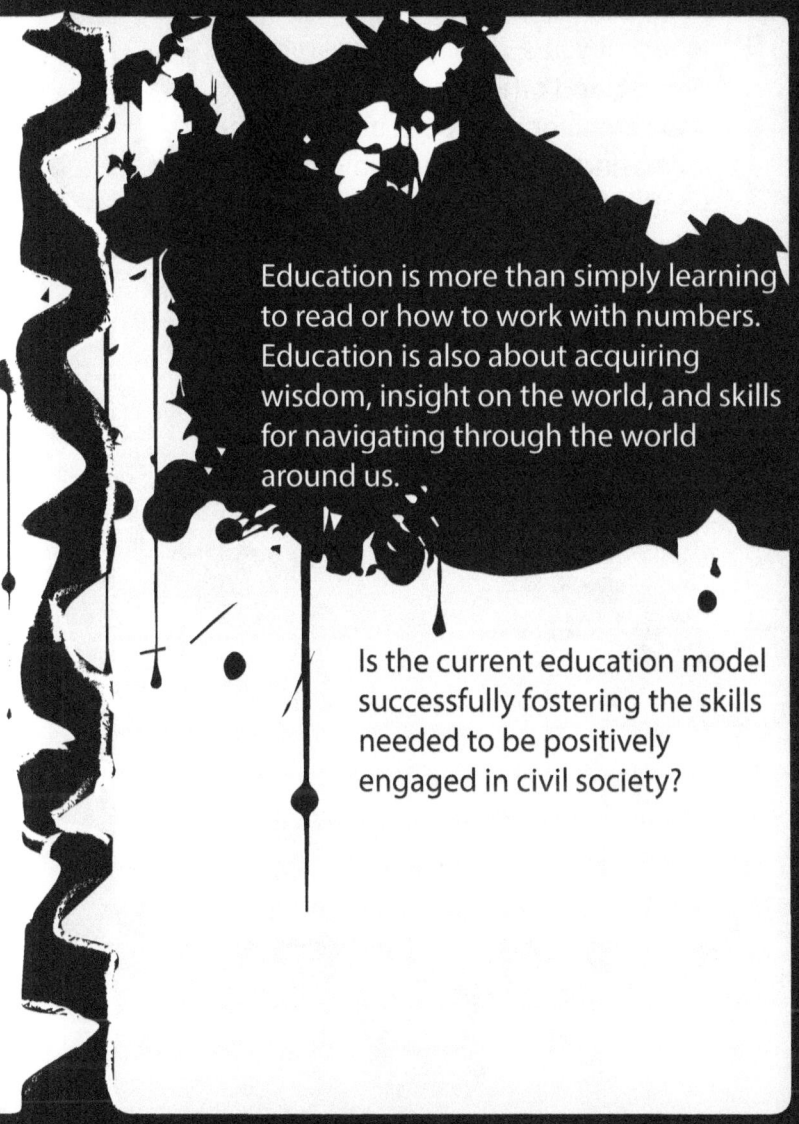

Education is more than simply learning to read or how to work with numbers. Education is also about acquiring wisdom, insight on the world, and skills for navigating through the world around us.

Is the current education model successfully fostering the skills needed to be positively engaged in civil society?

Send responses to twiza@newcitycommunitypress.com
A Community Writing Project of New City Community Press (newcitycommunitypress.com)

In recent years, through social media, protest, and other forms of petitioning and campaigning, youth have become increasingly involved in activism. The youth of today are organizing themselves and pushing for change and the rectification of injustices. Often when we think of 'activists', we think of famous names such as Martin Luther King Jr. or Nelson Mandela. But what about ordinary people such as these highly visible groups of youth who are organizing for change?

Can anybody be an activist? And what methods of activism do you believe are the most effective at bringing about social or political change?

Send responses to twiza@newcitycommunitypress.com
A Community Writing Project of New City Community Press (newcitycommunitypress.com)

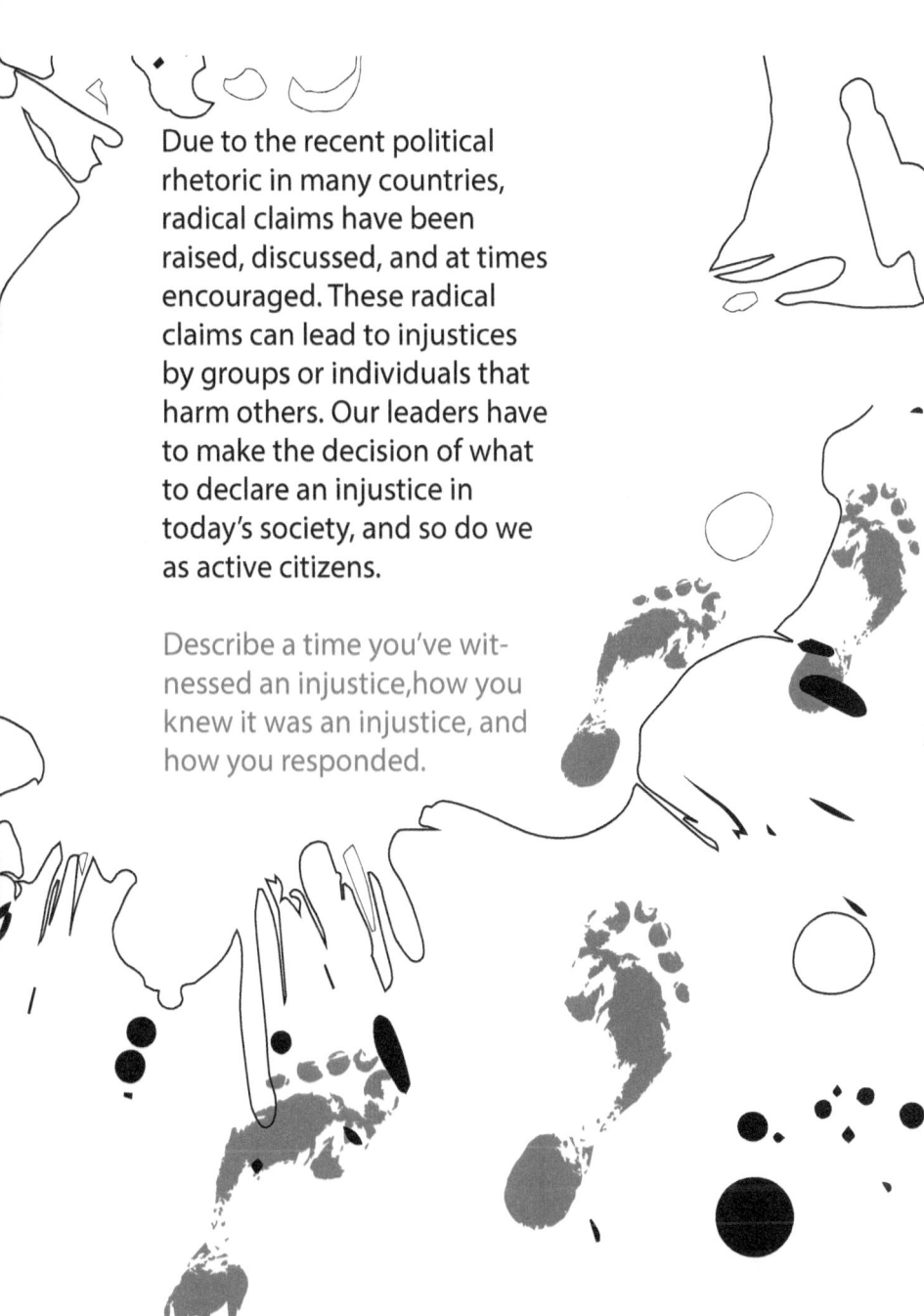

Due to the recent political rhetoric in many countries, radical claims have been raised, discussed, and at times encouraged. These radical claims can lead to injustices by groups or individuals that harm others. Our leaders have to make the decision of what to declare an injustice in today's society, and so do we as active citizens.

Describe a time you've witnessed an injustice, how you knew it was an injustice, and how you responded.

Send responses to twiza@newcitycommunitypress.com

A Community Writing Project of New City Community Press (newcitycommunitypress.com)

Of course, not everything went smoothly. After our initial outreach for the prompts, we received almost no response. During the course of the semester, we were also continually trying to find a digital platform to ensure we could talk with each other across international borders and time zones. Over the course of a month, however, we began to receive responses. Eventually, we had close to 300 students write to us from different locations across Algeria as well as from different universities in the United States – such as University of Utah, Michigan State University, Temple University, among others. In fact, we soon became overwhelmed with writing. As such, as noted above, the class in the United States soon became a weekly discussion group on submitted writing – evaluating it its fit to the book, considering what might need revised, corresponding with authors.

It was the initial hope to have Algerian students also work with us in evaluating submissions at each stage of the process, but history intervened in the form of Algerian protests for political reform.

Activating Civil Society
Our dialogues began by considering how education might prepare an individual to become civically engaged in their community. In the middle of these dialogues, Algeria began an effort to expand democracy and political rights in their country. The initial results of the marches and protests was the resignation of the current president and a call for new national elections. It seemed as if the goals of our book had emerged on the streets of Algiers.

Those of in Algeria became immersed in the daily energy and vibrancy of a collective call to enable Algeria to fulfill its historic destiny as a nation. They participated in deep dialogues about the future, participated in legal marches, enacted our values by taking care of individuals and communities engaged in these efforts. And they wrote.

They did not write as much, perhaps, in the planned weekly dialogues with the students in the United States. And perhaps, they did not write academic essays based on scholarly articles – which the United States students continued to do. Instead, they wrote a new grammar for what it means to Algerian with their bodies in the streets, their insights tapped out on our keyboards.

In a strange way, the initial framework of the project was shattered by the events in Algeria. Weekly conversations became monthly; group correspondence suffered; book deadlines were not often met. But here is where the initial trust and community of collective opening dialogues manifested their value. The Algerian students knew the United States colleagues supported their goals, were continuing the work required, and would welcome them back into the project when, hopefully, the civil goals were met, when they could return to a more traditional sense of a student. And that, in fact, is what happened.

Articulating Lessons Learned
The collective efforts of the Algerian people both interrupted and made clear the values of our proposed book. They also gave us the central metaphor through which to understand the writing chosen for inclusion: awakenings.

Many of the authors who have contributed to this collection wrote of transformative moments when they witnessed or were the target of oppression or injustice. In many spheres, religion, politics, education, gender, their personal experiences have helped to shape how these writers understand society. We see such stories as powerfully instructive.

Indeed, collectively, we have come to believe that one experience, lived by one individual, can shift the way we think about an entire group, structure, or issue. Such experiences can be terrifying, confusing, and definitely isolating. At first, these writers state, such experience can make one feel small, insignificant, and alone, to argue one person is incapable of righting such injustices. Indeed, these writer's attest that the work of understanding such moments as part of larger patterns in society is both frightening and empowering at once. Such insights place you within a community, but also show the extent of the struggle ahead. Ultimately, however, these writers demonstrate that such personal feelings can bind us together in a common effort for change.

And as these student writers have experienced such awakenings, they have also begun to develop a theory of how change occurs. Initially, change may be primarily personal, it is subtle, often undetected except in tiny gestures. Such change might move outward, onto social medial posts, finding a digital community of support. And these writers make clear that to become active in civic engagement means to use such digital resources and platforms to empower and educate ourselves and others. They argue that creating safe spaces for dialogue to happen is just as valuable as any other form of activism. (And here we might use our classroom as one such example.)

As students move outward, off of social media and into the streets, the work alters slightly. The effort becomes to find a vocabulary that can cross communities, fostered continued collaboration, withstand responses by those opposed to proposed goals of an expansive civil society. And, the writers argue, such work also takes courage. It takes the strength to lose what if valuable to you. To stare down racist agitators in your college town. To speak loudly to authorities who might not want to listen. Such are the insights, values, and experiences of the writers in this publication.

Through our time together, we have learned that the path to creating the ideal civil society in which democracy is realized and human rights are protected is unique to each society. We should not imagine our strategies and structures can be easily transported to different countries. Yet, we should imagine, must believe, that there can be a common end goal – an inclusive, open, and engaged civil society in which all are able to participate in the collective creation of their community. And despite the frustration out of which our book might have emerged, the oppression many of us still face, we are optimistic about the future.

Writing in the Moment
Our collective work emerged through dialogue, with each person coming into a recognition of the complexity of the past, the difficulty of creating a more equitable future, and the need for collaboration across boundaries. The writing chosen for inclusion in this book was selected for its ability to capture this complexity, this awakening to the future in which a multitude of voices would be heard and respected.

The writing, then, is deliberately unfinished, if by finished we mean a piece must invoke all elements of a genre, live within such boundaries, and provide articulated solutions to the problems addressed. The writing selected for our book crosses genres and expectations. An included essay might speak to traditions of academic writing, but veers off into personal anecdote, poetic language. Political moments are discussed, then compared to classroom art projects produced as a young adult. Theories of social change become enmeshed in stories of grandmothers, family's having to navigate war and civil conflict. The writing speaks in voices that are emerging, developing, and transforming civil space. The writing enacts a language of becoming, a struggle to blend personal moments into a set of public commitments. And in that way, it carries a power that transcends typical classroom discourse.

The writing is also deliberately utopian. Time will tell if the civil engagement highlighted in this book can achieve its goals – a Charlottesville free from racism; an Algeria enacting an inclusive civil sphere. We cannot promise that the individual goals expressed by the writers will come to fruition – achieving a college degree, creating a civil classroom, fostering tolerance in their community, transforming national dialogues - will occur. But we felt the need to highlight the courage and strength embedded in such efforts. We felt the need to combat visions which cast this generation as "less than" those that came before, "less than" up to the task of creating a better future. We intend to show a generation already undertaking such work.

The future, as they say, has already begun.

We hope you will join us in creating it.

Understanding the Structure of our Book
We have structured this book to reflect the dynamic which fostered its creation. For that reason, we have created three unique units: Education and Leadership; Civil Society and Injustice; Social Media and Activism. Each section begins with Opening Thoughts, which are excerpts from our initial dialogues with each other. These dialogues frame the central issues being discussed. Under the heading of Further Engagement, we then offer a writing produced by members of our project as well as those who submitted work from across our respective countries. Then, through Concluding Thoughts, we return to the insights of our fellow participants to capture at least some of the lessons of a particular unit. While the order of the units reflects the origins and growth of our own work together, they need not be read in order. We believe each can stand on its own as a way to explore the issues discussed. Finally, within each of the units, we have attempted to choose work which represents a variety of experiences, insights, and conclusions. In a project emerging from dialogue, then, we have not attempted to present a unified answer, but a landscape in which to foster greater conversation.

In particular, the following concerns are discussed:

Education and Leadership
The meaning and value of education is something deeply ingrained within all societies. As such, education plays a significant role in how individuals understand their role in particular cultures and the nation

as a whole. Education also shapes how an individual imagines their civic role in society, how they imagine their role in creating positive change. This unit explores how students experience public education as civic education. As such, the pieces speak to the successes, shortcomings, and necessary changes that the writers have experienced in education, as well as ways to enact these changes. Unique yet seemingly interconnected, the works also portray the current state of education across an international context. Given the role of education in shaping ideas and beliefs about the meaning of civic society and social change, this unit can provide context and meaning to the other sections of the book.

Civil Society and Injustice

There is a moment when what seems a personal experience of discrimination, oppression, is suddenly understood as speaking to larger social structures. Once understood, the injustices that too often structure society are exposed, actions are required. In this unit, the writers share their own experiences of discrimination as well as acts of support for those being oppressed. In the process, they come to understand the contours of injustice across college, community, and national borders. They begin to draw connections to what sustains such practices. Through this unit, what too often seems personal can come to be seen as political. And once understood as political, the possibility of change can be seen to emerge.

Social Media and Activism

The butterfly effect is an interesting phenomenon, where one seemingly small action can lead to a cascade of events, resulting in a result much greater than intended. Whether it be hitting "Tweet" on Twitter, stepping into a march in support for political change, these writings explore the personal and public changes that resulted from seemingly small acts. In the process, these writers take the reader into the experience of supporting Asylum seekers deposited by federal agents in cities across the country with no sustained support; of protesting Nazi activists on the streets of Charlottesville and the campus of the University of Virginia; and taking part in national efforts to create a broader civil and political society in Algeria. Throughout, a belief in a better future ripples through syllables on the page. As such, these stories should not be read as separate, but rather as one intertwining narrative on how injustice is tackled globally. How, perhaps, a generational vision is taking place across the globe.

1 EDUCATION AND LEADERSHIP

Passionate Words - Aspasia Tsampas

They told me I needed therapy.
Because I rolled my r's
and said *rrr*enember
instead of remember.

On paper I was perfect, they said,
but when I spoke it was "uneducated."
My mother, with her master's degree
but an accent thicker than the olive oil
on the groves of our ancestors before her,
apologized to me,

"I promise you will sound as smart
as you are, *agapi mou*."

At age 8, I went to speech pathology
A word of Greek origin,
pathos for passion
logos for words,

where my passionate words,
the most glorious link between
my proud identity as a Greek-American,
were beaten down until
I spoke *standard*.

While my tongue may have learned
to curb its fiery Greek accent,
my body *rrr*enembers.
And when I am angry or crazy,
it comes like an Ionian wave.

And I roll my r's
and say *rrr*enember,
because I will always remember.

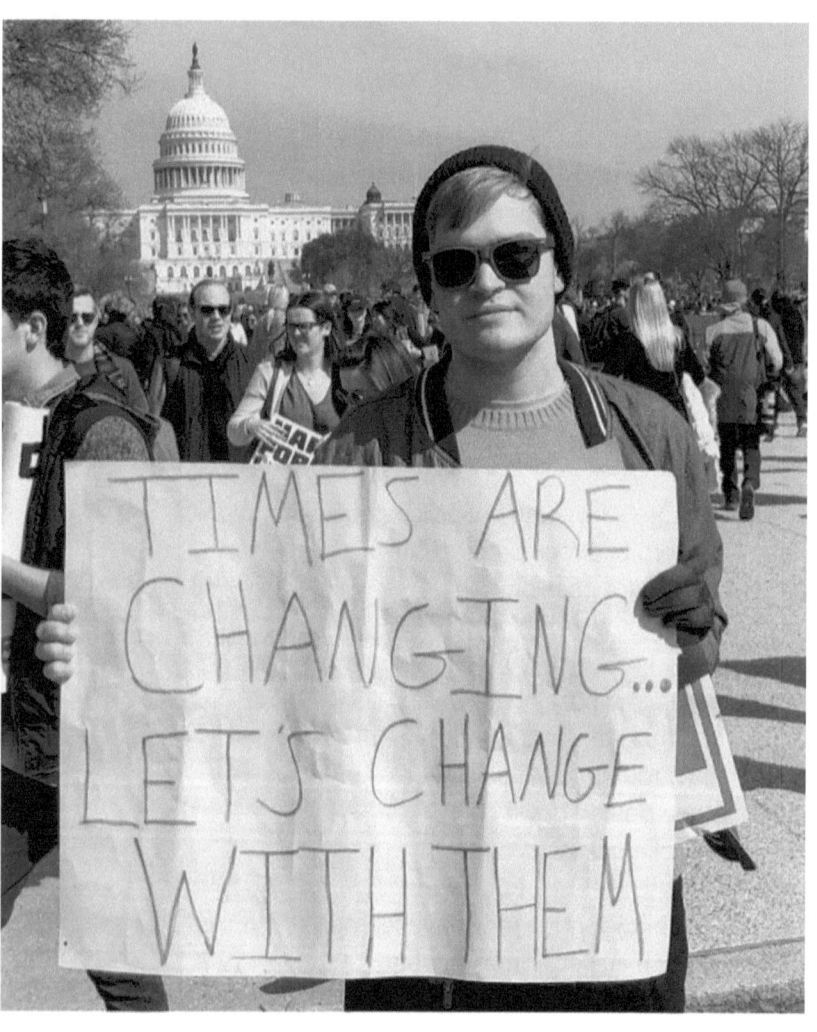

Dialogue

Chiraz Retimi
A leader in a basic definition is someone who provides guidance, directions, and has confidence in everything he does. Quite honestly, I think our educational system focuses mainly on memorization rather than developing critical and analytical thinking. In my country, good grades are a sign of intelligence, but the reality is an exam does not define our intellectual level. If a student believed that he does not have what it takes to fit in the "intelligence" box, he will lose an essential key to being a leader, which is confidence. Personally, my education did not prepare me to face the real world; I had to learn that by myself through personal experiences.

Samantha Owens
What you said about education being focused on memorization really resonated with me. I definitely agree with what you said about confidence being the key to leadership. I don't think that getting perfect grades in school equates to becoming a good leader. In the United States, I also think that when students don't excel at the typical memorization-based style of testing, it's easy to get discouraged and feel like you're not intelligent or have nothing to offer. I just wonder how schools could teach critical analysis skills more effectively. I think that many teachers want to spend time instilling those skills but maybe feel like they can't because those in higher up positions impose too strict of requirements onto them.

Chiraz Retimi
I am glad we are on the same page here because, honestly, I think that some teachers do not even realize how useless it is to give a "temporary educational base" to students and target their lowest levels of memorization and simple reasoning. Think about multiple choice questions. The answer is already in the given choices. The student only needs to dig deep in his mind, and he will find the answer easily, but he

will forget everything he studied because he does not need that amount of information anymore.

Not only is it easier to test students depending on their memorization skills, but it is also easier to teach them by memorization. Teachers, no matter if they know the subject or not, they are able to talk students through the context, show them conceptual links, or probably read a few words from the textbook and point to sections from it. They can then have the students repeat a short sequence of rules to solve very simple problems.

How can a teacher develop the sense of leadership in a student when she/he cannot even make the student appreciate the knowledge being taught? Making knowledge into something the student learns to consider as just an "obligation" to get done with in order to pass her/his test.

How can schools teach critical thinking and analysis skills more effectively? Well, in my eyes, it is all about thinking independently and accepting other points of view. There are some strategies a teacher could use in his/her classroom to raise these issues. Starting the session with a question that has multiple answers that makes students wonder about a topic—that is a great way to open up useful discussions and debates. Also, I believe that encouraging project-based learning can guarantee success in the real world, not only in school.

Chiraz Retimi

How can schools teach critical thinking and analysis skills more effectively? Well, in my eyes, it is all about thinking independently and accepting other points of view. There are some strategies a teacher could use in his /her classroom to raise these issues, starting the session with a question that has multiple answers that makes students wonder about a topic. That is a great way to open up useful discussions and debates. Also, I believe that encouraging project- based learning can guarantee success in the real world not only in school.

Bouchra Rahmouni

I think we share the same idea here. Many teachers in our country give their students a false idea that if a student memorizes and gets good marks, it means they are smart!

I think there should be a different way of presenting the lessons and testing students' abilities to prepare them for their future. Those subject matters we dealt with during primary, middle, and high school were beneficial—no one denies that is the case, but engaging students in the society's affairs and listening to their opinions would make a difference. A personality gets its full shape starting from childhood. If that means anything, then it is the necessity of discovering the inner energies of every child and instilling the right principles and values, including "leadership." That only can happen through education. I'd like to mention what Nelson Mandela once said: "Education is the most powerful weapon that you can use to change the world." It is through educating the others that we can make them leaders.

Meredith Gallagher

I feel the same way. I do not feel that current education systems do anything to address these social issues or prepare us to be good citizens and humans. What prepared me most for civic leadership was having a reaction against what I was seeing in my school from other students and teachers.

I grew up in a diverse school, but then I switched in middle school to a rural school. In my old school, my best friends were from all over the world, from Africa, from the Middle East. When 9/11/2001 happened, I had moved to the rural school. There I was confronted with so much racism and ignorance that I felt obligated to speak out against it. I fought back against all the ignorance through educating myself. I sought out religious texts and world perspectives to have facts to strengthen my arguments. I spoke out and disagreed with not just students, but teachers as well. I just could not fathom the hate I was seeing. We were just kids, but I was disgusted. To this day I feel lucky to have had that early exposure and opportunity to grow up around the families of my friends, Pakistani Muslims, Nigerians, and Eastern Europeans. I feel like I was inoculated against the hate that became infectious. So, while school didn't give me those skills or that drive, it did make me realize I was responsible to find it myself.

Further Engagement

Monica Mills

I once had two students, who I'll call Sharee and Alana. They were identical twins and were extremely smart. Yes, all of my students are very smart, but Sharee and Alana are special. They are geniuses if I've ever met any. Sharee desires to be an engineer, Alana, a doctor. I expect Sharee will design a hospital that provides groundbreaking accessibility while Alana will discover auto-antibodies that have the ability to cure the most intense pain. Then, they will win a joint Nobel Peace prize for their innovations that work in tandem to help those struggling with the most with physical pain.

I may be minimizing their abilities.

On the very first day of class, Sharee and Alana were the first students there, together, sitting next to one another, front and center. Their braces-filled smiles, their glowing mocha skin, and large springy curls left them conspicuous even when in a full room. But it was the way their excitement to learn was that of a child's excitement for recess that made them unforgettable. They came to class to learn as much as possible, use the knowledge to get into the best college, and start their careers.

One Saturday, I gave a test on solving quadratic equations. I combed the classroom as I always did while assessing my students. Sharee and Alana both did perfectly neat work. Their equal signs were always aligned vertically and each step was written in perfect mathematical notation. Mathematicians do their work with a precision akin to perfection, and the twins did work that I thought only existed in my nerd domain of numerical heaven. They both finished quickly and put their pencils down. While waiting for their classmates to complete their tests, I looked deeply into their faces in a moment that became incredibly defining for me. I saw in them an emotion one can only understand through experience. They were no longer 'first day of class' Sharee and Alana. Their excitement had turned to boredom. They looked as if they wondered about the point of this class and the work which they had to do. Their faces yelled disappointment in the most unique way. It was clear to me that they needed much more than I was giving.

Later, I sat with each test graded and stacked before me. Almost everyone received an A. I never thought I'd be so upset after grading such phenomenal work. A sense of frustration conjured in me, likely similar to what I saw on the faces of Sharee and Alana. With and without words, my students were telling me they wanted more than the college access math curriculum offered. And like always, they were stuck within a system that consistently fails students like them. This college access program was no different.

Math is a gateway to college. It can act as a barrier or it can be a window to a college degree. Once enrolled in college, students who didn't complete Algebra 2 in high school are significantly less likely to place into a credit bearing math course. This often decides whether a student remains in college or drops out. This is true, overwhelmingly, for low-income students and students of color. High school math is an absolute determining factor in college success and students who leave college because of it are disproportionately from the demographic that this college access program serves. So, where's the justice in teaching remedial math to college-bound, low-income students and students of color? There is none. It actually increases their chances of failure in college, consequently contributing to inequity, which threatens the justice that the program seeks to obtain. As Sharee and Alana sat in a remedial math class, Sharee's career as an engineer was in jeopardy.

White and more affluent students who wanted to become doctors would have a leg up on Alana. I vowed to right the wrongs of this injustice against a program that was definitely not serving the very underserved students I'd come to serve.

Many people have low expectations for students of color and low-income students. The reason: racism. The "bigotry of low expectations" continues to affect students long after high school graduation. College access programs do only what their name indicates: give access. Most do nothing to aid their scholars once they are in college. This suggests that college access programs are rooted in injustice, perpetuating the inequality and widening the opportunity gap. This realization was extremely difficult for me. I had to ask myself "What can I do?" I taught high school math for enough time and had seen this injustice before with many students. Schools fail students of color and poor students all the time. Students' needs aren't met at one level and that results in failure at the next level. It happens time and time again but is never less heartbreaking than before. Thus, I understood that inaction on my part would be too costly for my students and subsequently chose to rewrite the math curriculum for the college access program.

My associated class met only once a week, but what I learned was invaluable. Firstly, I learned of the true definition of activism, which isn't as complex as I previously thought. My professor brought many speakers into class who spoke of community organizing. Each story was different, but they all had one point weaved throughout their narrative: we all can be activists. Activism means one is using their own power to effect change, no matter how small. It can exist in the littlest things we do every day. With the college access program, I used my knowledge of teaching math to eliminate the soft bigotry of low expectations within my classroom. Simply teaching my students more challenging math increases expectations and teaches new knowledge. This is activism. Secondly, class brought forth a confidence that previously lay dormant within me. My class professor theorized knowledge and power in such a way that it completely altered my understanding of both concepts. I began to value my own knowledge and knowledge of other marginalized groups, something I had never done before. This instilled within me a feeling of power. I now understand that there are different forms of knowledge, power can look many ways, and power lies within everyone. My newfound confidence and theoretical understanding drove my activism.

On a micro level, I'm succeeding in my activism. Unfortunately, my actions don't eliminate the systemic societal injustices that rear themselves within well-intentioned systems like college access programs, nor on the global level where injustice can be even greater. With that said, I'd be remiss if I didn't acknowledge that the United States is far ahead of many other countries in the fight for educational equity. Currently, there exist countries where women are still not allowed to receive an education. Throughout the world, educational injustice runs deep for those with low economic means, people of color, and women. Just as injustice in my classroom threatens justice outside of my classroom, educational injustice to marginalized groups of people threatens their justice in society, and in so many cases, it threatens their existence. Society reflects education, and the world is an unequal place. As Horace Mann implied, fighting for educational equity is fighting for the equality of humanity because, as Dr. King understood, if injustice exists somewhere, justice is threatened elsewhere.

Alex Granner

Much of the education reform during the nineteenth century was focused on resolving discrimination and granting rights for minorities within school systems. Major pieces of legislation such as Title I (1965), Title VI (1964), and the Higher Education Act (1965) all focused on bettering poor schools, primarily schools with high minority populations. Much of this correlated with the African-American Civil Rights Movement in the United States during the 1950's and 1960's, which worked to promote equality. However, the composition of ethnic minorities within the United States has changed within the last decade. In addition to increased Latinx immigration, in recent years, the United States has seen a huge influx of Middle Eastern and North African (MENA) immigrants. The current education system is not built to accommodate these new students—nor, it seems, to have successfully rebuilt itself to recognize the skills African Americans bring to classrooms. As such, MENA students' culture, language, and religion are often seen as barriers to their success. In order to meet all students' needs, the entire system need to be restructured. Classes designed for students where Standard English is not the only language valued, where there is respect for religious practices, and a systemic acceptance of all cultures are necessary to make United States schools inclusive and tailored for the success of all students.

Melissa Mercado and Divya Pariti
It is difficult to understand how someone can dislike another person simply based off the pigmentation of their skin; however, it still happens. People make assumptions about others without even attempting to get to know them. We are lucky to have had little experience with racism personally, but that does not mean that we have not witnessed it at all. In fact, growing up in predominantly white communities, we've witnessed it quite frequently. Although our country has come a long way, racism is still a major issue and is prevalent not only in the U.S, but also all over the world. That is something that many people don't realize, and many people also have various misconceptions about racism. The official definition of racism is prejudice, discrimination, or antagonism directed against someone of a different race based on the belief that one's race is superior. Whether you've noticed it or not, acts of racism are still common occurrences, especially in academic settings. It's a shame that some students feel unsafe in school because of racism.

From our time in high school, we witnessed our fair share of racial injustices. Here are our stories:

My name is Divya and I am an Indian who was born and brought up in Naperville, IL. Naperville is not a very diverse community with 68% of its population being white. Ever since I was a child, I had to adapt to societal norms regarding culture. I distinctly remember when I was in second grade, I brought ethnic food from home and one girl told me that it looked disgusting and smelled weird. She then told me that I was the wrong color and that I didn't belong there. After that, I never took Indian food to school again. Though this was minor, it still impacted me in ways that I won't ever forget. My dad would pack me rice and I would make up excuses as to why I couldn't take it. I used to say that it was too messy or that it got too cold by the time lunchtime rolled around. These excuses continued to pile on, and I think, at the time, I believed what I was telling my parents. However, looking back on it now, I am able to see that I was just trying to preserve my image as the "whitewashed" Indian. As I grew older, I would try harder and harder to hide my culture and to act more "white" in order to fit in. If I had to go to the temple, I would say I had to go to church or make up a different lie. By the time I came to high school, I was very used to hiding my Indian identity. The one event I witnessed that impacted me the most was my junior year of high school. This boy came in with a Confederate flag wrapped around his body and he was wearing a "Make America Great Again" (MAGA) hat. I found out later on that he was suspended; however, the fact that he thought it was okay to promote those racist ideals made me very uncomfortable. Throughout high school, I witnessed various events of microaggression and subliminal racism such as this one; however, I was not completely sure on how to react to it. All I knew was that something needed to be done about these injustices.

My name is Melissa. Considering that I am half white and half Filipino, I've gotten used to being the darkest person in the room. It never really bothered me that much, probably because I've never really been a victim of racism. However, other people of color from my high school haven't been as fortunate. The high school that I attended had 28% minority enrollment. Because of this, it was very common for people of color at my school to feel out of place. The occasional racial slur would be said or a confederate flag could be on full display, and nothing would ever be done. I guess because discrimination wasn't ever directed toward me, I didn't notice how bad things were until my junior year of high school—otherwise known as the year that Donald Trump was elected president.

At first things were very civil. It wasn't a secret that the majority of my school was Republican and supported Trump, so if you had differing political views, you were automatically scrutinized, which is maybe why I wasn't very vocal about mine in high school. There was a group of people at my school that were often referred to as "The Hicks." Although they shared views with the majority, they were the ones who took it a bit too far. They constantly made rude, discriminatory comments, specifically toward Hispanic students. One of my best friends is Puerto Rican and ended up being one of the many minority students that received several threats leading up to the election. I even received a couple threats. Though mainly implausible, they were threats nonetheless. The threats varied in seriousness and extremity. Some were verbal or through social media. The day after Trump won the election was one of the only days that I was scared to go to school.

Thankfully, I wasn't on the receiving end of what "The Hicks" had in store for several people of color at my school. Not only did a confederate flag appear in the parking lot attached to a giant pickup truck, it also surfaced several times in the building. I was told many times that I was going to get deported, but that was the worst that I experienced, which isn't that bad compared to what other people at my school had to go through. My best friend approached me at my locker with tears in her eyes. I was in complete shock when she showed us her locker. It was vandalized with derogatory terms, threatening phrases, and of course, it was topped off with a sign that said, "Make America Great Again." My best friend wasn't alone; a few others were also greeted by a defaced locker when they got to school that morning. We immediately reported the incident, however, nothing was really done because there were so many people involved, and my school didn't want any more negative publicity than it already had. That was the first time I realized how big an issue racism was in my school. A group of kids at my school were openly racist, and our school did nothing about it. This angered me more than anything had in a while. I didn't know what to do or how to help, but I knew then that something needed to change.

Knowing that these events have occurred makes us realize that change is necessary in order to fix the discrimination that occurs in schools. While we know that it cannot be completely fixed, a plan of action would be to create more education about what exactly discrimination is and how it affects the majority of our population. Treating everyone as equals is very important, especially because adolescents are still developing, and it will help shape their views in general. This is a constant problem within society that needs to be addressed and advanced.

Gabrielle Hersey
Grade School

The last time this happened, it didn't end like this.
But then again, my life had never been easy.

My problems start in second grade:
    Kely asks me if I wanna ride bikes down the cul-de-sac.
    My memory skips ahead.

    A confusing blend of blurred colors and fast motions
    as rocks are being pelted from unseen directions,
    the laughter of the kids throwing the rocks is everywhere,
    Kely's shouting profanities I've never heard,
    and Mia's tugging me up the lane,
    white shirt pressing down on the gash across my arm.

    I'll never forget the way blood looks while slowly gliding
    across skin.

In third grade:
    All I know is when he pinched me and twisted,
    with all of his strength,
    it hurt

worse than that time I fell out of the pear tree pirate ship.
Kely was there, but she refuses to tell me.

In sixth grade:
    My friends break me up with the nicest guy I've ever met.

    Then pester me to tell them who I like now,
    until I start asking out anyone who'll listen,
    just so I'll have someone other than them to sit with at lunch.
    I pretend I'm okay when every single person says no.

    Remember the way scarlet can turn into a russet stain on my
    translucent skin?

In seventh grade:
    My best friend gets her boyfriend
    to rank the group of us on our level of hotness.
    I get a zero.

In eighth grade:
    I wrap my arm around Dani's shoulders
    like I've done so many times before.

    The bite she leaves doesn't fade
    until months later
    when I've secluded myself
    in the downstairs' bathroom
    with my sisters banging on the door,
    as I press a
    knife
    into my thigh for the fifth time.

    The war I fight every single day, is harder at night
    so I call Kely and ugly cry into the receiver.

    But I'm here.
    And I'm alive.

Djoumana Hadil Boughazi

Being in middle school and high school is a crucial part in the process of building of our personalities. It is around that time when we start figuring out who we are, what we want, and use it all to build our character, to become tomorrow's leaders. It all comes through the teachers and the curriculum. However, I would say that my middle school and high school education did not really support or have any significant contribution to building up my role as a leader in civil society. Most of my teachers were curriculum oriented and only focused on delivering the lessons in hand. They were mostly concerned in finishing the designated goals, a reality that has not changed for decades.

I think that the educational system itself is trapped in its comfort zone because school teachers and administrators do not think outside the box. This fact can be attributed to many reasons. Given the age gap, they cannot relate to students. They create schools which do not take into account students' opinions. It is a system that is very hierarchical. It seems immune to innovation. Unfortunately, we still use the same educational system, almost the same study materials, methods, and strategies to teach every single generation, despite the obvious thinking gap and despite the vast differences between them. Thus, it becomes almost impossible for teachers to add some new materials in order to keep up with what is happening in the world. This is despite many new studies that would help students and teachers work better in class, that would allow world events to be mentioned and discussed, and that would produce an evolution in students and their way of thinking. Of course, there are private schools that are keeping up with the world and developing new methods, but not everyone in Algeria can afford it. It's not very common, especially in smaller towns like my own.

Once I reached university, I had the chance to broaden my horizon. Even though the educational system and the curriculum at the university level are not really creative either, they do include a bit more perspective when it comes to knowledge. Some of my university professors use different and creative methods when teaching, methods which have a great role in shaping my leadership capacities even more. Many of them encourage reading, debates, and critical thinking, which is a key concept in building a creative ambitious leader—to teach her/him to think for themselves and see things from different perspectives. Being in university also allowed me to participate in national and international conferences, to see and listen to other people's ideas, stories, insights and positive criticism, and to be engaged in many activities, such as university clubs, extra curriculum programs, and even exchange opportunities. All of these are still helping me, and each plays a major role in preparing me to become a leader in civil society.

I strongly believe that active classrooms with enthusiastic teachers, whether in middle school, high school, or university, are needed in order to produce a generation of leaders who are willing to make a change. And even though, as a future teacher, I have to work with the curriculum in hand, since I do not have another one, I believe all teachers should all come up with creative ideas and strategies to spread knowledge and awareness in the classroom. If the teacher is "numb," so will the students be, and that will only create passive members in society. These students will grow up to be marginalized, pessimistic adults and teenagers who would rather sit back and let life pass by instead of making a move towards something great. Properly educated students would put great pressure on those who are in power by criticizing them and finding a solution to the problems facing their countries.

Joshua Farris

On December 1st, 2014, an email changed my life. I only read the first 3 words: "Dear Josh, congratulations!" I had just received a full scholarship to the University of Virginia (UVA). To me, this scholarship was my golden ticket to one of the top universities in the nation. I had been dreaming of this day for over seven years. It was a chance for a stable life. That dream energized me enough to attend two schools as well as work at both a local McDonalds and diner throughout my high school years. I rose at 5am everyday with purpose. I collapsed every midnight, struggling to sustain the pace.

Eight months after the letter, I excitedly left home and headed to UVA.

Unfortunately, I felt out of place the moment I arrived on campus. The marble exterior and Corinthian columns felt so different than the jaded mobile homes and brick apartment complexes I was used to back home. Making friends was also difficult. I remember being asked at a party the typical questions students ask, "What's your name? What's your major? Where are you from?" There was always that one question that eventually led down a rabbit hole:

"What do your parents do?"

"Well my mom's not working right now. My step-dad is a custodian, and my dad is incarcerated." I casually sipped my water.

"Huh?"

This typically led to a series of questions that I am comfortable answering, but they are uncomfortable knowing:

"Oh wow, can I ask for what?"

"Drugs, mostly Cocaine."

"Damn that's rough. What are you drinking?"

"Water." I sip.

"Why?" with a furrowed brow.

"Because I have a lot of alcoholics in my family, and I don't want to know if I'm one."

Then they always end the same way:

"Oh okay. Ya know, you should meet a friend of mine. Let me introduce you!"

For them, my story was novel. For me, my story was normal.

I sometimes forgot that fact.

I wanted to belong, have friends, connect, but not at the expense of my roots. It's part of who I am. I grew up in a small, rural, farming community in Shawsville, Va. With only around 1,000 people, even strangers were familiar. We pride ourselves on our mutual support, whether stopping to help someone with a broken-down car or to raise money for the sudden death of a loved one, we were always there for each other. Lack of money made us resourceful and creative in how we solved our problems. We made do with what we had, and that often encouraged our creativity. I see my community in myself.

I also see bits of my family in myself. I have my mom's resilient fire. No matter what happened to us, she always found a solution. If we needed coats for winter, she asked the Salvation Army. If we needed food, she would file for food stamps and find a food pantry. If we needed heat when it was cold, she would ask a church to pay our electricity. For all her flaws, my mom taught me to be resourceful and ask for help. My mom taught me strength.

I have my dad's charisma. My dad will talk to anyone. He makes even strangers seem like long-lost friends. For all his flaws, my dad is often generous. My dad used to work as a tractor trailer driver. When I went with him on trips, we often encountered beggars. Even if my dad didn't have a lot of money, he always bought them a meal. Through my dad, my blood courses with kindness, charisma, and creativity.

These roots helped me survive. In the ideal environment, my roots would allow me to thrive.

Soon after arriving at UVA, after all these opening conversations, I then began to search for a community that shared my roots. I found a student group named United for Undergraduate Socio-economic Diversity (UFUSED) which had an upcoming meeting. I remember dashing through a storm to attend. Drenched from head to toe, I arrived and found a classroom with about five students, two being the leaders. They did not discuss much, and the meeting ended shortly after. There were no more meetings. There was no community to unite.

Fortunately, I found solace in the dining hall workers. We often had similar roots. It wasn't always sufficient since I didn't see them all the time, but I always had someone to talk to during meals. My peers and professors may not get me, but they did.

Also, life in college with a full scholarship was not quite the ticket out of poverty I expected. In reality, I was stuck in between two worlds. Managing school and home was difficult. My family constantly kept suffering, and I kept supporting. I was used to handling my home life on my own. They called. I would respond:

They Call: The police invade at night, prohibit my mom from leaving to go to work. She was fired. They arrest my brother.

I Respond: I give money for rent until she finds work and to my brother for toiletries and food while in jail. Then I finish and turn in my paper.

They Call: My 13-year-old brother gets sick. He won't wake up. My step-dad misses work to take him to the hospital. He's fired.

I Respond: I pay for the electricity bill and for groceries while he finds work. Then I walk into my first class of the day.

They Call: The landlord learns of the police raid, ends our lease, and my grandma's house burns down.

I Respond: I raise $2,000 with a GoFundMe and then head to my part-time job.

Their suffering motivated me to work harder and achieve more. For me, there was more at stake than the grade. I had to learn to not only support them, but to advocate for myself at UVA as well as for those in similar situations. For instance, late one night, I was working on an assignment due at 8am the next morning. My dad called me from jail, wanting help. By the end of the call, it was 11:30pm. I had had too many late nights already. I finally relented and I emailed my professor, disclosing a bit of my life and, for the first time in college, I requested an extension. Thankfully he granted it. I discovered that asking for help is challenging, but it can be rewarding as well.

Sometimes, asking for help isn't enough. You have to fight for what you need. I remember being told one March that the Financial Aid Office (SFS) received my mountain of yearly required paperwork. August came around; classes began, and still no scholarship disbursement. "It's okay. It's late most semesters. Just be patient." I told myself. Until the registrar emailed me:

"You have 3 days to pay your tuition before being unenrolled."

ALL of my required classes were full. Once unenrolled, I wouldn't get back in. SFS said I didn't complete all of my documents. After showing them the confirmation from the previous semester, they said my request would require 1-2 weeks to process, as my case would have to wait in line. I didn't have that kind of time.

Fortunately, I remembered a talk the Dean of Students gave the previous semester. Dean Groves mentioned he starts his day at 7am by responding to emails. I emailed him that night and attached the email confirmation from March. I did nothing wrong, and while being at UVA was isolating, I was not throwing away my only opportunity for something more in life. The next morning, he sent it to the finance director and my financial aid was 'magically' processed. Magic requires privileged knowledge and connections. Many of us hardly understand our financial aid, let alone how to reach a dean. It was a lesson I had to learn.

I continued in my journey at UVA thinking I was the only one that encountered these issues. Then one March, I discovered a conference occurring in Washington D.C. for First-Generation and Low-Income (FGLI) college students. It was called AL1GN (Alliance for Low Income & First-Generation Narrative). Intrigued, I registered and attended. It changed my life. There I learned that I was not the only one that encountered the issues I faced. I found a community that could relate to my struggles.

I became so hopeful that I brought the conference to UVA. I knew I wanted to create a change before I graduated, and this conference was that change. The conference was my search for a community, for a place to belong. I wanted administrators to pay attention to us and know we were here. We needed their help. It's too soon to know if the conference created that change, and since I'm graduating and leaving this community, I may never know.

As I leave, I can only wish for the day when we have a community to share our experiences and the resources we have. One day, perhaps we'll have more advocates to demand for the resources we need. Maybe there will be collaboration between students, faculty, and administrators at all levels. I believe our unique traits do have value to the university: We have the discipline to get what we need. We persist in the face of struggle. We create solutions others think are improbable. Our own struggles endow us with empathy and kindness for the struggles of others. We need to feel valued to express them. Our roots ensure we survive. With support, our roots allow us to thrive.

As I end my four years here at UVA, I reflect on my experiences. I've gotten a great education, and I intend to use it. I lament not having a community for those that have similar backgrounds to my own. I think about the many that don't arrive to the finish line. I know my struggles are not my own, and I question how I somehow managed to navigate the struggles I've endured.

Our narratives are powerful, so let's share them to empower both ourselves and others to create change. With us, UVA is both a great and good university. Let's call on UVA for a seat at the table, and let's see if they respond.

Claire Song
Dear Younger Self,

Jimin, how are you feeling today? It's been awhile since I've talked to you, and I'm finally here, a place you could have never imagined: a day before my graduation at University of Virginia—over 2000 miles away from you.

I have been thinking a lot about you lately—about hundreds of questions you never got to ask our parents about moving into another country, how odd it was to move from a large city in Korea where everyone spoke the language of our family and friends, to a small parched land in Arizona that often hit three-digit zone temperature during summer. You watched our dad wearing a t-shirt and casual pants instead of a suit at the breakfast table. I saw our mother no longer playing a piano or humming her favorite lines of waltzes of Chopin. The house was silent all day. It wasn't until the night when she came home from work, the house was soon filled with the smell of steamed rice and the sound of Korean TV shows. Our lives were changing.

During our childhood, I never really thought about our parents' lives in El Centro, how small their world must have seemed, never extending beyond their home and their convenience store. Their one day was like the next. I translated the conversations from the same customers who come for house supplies, for morning snacks, and for afternoon soft drinks and candies. There was so little in this rural town that gave them pleasure. We struggled to find home in an agricultural town located 20 minutes across from the Mexican border. The town may be filled with minorities, but we were never a part of it, for not being able to fully speak Spanish nor English.

I often questioned their happiness, if all of this—leaving our grandparents and friends to live among strangers who can never fully understand our culture and language—was worth it. For the millionth time, our mother would say yes with a smile that softened her face. Eight years ahead of you now, the answer still has not changed.

I'm not exactly sure if I can give you the same answer, though. It was extremely difficult to see our parents give up on their lives in Korea, their family, friends, and careers. I watched them work morning to night, 7 days a week at a convenience stores because their college degrees in Korea did not transfer over to the US. I heard our dad dealing with his guilt of leaving his mother alone in Korea. I felt the wave of shame whenever our mom was treated with a condescending tone from the people outside of our home—grocery stores, banks, real estates, my school and sometimes, in our convenience store—due to her halting English.

For our parents, the American education meant a ladder outside of the well, like the ones they've used to escape from the poverty of their small rural towns in Andong, Korea. They knew what it was like to have their worlds turned upside down when they made their ways to a big city in Seoul. Sitting on a desk in a classroom one year after another, going from school to after schools and tutors, and studying 13 different subjects from morning until they went to bed. These were inevitable fates that my brother and I would have to face if we grew up in Seoul. When they traveled across the countries for their work, they saw there was a whole world out there. So instead, they took a leap. Their love, their tenderness, their visions, they gave to us.

For you, the American education meant a justification for your parents sacrifices. It was a means for you to defend your own happiness in your adopted country, for being the only one who found friends, community and home. The contrast was evident; your life was constantly changing, while your parents' lives seemed to be put on pause. The reason for your family's migration caused you a lot of agitation. At school you began to learn about Korea in English, written and taught by the foreigners. The stories of Korea seemed wrong, skewed and tailored to fit into the American textbook. At the same time, you were playing, learning and growing in the language of your neighbors. You were a part of everything, but never a full part of one. Whenever I stepped outside of my family: school, friends' houses, towns beyond El Centro, I was a foreigner, a shy Asian girl. Whenever I stepped inside of my family, I was an American who began to mix English words into Korean sentences.

We were the typical model-minority. We did well in school, graduating at the top of the class. We wanted to make our parents proud, to prove that their relentless hours at the store were all worth it. In the process, we lost our time to celebrate Lunar New Years and Chuseok, to go on family vacations and to talk about things that bring us joy. There is a huge empty space in our family photo album during my middle and high school years. We spent the majority of our time memorizing vocabularies to get used to the academic language written in textbooks and exams. We wrote several essays, analyzing the meaning of literature when we could barely comprehend the microaggression that surrounded us in our day to day lives. The passing experiences of racism in and out of school and the absence of parental rolls due to their work and language barrier robbed a lot of joys in our lives, but we tolerated. Because we thought this won't happen again, we are in college only once. It was a golden ticket to success and happiness.

We took up another identity in college, named Claire. You continued to make your parents proud, attending a prestigious college at University of Virginia with a full ride scholarship. Claire seemed to fit in better than

Jimin in a top tier college that was ranked a top 3 public school in the U.S.. People treated Claire better than they did with Jimin, more like a peer than a guest. For Claire, though, the meaning of the American education has changed a lot. You see, the education you thought of was solely based on the results: the grades, the college acceptance, the degree, leading to a career that will take care of you and our parents. I thought the education our parents' thought of was well-intended, yet naïve. I thought for them, thought having a degree would guarantee a life better than theirs; comfortable, fulfilling, and happier. But we barely knew the system of American education; about why you had to score higher than non-Asians to have a chance to get into the same exact college; about the gap of enrichment experiences even between first, second, and third generation Asian Americans who speak English, the language of academia within their household; about the impact of socioeconomic background on the difficulty of finding a community even after getting accepted to your reach school.

College was a promised land where I thought I would regain all the joy I had been robbed of during my transition into America. I thought I would fit right in since UVA had a larger Asian American population than my hometown. I thought I would automatically be more confident for attending college. I came into UVA being so sure that I would study sciences to be in the health care field because that was the most noble and respectable job I knew at the moment. I thought having a degree, a monetary stability and a display of wealth, meant that people would stop mistreating my parents for their skin tone and halting English.

Instead, I gained the vision to realize the disparity in accessibility of education, healthcare, and beyond between individuals with different racial and socioeconomic backgrounds. I learned problems within the system of education and healthcare, rather than in myself for not being smart or wealthy enough. I discovered my desire to use my privilege as a college graduate to connect people and to build a community rather than to reduce myself to fit into one.

Here's one thing I want to tell you: don't limit your vision simply to the end goals. It's not necessarily the name of your college nor the degree with a special distinction that will satisfy your soul. Rather, it's the knowledge and the action you take upon the desire. For the past year, I have been discovering my interests in various fields that I would have never known existed; I want to discover a way to improve the modes of communication by researching in speech-language pathology and dentistry. I want to come back to school to learn more about sociolinguistics and its impact on our social constructs. I want to mentor Asian and Asian American students to help their transitions, often at their vulnerable moments. I want to eliminate the fears of low-income families to reach out to their health care providers and build a community where they can seek both physical and psychological wellness. And I want to give my parents the education that they deserve and to allow them to gain the benefit of that education, freedom: the ability to read signs and to travel alone, the strength to combat racism, and the courage to find a community.

It's this desire to act, powered by the knowledge that you gain from education. And in a sense, this is the exact privilege and freedom our parents wished upon us.

It's surreal to be writing this to you as I am about to finish up my undergraduate degree just in 4 weeks. I feel a vague twinge in my heart every time I think of you. You thought you would never make it out of that small town. I've been in your shoes, and I would never wish that pain of transition on anyone. The teenage years are hard-enough time as it is, and now you've got to learn a new language to an academic level, a culture to make friends, and a strength to parent yourself. There is only one way out of the pain, though it's not for the easy or faint of heart: learn, move a muscle, change a thought. When you feel like you don't belong to any community, know that you have the ability to make one.

Love,
Claire

Taylor Blackley

I feel that while our current educational model is sometimes fostering some of the skills necessary for engaging positively in civil society, it is often neglecting others. There are several issues within academia which make it inaccessible and out of touch. Sometimes it seems as though education, at a public and private level, is geared toward a certain type of student and outcome and limited by this assumption. Also, a lot of stories are left out of public education. Why is it that I am only now learning the histories behind some of the bitter racial divides that exist in US society? These stories should be part of more than just a liberal arts education. To engage students in a way to foster their positive involvement in civil society, these issues must be introduced in a sensitive, productive way. People need to learn how to discuss topics that are controversial in a manner that is respectful and just.

Jayden Williams

Mel's Café is my escape from college. Physically, since it is off grounds [away from the University of Virginia], but mentally too. I can enter and look around and find familiar smiling faces. The atmosphere in Mel's is equivalent to a black barber shop. You can go there and feel accepted and feel like you're a part of the community. Since Mel's Café is so historic, when you are there, you feel as if you are a part of the history. Charlottesville has had a lot of renovations but Mel's has always stayed the same. One of the most devastating "renovations" ("urban renewal") in Charlottesville's history was of Vinegar Hill. Mel himself used to live there, and the café he created resembles that feeling of an old, thriving black community.

I tell this story to make the following point: Since I was admitted to the University of Virginia, I was initially under the impression that my previous education had pointed me in the direction of succeeding in life. As an African American, I am learning I have not been exposed to my history in this country to the same extent of white Americans. As a result, I feel like the education system has prohibited me from creating accurate insight about the world around me. Recently, there have been times where I have been exposed to African American history through peers or the internet. I have wondered how these events never been mentioned before in classes? One example is Vinegar Hill in Charlottesville Virginia mentioned above. Vinegar Hill was a thriving black community within the segregated city. It contained a school, houses, and many flourishing businesses. The white part of the city was infuriated that more people were going to the black-owned businesses for goods instead of white-owned businesses. So, in retaliation, they destroyed the community based off of an "Urban Renewal" initiative which destroyed around 30 black-owned businesses and forced approximately 140 families to relocate, the majority of which were African Americans. (See Smith, https://timeline.com/charlottesville-vinegar-hill-demolished-ba27b6ea69e1.

I learned about this history as I was sitting in class about to leave. My teacher was telling the class that she had to leave early to go to an event at the African-American Heritage Center at the Jefferson School, where they have an exhibition of images of Vinegar Hill before residents were forcibly displaced. This resulted in many confused faces. I immediately felt embarrassed. Not only because of my lack of knowledge about Vinegar Hill, but because I have lived my whole life no further than 40 miles away from the city. Later that week, I was eating at Mel's Café, and I was thinking about the tragedy that occurred. The repeating question I asked myself was, "How could I have never heard of this?" After thinking about all of the other countless local and less important historical facts I know, I realized that it's not my fault for being so clueless. It's the fault of my previous schooling and its inadequate curriculum. It seems as if, when it comes to African American history, important events such Vinegar Hill slip through the cracks. It's blinding myself and others from being able to truly see the world. I used to walk into Mel's and only think about the great food and inviting culture, but now, I gratefully see the bigger picture that encompasses the journey this building and community has gone through. If only students were taught an equal curriculum, then would we see less of these unexpected moments where we feel as if we have been robbed of the truth.

Khadidja Khellid

In Algeria, enrollment in education has long been a privilege enjoyed by men, who have historically had higher rates of enrollment, higher literacy rates as adults, higher diplomas obtained, higher levels of education by age, and so on. Years after independence, the level of education has changed. Free and compulsory education for children up to 16 years old did not only prove to be enough to provide basic education for all children, but once they entered the school system, girls were also found to be more likely to take full advantage of their education and continue their studies into high school and university. Since the new millennium, this phenomenon has become increasingly evident in the records of the Ministry of Education and the National Office of Statistics. This imbalance between men and women in terms of educational achievements is now clearly tipped in favor of women. In high school and university, the graduation rate for girls far exceeds that of boys, which has a strong relation with the movement of Algeria toward a more open network of civic participation. The Algerian woman had always proved herself to an active element in civic society and, now, she is proving herself to be a strong leader in society. While I will not argue that Algeria is a perfect society, I will try to show the progress women have made and highlight the important work to be done.

Algerian woman as a Highly Educated Element in Society
As is the case with other patriarchal entities in the region, Algerian society was a world dominated by men, a world where a woman had an inferior status from birth to death. In the aftermath of the Independence struggle, after 132 years of French rule, the state had found itself existing within the ruins of the colonial system. The vast majority of the population was illiterate. According to the 1966 Censuses (ONS, 2011), 75% of people aged 10 and over could neither read nor write. This percentage was 85% for women compared to 62% for men (1). The government actively worked to change this situation. By the 2000s, Algeria succeeded in reaching some of these objectives. The government policy that has undoubtedly been the most important was universal access to education, which was made compulsory and free for

children between the ages of 6 and 16. This has been most beneficial to the improvement of the status of women. Girls now received the same primary education as boys and then went on to succeed at universities. (Figure 1). As a result, some women were able to leverage this new status to maintain a newly found independence and became actively involved in the development of the new state.

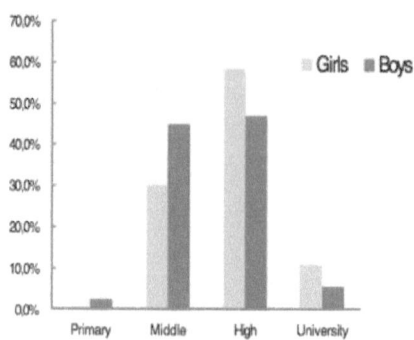

Figure 1: Proportions of unmarried persons aged 15-19 attending school in 2002, by level of education   (2)

This can be seen in the history of women within my own family; myself, my mother, and my grandmother, three generations of women who have experienced the educational system in Algeria. For instance, my grandmother is 76 years old. She did not get any significant educational access. She passed through part of the colonial education system, but since that time until today, she is an example of a house woman (Figure 2) .

Figure 2: The Grandmother

My mom was born in 1963, a year after the national independence. Although the conditions in Algeria were poor at that time, my mom was one of the few girls in my hometown to attend school. When she did not pass her Baccalaureate exam, she was allowed to attend other institutions. Indeed, she continued her study at a Professional Formation Institute (Figure 3).

Figure 3: My mom in the Professional Formation Institute 198

Yet, when she entered the workforce, social norms constrained women when choosing professions. Due to this, many female professionals ended up working in fields such as nursing and education, which were considered more socially acceptable and gender appropriate. As my mom completed her studies, she became a teacher in a vocational formation centre (a centre for those who could not join college). After 32 years as a teacher, she took her retirement in 2019.

Figure 4: My mom's first days at work 1986(the right) / My mom's retirement 2019(the left).

By 2005, when I started school at the age of 6 years old, educational access had changed significantly. As with any Algerian child, I started my educational process in primary school in 2005 at the age of six. In the fifth year of primary school, each pupil has to pass a national exam BEP (Examen du Brevet d'enseignement Primaire/ Examination of the Primary Teaching Certificate). Each pupil that receives at least 5 out of 10 is allowed to move up to middle school. I received an 8, which was an unprecedented success for a girl in my family.

Middle school in Algeria lasts for 4 years. From 2010 to 2014, I was studying hard and as a result getting good grades. In the fourth year of middle school, each student should pass another national exam called BEM (Examen du Brevet d'enseignement Moyen/Examination of the Middle Teaching Certificate). Any student who gets at least 10 out of 20 is allowed to move to high school. I got 16 out of 20. I then went on to high school. In the third year of high school, each student should pass another national exam called the Baccalaureate exam (BAC). To be able to get an acceptance to college, students need to get a GPA equal or above 10/20. I passed my BAC exam in 2017 and I got 14 out of 20 (Figure 5).

Figure 5: My last days in high school with my friends and my best teacher 2017

Passing all these 12 years in studying and moving from one phase to another is something that's possible for any Algerian student. The only difference is in getting good grades. Getting 14 out of 20 in my

BAC exam allowed me to have more options in choosing what I would study in college. The higher your score, the more options available in college. My success allowed me to attend The Teacher Education Institute, which is considered by most Algerians as better than any normal university. Here I'm getting prepared to be an English teacher of high school. My study lasts for 5 years, which means now that I have 3 more years to finish my studies.

Yet, social expectations seem to have changed only slightly over time. Looking back to the recent ten years, the Algerian woman has become free in choosing her job regardless of the traditions of society. The Algerian woman today is not only defying man and society, she is also challenging herself. Yet, she is struggling to balance work and home life because her new position as a female worker has not changed her traditional responsibilities toward her home, husband, and children. What is noticeable is that Algerian women have always shown their capacities and willingness to be professional at work while at the same time be there for her home.

Figure 6: My presentation in Mr.Hachelaf's session December 2018

Algerian woman as a highly civically engaged element in society
What is next after a woman has completed all of the tasks of society, the degree is earned, the career has been successful, the relationships are established? What is the future of these educated women? I believe the focus will be on identifying her interests outside of her work and family requirements. This is an important step in her identifying opportunities for civic engagement, "the ways in which citizens participate in the life of a community in order to improve conditions for others" (3).

From personal experience, I can state that there were opportunities for me to be more active and more civically-engaged as a student in college. I participated in different activities and events. I was appointed as the Deputy Secretary General of a cultural club in our college. I participated in organizing some workshops dealing with reading and health. I organized some volunteering campaigns for patients. I also participated in making the first street bookshop in my hometown (Figure 7). More than that, I am working with one of our Twiza members, Chiraz, to make free summer classes to teach English for primary school pupils to change French culture with English.

Figure 07 My participations in different events.

In fact, the National Assessment of Educational Progress Civics test results indicate that girls perform as well as, if not better than, boys on civic knowledge tests (4). Today's Algerian woman, as all the world's women, is moving ahead of her male counterparts on many indicators of civic engagement, including volunteering, membership in community associations, and voting. What is evident is that women are more likely to engage in grassroots community action through volunteering and through community-based organizations. Women also show a stronger desire to help those who are in need than men. For instance, in my hometown, a lot of Voluntary Charitable Associations are based on the female presence. In Ramadan, the ninth month of the Muslim year during which Muslims fast from dawn to sunset, Algerian women, especially the youngest, are competing in participating in "Mercy Restaurants" that are known for providing food for wayfarers and workers who cannot go home.

Yet, women's civic participation is not only limited to kitchens. We can also notice that young women are involved in all aspects of civic society, from being active in their society by leading specific associations of different purposes (education, social training, sports, music, and so on), to moving forward in participating in international events where they find themselves representing their country and their culture. For instance, women are active in "Learn In," an association which is representative of an international foundation accredited by the British Council in Algeria which is led by an activist woman, Ms.L.Anissa, as well as representing Algeria in the international forums like the debating competitions that have taken place in Qatar.

Algerian women are also trying to be closer to politics, although their presence in this field is lower than men. Still, there are examples where a young woman who gets involved in the community receives support, encouragement, and mentoring to become a political leader who can change laws, policies, or systems to benefit more people. As I am present in many civic events, I am present in political matters. In the Parliament elections of 2017, I was an organizer of an election campaign for one of the candidates in my hometown.

There is no better example of women's political engagement than the tumult that is happening today in Algeria with women often in the frontlines. She is protesting hand in hand with men to change the conditions of the country as they wish it to be. Her presence is not only direct but it can be also indirect, depending on each one's capacities and abilities. She is present even in the simplest ways, either with preparing sweets and cakes for demonstrators, or distributing water to them from balconies, or even opening the doors of her house to the press in order to cover the events.

And as with any Algerian woman, I'm always present.

Figure 8: Algerian woman in today's protests

References:
(1).Office National des Statistique (ONS,2011)/Journal of Education & Social Policy Vol. 5, No. 2, June 2018
(2). Journal of Education & Social Policy (year) Vol. 5, No. 2, June 2018 doi:10.30845/jesp.v5n2p10/ page 16
(3). The Center for Information & Research on Civic Learning and Engagement

Shelby Wayment

I think that throughout my experience with higher education, I have been taught to question my surrounding world, and in doing so, I have learned the skills necessary to be engaged in civil society. I have even learned the necessary skills to protest against policies and actions that I disagree with—for example, my roommate and I organized a silent protest on the steps of the Utah State Capitol our freshman year.

I believe some of these skills that I have gained come through the respective majors and minors I have chosen. The combination of these classes created a unique combination of classes/skills for me where I have learned more about our government processes and how to effectively speak up, while the rest of my classes have taught me to challenge and question our surrounding world. I believe all of these contribute to an ability to positively contribute to civil society. I believe that you should have the ability to question the world around you, but also the knowledge to understand how to challenge your surrounding world. These are skills that I do not believe I would have if it had not been for my experience in higher education.

However, while my experience has fostered these skills successfully, I think that our education model as a whole is largely inaccessible. Tuition costs are high, and with rising costs of living while wages continue to basically stagnate, college is largely inaccessible to much of our population. I think our education model could be used to successfully foster these skills, but as it currently works, I think it only provides these skills to a select privileged few.

Hachemi Chaima

I am already familiar with terms like leadership and leaders. I grew up listening to stories about leaders. I also have my father as a vivid example of a leader. Thus, I can tell that my teachers in middle school did their best. For instance, my teacher, Bedarnia Mbarka comes to mind. She is a real example of a leader. She tries to awaken the leaders inside of us, but not by lecturing or dictating ideas and tips.

She is that type of leader who asks us to observe and work with her. In fact, all my teachers wanted to shape good citizens. They always helped me and encourage me to speak in public. In addition, they used to make me work in groups. They wanted me to participate, to lead, and to follow. I remember all of what they used to say and all of what they used to do. They were united and worked together. They wanted me see the model in front of me. They showed me what is meant by "us." At that time, I did not realize that because I was not that aware of what they were doing or saying. Today, whenever I read something about leadership—be it an article about its characteristics, activities, things to be said or done, or a book—I just smile to know that once upon a time, I had great teachers.

Concluding Thoughts

Bouchra Rahmouni
I just want to add that, for me as a future teacher, I will work on giving my students the chance to think the way they want and express themselves freely because my mission is going to be guiding them and not imposing my own thoughts or those programmed lessons on their minds. I believe that there are some other subjects as important as math or science to teach people out there, including something my teacher, Professor Hachelaf once mentioned which is treating students as citizens and not future citizens. Here, for example, speaking classes can be organized in which teachers listen to everyone's thoughts and opinions, because knowing from where they are coming from leads to a better result concerning preparing them to be leaders and good citizens.

2 CIVIL SOCIETY AND INJUSTICE

Justice shall prevail / The love of a patriot
Mahieddine Ouafi

Independence feels senseless;
Everything after was nefarious. Glorious,
Is our country, but shrouded in darkness;
We lost sight, but we were not oblivious.

A proud patriot with no copper of his own;
Love and Honor are his only wealth.
Only stones, while corruption sits on a throne.
Alive, but despair shattered his health.

A mellifluous tone chanted in his head;
Voiceless sounds, yet eloquent.
Unleashing his courage and erasing his dread.
To injustice, he shall not stay obedient.

The proud man walked like a bart.
With millions of his compatriots, he marched.
A new revolution was meant to start
To cleanse the flag and glory they had smirched.

The patriots roared fearlessly at their foes.
Soon, corruption shall withdraw and depart,
Because very little did they know:
Determination dwells in the patriots' hearts.

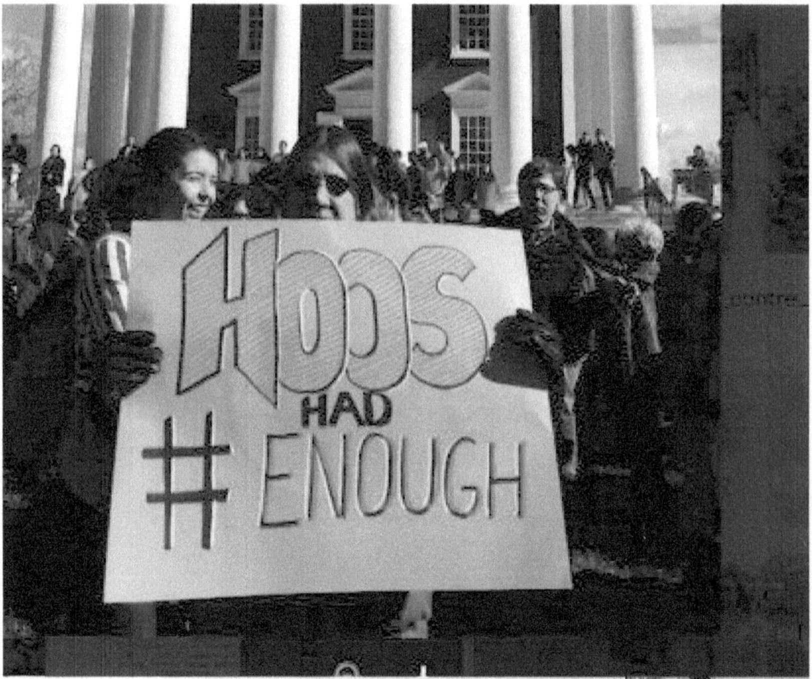
HOOS
HAD
#ENOUGH

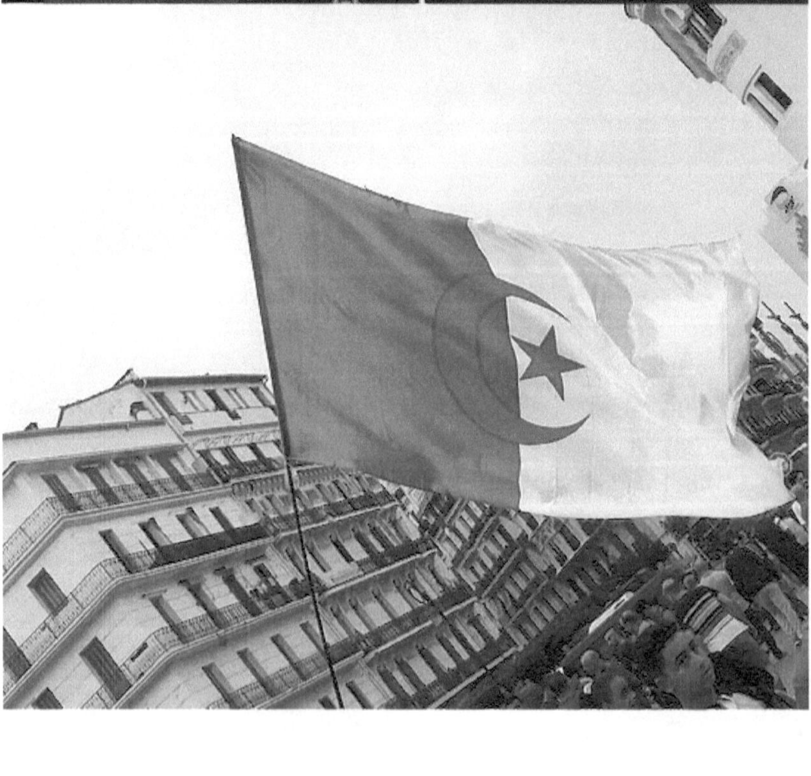

Dialogue

Chaima Hachemi

Before talking about the civic society, any society should have the right to a civic space that allows an individual to talk on behalf of their people.

Samantha Owens

I think the basis for civil society should be that it is inclusive. There must be spaces for all within civil society in order for it to be a well-functioning space. I think it's important that people have open dialogue that crosses boundaries of gender, race, sexuality, and ethnicity.

There are many human rights that I think everyone should be able to claim. Obviously, everyone should have the right to clean water, shelter, and all the other basic necessities of life. Some other human rights I strongly believe everyone should be able to claim include the right to education, the right to actively participate in government, the right to free speech, the right to freedom of religious and ethnic practices, and the right to autonomy of one's own body. I believe that everyone should be able to claim these rights because oppression and force are not conducive to progress. The best ideas, leaders, and relationships grow from freedom, at least in my opinion.

Nadjet Boucherit

As far as I can see, a civic society should be the community of principles ,values, virtue, and ethics that call for goodness away from the values of vices, antagonism, and hatred. They should be in harmony with the principles and values of all heavenly religions. All human beings are born free and equal and should be treated the same way. Everyone can claim their rights regardless of language, religion, and race, as well as the right to recognition as a person before the law, the right to public hearing, the right to privacy, and the right to asylum.

Allaoua Hisham Khalil

I agree with almost everything mentioned; however, I think most of what you have said is already established. I think you have taken the first step in this conversation, and the second step would be refuting arguments of those who hold the other point of view, as I suppose that none of us here disagrees with any of what you have said. Oppression and force were always the reason dictatorships fell not long after their rise. The main reason was that such societies never caught up to how the world has progressed or caught up to the fact the world respects human rights and was learning to be inclusive.

Aissa Seddiki

"Preaching without taking serious and practical steps is merely another maze designed for people to waste their efforts on the wrong channel." All that you said is true, yet it does not manifest in the real world.

Najwa Harizi

#equity, #peace, #integrity, #reciprocal_respect and #freedom. It is commonly acknowledged that "actions speak louder than words," and this is totally true. In this sense, civilians must not only recognize certain values and principles, but also work to apply them. As such, civic societies must stand upon sound philosophies and policies. They should be well-oriented and directed by an efficient organization as well as effective conventions and traditions. Civilians should share common responsibilities and basic rights. Such rights involve the right for a decent life with an access to good education, medical care, and other public services. The public should also have religious and political freedoms: the right to freely practicing religious rites as well as the right to vote.

Furthermore, I think #security is above all the most substantial human right, along with human recognition, respect, and equality. Men, women, children, the youth, and the elderly all have the right to enjoy a peaceful and safe life with no wars, threats, or assaults. As human beings, people in global communities merit respect and equal treatment without prejudice or discrimination in terms of skin color, race, gender, or religion. Earning such vital rights, I believe, leads to civilians accomplishing their duties with both excellence and pleasure, leading in turn to a flourishing society. All in all, I think the basis for strong civic societies interconnects with human rights and duties. It is more or less an interactive and complementary relationship.

Aissa Seddikki

Can we as citizens achieve such ideal society? I do not know why I am the only one who senses the world in black and white. Great words! High optimism. Congrats.

Najwa Harizi

Surely, we cannot reach the perfect image of a society, but what I wrote is normally the natural, ordinary case. Still, I don't know why such basic merits can't be adopted by universal communities and why such rights seem out of sight.

Madhu Napa

A civic society is a collection of thoughts and ideas expressed by a community and is somehow unified through some underlying commonality between the members of said society. These ideas are ideally expressed without fear of how they will be received by others. Instead, the people should work together to integrate each other's opinions in a way that can better serve the environment that they are in. The unifying factors can be nationality, beliefs, or even proximity. A good civil society should have nestled unifying factors, so that more diverse ideas can emerge from the community. The more varied the background, the better the overall picture is of the issue at hand. For example, if the only common feature between members of a society is the fact that they all like ice cream, then when deciding what flavors to sell in the ice cream shop, it will be harder for the community to decide. But, if the society has some members who like chocolate ice cream, and some who like vanilla, then there is a narrower and streamlined approach to the ice cream shop dilemma.

Human rights are basic rights that stem from necessities in life. Humans have the ability to formulate opinions, so they should be able to express them without prejudice. At the bare minimum, basic heath rights, like clinics or emergency rooms, should be a given, so that the members of society can stay healthy. Access to food, water, and shelter should also be a given, because without these things, it would be very difficult to survive. The ability to get an education should also be available to people, if not then at least to a certain level, because humans are naturally curious and would benefit from feeding our brains with knowledge. It is with human rights that a society is at its peak.

Aissa Seddikki
It's been such a great time spent reading these posts, yet it seems that I am not in the same basket you're in.

First of all, all that I am going to say is only valid to be applied to Arabic societies, for I have never had an experience out of the Arab context. "Make your dog hungry, it follows you."

This statement was made by one of the biggest and most influential politicians in Algeria. Through it, we can honestly and courageously raise a number of questions. For example, are we really enjoying the free will to express our collective interests? Here, of course, I mean clearly whether these on-going demonstrations in Algeria (2019) are truly run by the pure will of the people, or if it is a game being played again and again by other players that want to add their decoration to the current scene.

As a big fan of the conspiracy theory, I strongly believe that no single individual within an Arab social fabric can impose him/herself over the will of those at the top of the power hierarchy. Moreover, nor can he/she claim different rights other than the essential basic ones. "Essential basic ones," here, means the right to safe sanctuary, clean air/water, school, and speech freedom. Hence, I cannot hide my deep concern that someday we will be obliged to put meter above our shoulders to

count how much air we breathe, so that we pay later.
All in all, civic society is merely the biggest lie made by politicians for keeping the audience competing one against the other and forgetting about their legitimate right to choose who leads them as a servant more than a president. We are just controlled by the massive censorship that surrounds us each moment we rise up to claim certain needs—not even rights!

I wish my humble words would be clear.

Meredith Gallagher

Aissa, I cannot claim to know what your pessimism in the system feels like or the experiences that led to its development; I do recognize it. American politicians are also well-versed in tactics that leave poor and middle-class people at odds to keep them distracted. Some even say that the idea of the "American Dream" is the basis of crime because people either become disillusioned when they realize how unfair the system is to them, or instead, some are so desperate to achieve that dream that they try whatever possible to reach it. People I know bought into the rhetoric, always complaining about other people taking handouts and abusing the system, but they themselves had worked hard and got nothing for it. In reality, they were only a tiny bit above those people they were convinced were hurting them. They could actually have benefitted from some of those programs like affordable health care, education financial aid, etc., but they were so caught up being angry that they missed out. So, I totally get how it can be so disheartening and how a person can feel so useless they become pessimistic and distrustful without any hope of change.

Aissa Seddikki

That's true, but our Algerian policy is so different. Politicians play within a paradoxical context.

Meredith Gallagher

I agree that no society is born perfect. I think that is a good way to describe that current imperfection isn't a reason to give up; it is a reason to keep going. If we look at something like the UN's Universal Declaration of Human Rights, it might seem out of reach, but as long as communities or countries continue to strive to improve themselves attain rights for their people, there is something to applaud.

Chaima Hachemi
Yeah, this is the point to be made.

Further Engagement

Chiraz Retimi
All credit goes to my religion, "Islam," to forming who I am today—the independent, the understanding, and the well-spoken person. These are all characters of a civic leader. Islam has raised a sense of responsibility in me. No one is to be blamed for a mistake I have made. The Quran says, "And no bearer of burdens shall be made to bear another's burden." It taught me that all humans are equal. In his farewell speech, our prophet Mohammed affirmed that all people are equal like the teeth of a comb and that no Arab is superior to a non-Arab. Nor is a white person superior to a black person, unless by virtue of personal integrity and moral rectitude.

So, I do not pre-judge people based on personal standards. I do not take sides when I deal with people. All humans have the same rights, and there is no difference between them. Also, accepting and respecting people's point of views is one of Islam's most essential principles. Not imposing my opinion on people and trying to be as open-minded as I can are keys to becoming a civic leader. Not shaming people's different mindsets and perspectives, as well as being receptive and gracious to any constructive criticism is crucial to form a civilized society. Abu Bakr al-Jazaeri said, when he began to speak at his inauguration, "If I do the right thing then help me and if I do wrong then put me straight. Truthfulness is a sacred trust and lying is a betrayal."

Also, it is important to be out-spoken and have no fears when it comes to telling the truth, when needed, because sometimes people's response can be intimidating, but the messenger of Allah said: "Let not any one of you belittle himself. They said: O Messenger of Allah, how can any one of us belittle himself? He said: He finds a matter concerning Allah about which he should say something, and he does not say it, so Allah (mighty and sublime be He) says to him on the Day of Resurrection: What prevented you from saying something about such-and-such and such-and-such? He says: It was out of fear of people. Then He says: Rather it is I whom you should more properly fear." This event was related by Ibn Majah with a sound chain of authorities.

In short, Islam has made me a better person through teaching me responsibility, humility , acceptance, respect, and downrightness. These are all characteristics of a civic leader.

Victoria Hunter

I remember one time during my senior year of high school, I was on the Shakespeare team with the Jean Massieu School for the Deaf and Blind. This was my second year on the team, and we were going to Southern Utah University in Cedar City, Utah for a competition. I am not deaf myself, but all the actors are deaf. The hearing people, like myself, voice what the actors are signing. At the competition, the deaf actors would be on stage while the three of us voicers were just off to the side, so we weren't seen, but we were heard. I had a great time every year and I loved all of my teammates. We all worked so hard each year to be at this competition.

We would perform for three judges. Two judges were wonderful and so sweet. One judge even cried at our performance because he enjoyed the merging of the two cultures. However, one judge was not amused with the idea of Deaf actors. I don't think this judge realized that all three of us voicers could hear her talking during our performance about how she doesn't like all the hand movements from the actors (which is how they sign their lines). She stated that Deaf people cannot be actors because no one would ever understand them. I know that she was not talking about me, but she was talking about friends with whom I have grown really close. It was not easy to sit back and let it happen.

At the end of the performances, myself and another voice actors spoke to the judge about what was said about our friends. The judge stated we could never place in this competition with deaf actors. We talked to our teacher, who spoke to the competition leadership. We received an apology but also stated they could not do anything about it. In the end, we finally got our score sheets back. The two judges who were kind had marked us incredibly high, one even gave us a perfect score. However, the other judge had marked us extremely low and most of her comments were rude towards our Deaf actors. Fortunately, with the high remarks we got from the other judges, we still placed second.

Despite this, I will never forget hearing her talk about my friends the way she did and we all know that the way she graded us was based heavily on the fact that she did not like Deaf people being actors, which is entirely unfair. Outside of talking to the people in charge of the competition, there wasn't much else for us to do. Unfortunately, this is the world in which we live. We should continue to strive to improve it, but never forget that it is full of imperfect people. We need to stick up for those who may need our help.

Perris Jones
A short story (based on too-often-true events):

It started out a normal day, Justin, my oldest went to high school, and my two youngest, Mary and Antonio got up and went to school a little later. My husband and I went to work shortly after our youngest departed; everything was as it should have been, peaceful. Now, 3 o'clock is upon us, and Justin arrives home from school. I ask what he wants to eat for dinner, and he responds saying his favorite dish, Shrimp Alfredo. Since I love to cook for my son, I agree and send him to the grocery store a couple blocks away to grab some cheese and extra pasta noodles. Once I send him on his way around 3:30 pm, I begin preparing for dinner. Soon, Mary and Antonio return and begin doing homework after a short conversation with me about their school day. Around 5pm, my husband arrives home hungry and tired as always. As I continue cooking, I begin to subconsciously think to myself that it has been a while since Justin left, but I provide myself with some reassurance, thinking that he does get side tracked, so I think nothing of it. When I finish the shrimp and sauce, I join my husband and the kids in the living room as we await the arrival of Justin from the store. As we wait, we turn on the television for the nightly news, and the headline is about a shooting that has taken place a couple blocks away from us.

Almost as if the headline was a cue, there was a knock at the door. I went to open it, and there were two officers standing with terror-stricken looks on their faces. The elder of the two officers said, "Ma'am we have some news to tell you, you may want to sit down." I could tell from the looks on their faces that my baby boy was the victim of the bullet on the TV. I dropped to the floor screaming in agony, mourning, and confusion. I refused to believe he was the victim; in my mind he couldn't be—I had just seen him, and now he's gone? No, I refuse to believe it. Justin wasn't a criminal. He never committed any injustice, but he was the victim of one. My husband picked me up and sat down on the couch, holding me as the officers explained. I found myself staring at their lips as they moved. As they talked, I found myself drifting off, thinking of my son.

Then I picked up on the words " an officer mistakenly shot him." I immediately became outraged and asked why? Why take my son's life over an accident? No answer they gave to me could have made my anger relent. They kept saying that he appeared to be one of the guys that they were after for drug charges, and that when they tried to pull over to confront him, he ran, so they thought he was guilty and shot him. But I knew that wasn't the reason. I knew they shot him because of the color of his skin. Therefore, I asked one question,"If he was a white man and he ran, would you have shot him or would you have yelled 'Stop' and chased him down?" The officer responded, "I would have yelled 'Stop' and ran after him." At that point I asked the officers to leave my house, as I saw that the color of someone's skin speaks louder than that of the colors that lie within.

A true story:

Vanessa German, an artist from Pittsburgh, has a piece of artwork that portrays a violin on top of a boy's head among other objects. In this piece, she drew inspiration from a young man that happened to be her friend, who was taking a walk from his house to the corner store only a few blocks away when his life was changed. He was a queer African American who had an extreme gift with the violin. His parents spent the majority of their earnings to send him to a private school in which his talents could flourish. On his way back from the store, police officers, not on duty, claimed to have viewed him as a suspect they had been attempting to find. They started running after him, and as a gay, black teenager in the hood seeing people chasing you, of course, he ran. When he was caught, they beat him to the point that it crippled him. He was so badly beaten that even when he recovered, he could no longer play the violin. Vanessa German puts the violin on the head in this art piece as a statement to say, if you saw the rainbow of attributes and the personality that was inside him, the beautiful array of talents he had, would they have beaten that person? She ventures on to say "No," to which I agree. This country has a history of judging a person on the color of their skin rather than the contents of that which lies within. Especially in the case of black men and women, we simply can ask when will it end?

These fictional and true stories present events that ask the listener to consider the value of human life and its significance. In the calendar year of 2018, police officers took a life 342 days out of 365. "There were only 23 days in 2018 where police did not kill someone" (Mapping Police Violence). There is no reason that anyone could give to get me to believe that 342 people deserved to lose their life. What gives the cops the right to take someone's life? The color of their skin? The location in which they live? How many tattoos they have? If their teeth have gold on them? If their pants sag? What gives them the right?

An article entitled "Mapping Police Brutality" states that black people are three times more likely to lose their lives to police officers. Of the people killed by police officers in 2015, 30% of the African Americans killed were unarmed as opposed to 21% of Caucasians. Despite these few facts, people will still try and deny that there is racism and stereotypes lurking throughout this nation. A study showed that 13 of the 100 largest U.S. police departments kill black men at higher rates than the U.S. murder rate. Despite these overwhelming truths, 99% of the cases involving these situations result in the officers walking free. If a black man had murdered these people, they would have been locked up, or even worse things could have happened to them. But in this country, we choose to honor the villain who portrays himself as the victim.

In the midst of a world that chooses to look at situations such as the injustices against minority races with anger and hate, we must find a way to see the change and work toward it. The more that we get mad, the worse things will get. The old saying of "you can't fight fire with fire" is true. The fire will only rage on if violence is the answer to every situation that pops up. Trayvon Martin, a young man who was fatally shot and killed while walking down the street, seemingly was the case that made the pot boil over. His mother, Sybrina Fulton, decided to try and promote a change rather than respond in anger. She began speaking following her son's death to get people to lose the hate and the anger and build a tolerance for when things of this nature happen. Of course, there will be anger, and there will be negative thoughts, but the more those thoughts and emotions can be contained, the more that we can begin to move toward a different future. Sybrina Fulton stated during one of her speeches, "We are all in this country together and we need to learn to get along together. Regardless of what somebody's race is. Regardless of what somebody's sexual orientation is. Regardless of the color of their skin" (Koin 5). Like every relationship, there has to be sending and receiving; we must have both sides of the spectrum advocate for change, not just one. We must make a conscientious effort to move beyond the view of white and black and move toward a view of brother and sister. We must come to realize that you are just like me, and I am just like you.

Erynn Brantley-Ridgeway

#JusticeMeans equal opportunity for all people, no matter their abilities, color, or gender. I am a woman, a black woman, and I should have the same opportunities as a white woman or a white man. Women shouldn't have to fight for a seat at the table; blacks shouldn't have had to fight for the right to vote. People shouldn't have to fight and protest for justice when in fact, justice is what America is all about. But the truth is, it's not.

#JusticeMeans giving people the punishment they deserve when they break the law, such as a police officer taking an innocent life. Cases like those do not get justice. Without justice, there will be no peace. The government doesn't want an uprising—they don't want marches or sit-ins. They don't want people marching and shouting in the streets with their fists in the air. They don't want people to retaliate against those who have done them wrong. If they want peace, why do they not bring justice? #JusticeMeans taking a stand against those who are wrong and doing something about it.

Kristian Cavender

Justice means equality amongst everyone no matter the circumstances. The justice system in our society is messed up and needs to change. Consider that, in our society, the rich and the powerful can get away with most things, whereas the poor and people in poverty will take the blame. Then there is discrimination and prejudice in the prisons. Black citizens are being incarcerated at more than three times the rate of white citizens. This is a problem caused by our society that put this system in place, a system which caused the number of prisoners to increase rapidly. Even when any prisoner is let out, most of them have

WE KEEP US SAFE

no money, nowhere to go, and only the clothes they wore the day they went to prison. They are just let out to the world with no assistance and no job.

Shelby Host

Community
"All immigrants" they said
"My money" they said
"Un-American" they said
Why do we listen
To the things that they said

That's wrong I thought
Not facts I thought
That's prejudice I thought
I decided to say
The things that I thought

"Not all" I said
"Our money" I said
"Citizens" I said
Can you please listen
To the things that I said

Hardworking they are
Just starting they are
Discriminated they are
Why can't you see
All the things that they are

Injustice they face
Killing they face
Bans they face
You don't even know

The things that they face
They can support
They can change
They can engage
They can do things
That keep community

I have talked
I have engaged
I have defended
I have done things
That support community

They have talked
They have engaged
They have defended
They have done things
That support community

I have learned
I have opened my mind
I have humbled
I have done things
To learn community

We learn
We grow
We reflect
We do things
To learn community

Samantha Owens

I grew up in a small town in Wisconsin, right on Lake Michigan and about half an hour north of the state's largest city, Milwaukee. As a child, I felt safe and supported in my little suburban bubble. Anywhere I went in town, there was always a familiar, smiling face. The community was tight-knit and everyone seemed to know each other and the ins and outs of each other's lives. We congratulated each other on our successes, mourned each other's losses together, and stepped in to help each other in times of need. Some of my earliest memories include helping my mom cook and deliver meals to one of my childhood friend's family when his mother was diagnosed with breast cancer. I remember going over to my elderly neighbor's home on the weekends to help her with her garden once she could no longer bend down to pull the weeds. To my young self, Port Washington, Wisconsin was a utopia. Life couldn't get any better. But as I started to get older, I began to realize that my hometown wasn't as faultless as I had seen it to be.

My town was predominantly white, politically conservative, and, most importantly to the town's identity, Catholic. I attended church with my family every Sunday morning, and on Monday nights, from the time I was starting kindergarten until I was a junior in high school, I attended weekly Catholic education classes. During the early years, I saw nothing worrisome about the education I was receiving. We talked about Jesus and Noah's Arc and who God was. We learned that God loved everyone equally and forgave everyone who strayed from his path. This happy, shiny picture was my concept of Catholicism until I entered seventh or eighth grade. When I started getting older, the catechists who taught my religious education classes began to delve deeper into the official doctrine and history of the Catholic Church.

With each year older I got, the seemingly more devout and fanatic my catechists seemed to get. The members of my church who had taught me about the love and forgiveness of God when I was a child were now changing the message. God's love and acceptance suddenly had conditions. Living only a half hour away from Wisconsin's largest, most liberal city, I had always had exposure to alternative ideas. My mother had also worked extremely hard to ensure that I lived my life with a kind and accepting heart. With those influences opposing my simultaneously Catholic upbringing, I sat in class each week growing increasingly angry, confused, and internally conflicted. I had always believed that the right to choose who you love was something that should be afforded to everyone. I saw no issue with non-heterosexual relationships. But now, adults that I trusted were insisting that it was sinful and abhorrent. I also firmly believed, especially being a woman, that the right to have an abortion was one that should lie solely in the hands of the pregnant woman. But now, powerful men with high ranking church positions were telling me that it was an unacceptable decision.

I tried to speak out. I would raise my hand during our discussions to offer an opinion or to ask why God wouldn't be okay with such things if he supposedly loved and forgave all of his believers. I fought with all my being to make my voice heard and to get through to the adults in power within my parish, but it was no use. I was shot down with every attempt to state my concerns. I was told blatantly that my opinion was wrong. I was told that it wasn't my place, as a child and as a woman, to hold such a blasphemous opinion within the church. My spirit grew weaker and weaker until I had nothing left to give. Every night after class was dismissed, I would go home and cry to my mother who, despite her affiliation with Catholicism, had always taught me about the importance of standing up for those who are different and to accept others no matter who they are. I couldn't justify my belief in a system of religion and in a god who wouldn't love people simply because they live their life a certain way that the men in power don't agree with. I asked myself daily, why should the elite men of the church get to dictate aspects of others' lives that do not directly affect them in any way?

Me against the entire Catholic Church: I knew I couldn't win that fight. I decided, sitting in religion class one week, that I needed to focus on helping myself and others to embrace their identity as an individual with valid opinions and feelings rather than as a subject of the Church.

For me, being an outlet for people with different needs and priorities than what Catholicism allows was a drastic change. Nobody had ever provided me with that kind of support, and I wanted to be the one in my community to create that space.

Religion fostered my ability to be a civic leader in a roundabout manner. Catholicism never empowered me in the sense that I felt loved, included, and listened to. I tried to be a leader within my tiny bubble of the parish, but I was never able to get through to anyone. Rather, Catholicism empowered me by challenging me to define my beliefs and opinions for myself. Because I didn't agree with the official stances of the church, I was able to thoroughly and independently form my worldview. The feeling of being completely alone against a massive entity like the Catholic Church made me more determined than I otherwise ever could have been to be a leader in civic society. Through my relationship with religion, I realized that being a leader in civic society isn't strictly about changing or 'taking down' powerful systems. It's also about starting dialogues, providing support, listening to one another, and creating safe spaces.

I realize that I'm one of the lucky ones. I was raised within a Christian faith within a widely Christian country. While my decision to leave the Catholic community made me feel isolated, it was relatively easy for me to find others who were turned-off Christians and now identified as not-religious. My new status, while not valued in my hometown, is a position that the general public respects in American society for the most part. Having Christianity as my starting point automatically and unfairly, gives me privilege.

The United States, in theory, highly values and protects religious freedom. In the very first amendment of The United States Constitution, freedom of religion is guaranteed to every citizen living within the nation. It is required of Congress that no religion is favored over another in law and that one's individual religious practices are not restricted. On a legal level, we are protected from unfair treatment on the basis of religion. While I am grateful for these protections and believe that all people should be afforded these protections as well, I do not believe that the conditions written out in our constitution do an adequate job of ensuring that all citizens' religious freedoms are protected.

In American society, there is a quite transparent and obvious public preference for certain religions over others. These have shifted throughout history, but as the nation stands now, Christianity and Judaism are typically shown a level of respect and freedom which other faiths such as Islam, Sikhism, Buddhism, Hinduism, and many others are not always afforded. There is a noticeable fear of the "other" that permeates American culture. This has always existed to some degree, but I believe that the attacks of September 11th, 2001 have a lot to do with this. The attacks on the World Trade Center were carried out by Islamic extremists: outliers.

The individuals who launched the terrorist act on the United States are in no way representative of an entire religious group, but the media and some of the legislation and military action that followed 9/11 instilled a fear in much of the public that was, and still is, difficult to reverse. Because many people in America at the time lacked a basic of understanding of Islam, they were easily swept into the frenzy. A lack of education and visibility surrounding non-Christian faiths in the United States has led many other non-Christian religious groups to be lumped into the group defined as "other" that many view as dangerous. An example of this problem that I've found especially prevalent recently has been surrounding immigration laws.

The ways that I and others combat this issue is mainly through education. If Americans become better educated in regards to non-Christian faiths, something that was once "different" and "unknown" will become normalized. It is important that regardless of what religion somebody practices, they are guaranteed the same rights and protections that every American is promised. Even outside of official legislation and government policy, respect should be afforded equally to everyone.

Once the confusion is taken away from some of the religions Americans are less exposed to on a daily basis, I think that religious freedom can truly be reached.

Meredith DiIoia
Religious Freedom: A Universal Right Denied to the Uighurs in China

Uighurs are a Muslim community in China that are being forced into concentration camps under the pretext of "de-extremification training centers." As a result, the Uighurs are becoming a minority in the one area where they were allowed to be themselves: "The Uighurs. . . number about 11 million in western China's Xinjiang region. They see themselves as culturally and ethnically close to Central Asian nations, and their language is similar to Turkish. But in recent decades, there's been a mass migration of Han Chinese (China's ethnic majority) to Xinjiang, and the Uighurs feel their culture and livelihoods are under threat" (Hughes). The Uighurs are not wrong to feel like their livelihoods are under threat, because they are. The Uighurs are involuntarily being taken from the security of their homes to cruel and brutal prisons. Their right to practice their own religion has been stolen from them by the Chinese government. There have been multiple cases about the horrors that have occurred inside the walls of these "training centers." There are a multitude of stories about people whose lives have been affected. Cases like these though, have not nearly received the publicity or public outrage that they deserve.

Background and Current Abuses
The recent rounding up of Uighurs began in 2017. The "Uighurs abroad grew alarmed as friends and relatives at home dropped out of touch, first deleting phone and social media contacts and then disappearing entirely. Uighur students who returned or were forced back to China after studying in foreign countries likewise vanished upon arriving" (Millward). With such disappearances, questions have arisen among family members. With the threat of the Chinese government overhead, however, it can be difficult to find out exactly what occurred. For instance,

Aydin Anwar has been unable to discover what has happened to his Chinese residents from her location in the United States. Yet, thanks to her father's experience as a Uighur rights activist, she does know about the dire proceedings that take place in these camps. Her father told her that "People in these camps are forced to renounce their faith, adopt atheism and pledge allegiance to the Chinese state as a god." She also knows that there is "lethal injection, forced sterilization, torture, bodies being cremated to destroy evidence. These are all signs of a looming genocide" (Shenoy).

Tiram lived In the Xinjiang region. His sister, Zohra, was sent to one of these "re-education camps" in 2016 after a family trip to Turkey. After paying the Chinese government around three thousand dollars to be able to communicate with his sister, Tiram was able to visit her in the camp. Tarim was shocked by what he saw when he arrived. Zohra and the other three thousand were trapped behind a mass of towering sixteen-foot barbed wire walls. Tiram stated "Zohra was not her usual self and said that she looked pale. Dark spots formed around her eyes, which welled with tears . . . Zohra told her brother that she needed to complete some 'lessons' and undergo a test afterward. If she passed the test, she would be released" (Regencia). Unfortunately, Tiram never found out if she passed the "test" or even when the "test" would take place. Instead, Tiram had to escape from Xinjiang to Turkey to try and evade the Chinese government because he had visited his sister. He still lives under constant fear because of the danger that defying the Chinese government poses. Yet, because of how urgent the threat to the Uighurs is, Tiram has continued to have the courage to speak out: "But the world has to know what the Chinese government is doing to the Uighurs. Even the dogs have more rights than the Uighurs in China" (Regencia).

Sayragul Sauytbay, a worker in the camps, knew that what was happening was obviously a crime against the Uighurs: "She told the court how she had been transferred the previous November from her school to a new job teaching Kazakh detainees in a 'training center.'"

She stated, "They call it a 'political camp' . . . but, in reality, it's a prison in the mountains." There were 2,500 inmates in the facility where she had worked for four months and she knew of other such camps. There may now be as many as 1,200 such camps in Xinjiang, imprisoning up to a million people, including Kazakhs, Kyrgyz, and especially Uighurs, who make up around 46 percent of Xinjiang's population" (Millward). While everyone can agree that what the Chinese government is doing is horrible, there is dissent among Uighur activist groups over what actions to take.

A member in Ayden Anwar's activist group, Salih Hudayar, voices his concern about the split: "The only way we can ensure our freedoms and human rights is by restoring our independence and that's the only way we can ensure our overall survival as a whole." But calling for independence is controversial among older established Uighur groups. "They say it's unrealistic," Hudayar commented, "or that the international community will stand against it, the US will oppose it — which is nonsense." The disagreement is causing a split. The new group has been shunned by established Uighur organizations: "The fact that they weren't willing to work with us is what caused us to come out as a different organization," (Shenoy). This division between the groups shows why the United States needs to step into this human rights issue. The fear of unrealistic-ness that the older group claims exists can be easily diminished by the United States taking a stand and enacting economic sanctions against China. This will back up the universal truth that religious freedom is an all-inclusive right.

Proposed Actions
Religious freedom is a universal right that every single human on earth is entitled to according to the United Nations Universal Declaration of Human Rights. It states, "Everyone has the right to freedom of thought, conscience and religion; this right includes freedom to change his religion or belief, and freedom, either alone or in community with others and in public or private, to manifest his religion or belief in teaching, practice, worship and observance" (United Nations). Thus, the Chinese

government's attempts, through camps, to convert the Uighurs violates a multitude of humanitarian laws set forth by the United Nations, such as Article Five (No one shall be subjected to torture or to cruel, inhuman or degrading treatment or punishment) as well as Article Nineteen (Everyone has the right to freedom of opinion and expression; this right includes freedom to hold opinions without interference and to seek, receive and impart information and ideas through any media regardless of frontiers). Viewing the crimes against the Uighurs as a direct violation of religious freedom, which is an international right, allows the United States government to step in and create a punishment for the actions of the Chinese government.

The United States needs to make a clear stance that these abuses will not and should not stand. So that China will feel the most pressure to stop these camps, the United States should enact tariffs on electronic equipment, machinery, and steel products, which are what the United States import the most from China (World's Richest). The total of all those imports equal to 289.9 billion dollars (World's Richest), which would easily send a strong message to the Chinese government about how the United States feels about China's "re-education camps" for the Uighurs. The recent trade war between the United States and China proves that tariffs will have serious consequences against China. China has already started to feel the impact these tariffs have: "China's National Bureau of Statistics said the non-manufacturing purchasing managers index fell to 54.0 in July from 55.0 in June.

The index covers such things as retail, aviation, and software as well as real estate and construction activity. Meanwhile, the manufacturing purchasing managers' index was 51.2, its weakest since February" (Wallace). Meanwhile, the United States economy has not felt a huge impact from the trade war: "U.S. GDP growth hit an annual 4.1 percent in the second quarter, the fastest growth in four years. The S&P 500 stock index is up almost 14 percent in the last year, while the U.S. Dollar is booming against other major currencies" (Wallace). This research serves as concrete proof that the United States is in a strong position to use the tariffs as an economical way to create change for the better, for the lives of the Uighurs. Furthermore, the introduction of these tariffs, which will be under the demand that they will not be lifted until the Chinese government disbands the concentration camps, promotes a campaign of religious tolerance, and reimburses the Uighurs who have suffered so cruelly under the Chinese government's control, the tariffs will be another way the United States will incite change. Once the United States takes this affirmative stance, first world countries like England, Germany, and Japan will also hopefully take similar actions and solidify the unity of the concept of universal human rights and religious freedom, specifically.

Without urgent interference from strong governments with a global reach, the safety and lives of the Uighurs are in peril. The United States specifically must have a major role in stopping the persecution of the Uighurs. The way they can do that is by creating tariffs on the top types of imports from China. This will make China hurt economically so that they will dispense with their concentration camps and the attacks on the Uighurs. Religious freedom is a universal right that is vital for every human's life. It is vital that countries like the United States maintain a strong stance in support of religious and human rights as well as use their power to end such abuses.

Works Cited
Albert, Eleanor. "What to Know About Sanctions on North Korea." Council on Foreign Relations, Council on Foreign Relations, www.cfr.org/backgrounder/what-know-about-sanctions-north-korea.
"Documenting Numbers of Victims of the Holocaust & Nazi Persecution." Documenting Numbers of Victims of the Holocaust & Nazi Persecution, www.jewishvirtuallibrary.org/documenting-numbers-of-victims-of-the-holocaust.
Hughes, Roland. "China Uighurs: All You Need to Know on Muslim 'Crackdown'." BBC News, BBC, 8 Nov. 2018, www.bbc.com/news/world-asia-china-45474279.
Millward, James. "'Reeducating' Xinjiang's Muslims." The New York Review of Books, The New York Review of Books, Jan. 2019, www.nybooks.com/

articles/2019/02/07/reeducating-xinjiangs-muslims/.

Regencia, Ted. "Escape from Xinjiang: Muslim Uighurs Speak of China Persecution." GCC News | Al Jazeera, Al Jazeera, 10 Sept. 2018, www.aljazeera.com/indepth/features/escape-xinjiang-muslim-uighurs-speak-china-persecution-180907125030717.html.

"Rohingya Crisis." Human Rights Watch, www.hrw.org/tag/rohingya-crisis.

Shenoy, Rupa "As Families Are Lost to China's 'Re-Education Camps,' US Uighurs Are Split." Public Radio International, PRI, www.pri.org/stories/2018-12-19/families-are-lost-china-s-re-education-camps-us-uighurs-are-split.

Top Oil Importers, www.worldsrichestcountries.com/top_us_imports.html.

"Universal Declaration of Human Rights." United Nations, United Nations, www.un.org/en/universal-declaration-human-rights/.

Wallace, Charles. "Trade War Hurts China While U.S. Economy Booms." Forbes, Forbes Magazine, 31 July 2018, www.forbes.com/sites/charleswallace1/2018/07/31/trade-war-hurts-china-while-u-s-economy-booms/#383c94275b64.

Westcott, Ben. "Chinese Ambassador Threatens Retaliation over Possible US Uyghur Sanctions." CNN, Cable News Network, 28 Nov. 2018, www.cnn.com/2018/11/27/politics/us-china-uyghur-cui-tiankai-intl/index.html.

Nour Elhouda Belakhdar

To be yourself as a woman in a world that is dominated by the male population is very difficult. No matter how hard you work or how sincere your intentions are, you would never be given credit like men. It is a sad fact, really. I acknowledge there are some tasks that a woman can't do, but what about those we are able to do? Sometimes we do the same job a man does, with the same number of working hours, the same outcome, but we still don't get rewarded or praised like the males, which is just unfair. Most men feel superior to women because they consider us weak and not intellectually equal to them.

Men say the "fairer sex, the softer sex" like they are cursing us, branding us for something that, if looked upon from a different perspective, is actually normal, natural. As for harassment, women are always the ones who are blamed for this act. We are always the ones "at fault." It seems that, globally, even rape is regarded today as not that "important of an issue" anymore. I think the only way to solve all these problems of sexism and harassment is to treat it as a disease. It needs a diagnosis, prognosis, and preferably a cure. Some men out there can do with a dose of medicine.

I know and I've heard of many examples of women being assaulted and harassed, of women becoming victims of abduction by some men in the street—thankfully, the women were rescued. An important issue in such stories is that the women in question did not file a complaint to the police. Most of them could describe the assailant perfectly, but they don't go to the police because they are afraid. They know that the man in question can get back at her, do worse things, and no one would be the wiser. We are, in some cases, really afraid of some men because they are physically stronger than us. Men know that, and sometimes they use it against us because they know in most cases we can't retaliate—especially when they give you that smirk which says, "I can hurt you, woman and you know it. I dare you to act on it." It is the bitter truth.

Bouchra Rahmouni

The history of Algerian women in politics goes back to the beginnings of our history as a modern nation. Indeed, women's leadership in Algeria is a long one, starting from the Algerian revolution that started in November 1, 1954. The nation witnessed remarkable participation of women in the war, such as Lala Fatima N'soumer, Hassiba Ben Bouali, and Djamila Bouhired, as well as so many others who contributed and had important roles in the revolution.

After Independence, women started voting, and in 1984, Algeria witnessed its first female minister, Z'hor Ounissi. Ever since, women's rights organizations and associations have worked hard to prove that women are able to work and are capable of taking part in the "leadership world." Still there is also the case of Louisa Hennoune, who was the first Algerian and Arab woman to run for president in April 2004 but lost to Bouteflika (the previous president). She tried again in 2009 and 2014 but also failed. Her main goal was to separate religion from politics, which is a thing that Algerians rejected. She faced harsh criticism over her program and ideologies. Yet, I think Hennoune lost because she was a woman.

Algeria is a Muslim country. Everyone practices Islam, and the religion is strongly connected to politics. So, speaking of women in leadership is hard to discuss. Religious individuals claim there are Islamic rules that do not allow a woman to lead a nation. Women, in this Islamic viewpoint, are better staying at home. Moreover, women do not have to go for work because it is the man's duty. He must work for his family. This is seen as part of making life easier for women because women are seen as not as strong as men. There are also additional customs and traditions that are not strictly religious but also consider women to be modest, shy, and demure. Such Algerians also think that women are weak and cannot handle the pressure of working outside as men do. Taken together, all these beliefs support the idea that staying at home guarantees women] a decent life. For this reason, many Algerians believe that a woman should stay at home to take care of her husband and children. She should stay away from the problems of external life that the man must endure.

I think that the real problem lies in how people misunderstand the religion of Islam. Some religious individuals use some verses of Quran against women in order to prevent them from taking leadership positions. I am not an expert, and I may not be so religious, but I can see that most men here misunderstand what Islam truly says. Islam does not fully prevent women from having a job. It says that a woman should not lead a nation, yet we can say that women have held leadership roles in Algerian history. Indeed, Islam honored women and made them a support for men since the time of the Prophet Muhammad (pbuh) and the dissemination of the Islamic message. Taking on leadership roles is a form of such support. Finally, many of these cultural traditions against women are no longer as sacred as before; some mentalities changed, and women stood for their rights.

Yet, it is important to add that, despite all the laws and newly declared rights, women's participation in the labor force is still weak. Recently, the Minister of Solidarity declared that only 20% of the labor force consists of women. Women, however, obtain more education than over 80% of men. Again, I believe this has to do with women not being respected as leaders. An article I read stated that 47.8 % of the Algerian population strongly agree that males make better political leaders than women; 21% think that university education is more important for boys than for girls. This shows that some people in Algeria do not welcome the idea of female leaders in their country in either the workforce or government.

I personally experienced the case of being a female leader and experiencing these negative attitudes. I was a member of a club in my school. When the president graduated, they needed a new person to lead, so I was chosen. Some old members did not like this fact and quit. Then male students would not join because a girl was leading their club. All the members were girls. I heard so many negative comments from the beginning, and I had to endlessly prove myself. We started working and making efforts. Then, when the club organized successful events, many students, including males, showed interest in joining. We now we have over 10 male members. The idea is that students in my school do not believe in women's capacities until they're proven wrong. This is just a simple example of the obstacles that women face on their way to leading.

To get into leadership positions, 'Algerian feminism' has become a movement that is fighting for equality between men and women. This movement, recently started working on spreading some ideas that stand for women's rights. This has made them speak more freely about their concerns, such as being equal to men in everything. Women are now organizing meetings and debates in which they defend themselves and their opinions. The Algerian feminism's main goal is giving women the freedom to be and do whatever they want. They want to see more women in leadership roles, which is a commitment that brought women's support to their efforts. We have seen feminists protesting alongside all the Algerians against the current political system in what is known as the movement of February, 22. One of the things they want is to see more female leaders.

Other women, such as Nadia Ait-Zai, who is a professor of family law at Algiers University and an expert in the domain of politics, speak for including women in politics. When new laws were declared in 2012 that promoted women's participation in local and national politics, Ait-Zai described them as 'courageous.'

In addition to Ait-Zai, there are many other women who fight daily by creating associations and clubs, as mentioned above. There are women who write to prove to the society that women can do anything, that there is no difference between men and women when it comes to leadership. They are making remarkable achievements because there was a time when no one could even express their opinion. Now they use social media, and they meet to discuss their issues. While she has lost elections, we now also have a woman leading a political party: Louisa Hennoune.

Still, there are differences among women who argue for political and civic rights. The ideologies and the goals of these movements differ. Some aim to create chaos, others productive change. I guess the women who should be supported are the ones who have the capacities to lead, to make a difference, and do good for their country. We have seen all too recently that there are some women of power who are not trustworthy. This makes people believe women should stay at home. I still believe that such a cultural change was never meant to happen in one day or two. It always takes time and efforts. But the effort must continue.

I would end by saying that there are some positive results of fighting for women in leadership in Algeria. Mentalities started changing, and women are trying harder to prove their capability and readiness to take hold of the torch to be leaders in universities by leading clubs, by being ministers in governments, and by being teachers in classrooms. There is still a long way to go, but I believe my country is beginning to learn that being a leader has nothing to do with your gender. It has to do with your capability, responsibility, personality, and credibility.

Concluding Thoughts

Fouad Cherif Belferd
In my opinion, I think the basis for a civil society should be open-mindedness, which means that everyone must accept others and accept their differences in terms of gender, ethnicity, religion, and culture. As such, we need to create leaders in society who fight for other's rights, such as the right for education, freedom of speech, and religion. I believe that these are the first steps in forming a civil society.

Allaoua Hisham Khalil
The role of leaders in defending human rights is crucial. Thanks for bringing this up, I was going to say it too.

Fouad Cherif Belferd
A role that has been left empty in this society for the past 60 years or so.

3 SOCIAL MEDIA AND ACTIVISM

Sophie Beckman

Poem for Grace Lee Boggs
The time has come for a new dream.
A readiness for change.
Revolve
Like hands circling a clock
Put together and assembled by younger hands
None old enough to call it
Man-made.
Flown across the sea while the Earth
Revolves
Keeps time according to a suggested beat.
A ticking unlike our hearts
Whose beats pound with the tender tenacity of a mother
Soft enough to protect the fragile fragments of her baby's skull
Strong enough to vibrate the soil that only men have turned
A battleground.
Capable, constant, everchanging
How she evolves
She turns the battlegrounds into botanical gardens
Each on an act of resistance, resilience, restoration
Though her wristwatch revolves in circles
It does not match her soul's revolution
Our soul's evolution
The everyday rebellions and the collected catastrophes.
Propelling us into a new hour
On a clock unlike our wristwatches
"What time is it on the clock of the world?"

Original Artwork by Hind Belakhal

Equality and Justice

Dialogue

As part of this project, we solicited Algerian and U.S.A. activists to discuss the role of social media and activism. We decided to mask their identity to allow them to speak freely about the current political moment without fear of reprisal.

Algerian 1
Social media has a great role in our lives in general, but it can both improve or hurt society depending on the way of using it. In my country, social media is playing a huge role in guiding the society, especially now, since there are many protests happening all over the country for political reasons.

Algerian 2
I think that social media improves as much as it harms the society. It is a double-edged sword.
On one hand, any ordinary citizen may find his ideas and opinions heard and can talk freely with anyone. This creates fruitful discussions and dialogues that lead to a proper response to the issue.

On the other hand, social media has a hand in spreading false ideas. It sometimes leads to a mess in society like what happened in some Arab countries some years ago. In my country, I think social media has contributed positively to the movement that started almost a month ago.

People have united their words. Everyone's opinion is heard. Many public sites have been created to show how to organize protests and marches. I think that the idea is that people can use social media the way they want, either positively or negatively.

Algerian 3
Looking back on what would influence people of my community: Some years ago, we could notice that, regardless of the quantity and the quality of direct speeches and debates, they were more influential.

Today, people don't trust other's speeches as much. They trust and get easily influenced by social media.

This influence by social media has both positive and negative effects. I can give an example from what is happening in Algeria. From the day these protests started one month ago until today, the protests have emerged from social media. The Algerian population is about 42 million. We can say that at least 20 million are protesting. That means that social media influenced all of this population! During these protests, social media is also playing a double role. It acts as alternative journalism, since real journalism is not present as it is supposed to be. It also plays the role of informing demonstrators by explaining complex political concepts as well as presenting various possibilities and suggesting some solutions.

Yet, we should be aware that, as much as social media can build a real civic society, it can destroy it. Social media can be used in a wrong way, by wrong persons, to achieve wrong ends. What comes to my mind is the latest invitations to take part in the civil disobedience by certain parts of society, as well as the absence of specialists to make the people aware about the seriousness of the matter. That can lead us into some serious problems.

Still, I can confirm that social media is the way that will lead us to the change we want, as long as we keep using it in this positive way.

U.S.A. 1

I agree that there are negative sides to social media, but through encouraging open dialogue, the positives far outweigh the negatives. Sure, some people use social media to spread misinformation or backwards ideologies, but the beauty of the internet is the ability to discuss and fact check these issues at any given time.

Social media also brings light to issues about which the majority of the public would have otherwise remained unaware. The internet allows you to interact with and learn from people you never would've had the chance to speak to, helping you see the world from a different perspective. If it were not for social media, we wouldn't be having this conversation right now. I know for certain that I've learned a lot from things I've read on Twitter or Reddit. These sites have changed the way I view the world and provided me insight I know I couldn't have easily obtained from elsewhere.

U.S.A. 2
I also agree that social media can be a really positive tool that encourages open and productive dialogue. But the thing I struggle with in this conversation is the fact that one can very easily isolate themselves on social media so that they only are exposed to information and viewpoints that support their pre-existing views. It is easy to stick to sources that are comfortable to you. When we do that, our opinions can be made even more extreme or one-sided. Another negative of social media is that it is difficult to distinguish what is fact from what isn't.

Misinformation spreads quickly and can be taken as truth by large masses of readers. If you can partake in dialogue on social media while at the same time bearing in mind that not everything you hear will be true and that it's important to hear alternative viewpoints, then there are great possibilities for what social media can facilitate.

Algerian 4
Social media has been a great help for people to reach out to crowds and to make their voices and ideas heard, especially when it comes to organizing movements. We've seen some of the greatest examples lately in our country, Algeria. It also helped a lot of people who were marginalized and afraid through giving them mental support like the #MeToo movement, which has helped not only women, but also men to come together, support each other, organize committees, marches, and even donations for others. Social media plays the role of an international platform with no borders in which everyone can be heard and any ideas can be shared and discussed.

However, it can also be an issue. Many people misuse social media to spread fake news and sabotage the great works that other people may have accomplished. Others may even take advantage of a certain situation and use social media to add fuel to the fire instead of seeking a solution. They encourage others in the opposite direction. We can use the situation in Algeria as an example as well. Many people are doing great work organizing the marches, taking the people's opinion into consideration and sharing ideas and solutions, while others, luckily a very small minority, are trying to sabotage this movement and create a riot. So, I believe that social media is a great tool, but only when we know how to use it. Because in the wrong hands or if misused, it can be a huge destructive tool.

U.S.A. 3

I think the main reason the arguments are so strong on each side resides in the inherent power of the open and unregulated nature of social media. Never before in human history has there been this kind of access to self-publication. There is usually a go-between. We were limited by the capacities of physical space and word-of-mouth. Our new "hybrid embodiment" allows us to move as far as others are willing to listen. Any system which enables this comes with the possibility of corruption and hijacking, as it is engineered so as not to have any checks or balances (such as an editor for a publication, etc.). This means that we, the public, must provide our own checks on movements and patterns of use that we find unsavory. The spread of fake news, echo chambers, and digitized fascism have all gained traction, but the same tool they use to embolden themselves has also been used to destabilize them. All in all, the benefits of instant communication and global connectivity are too large to ignore, despite misuse of certain elements of social media. Information is power, and nobody can dispute what social media has done to support this.

U.S.A. 4

Social media has hurt the ability to have productive dialogues in a civic society. Whether it's Twitter or Facebook, society has a major problem when it actually comes to discussing issues. Instead of promoting solutions or highlighting the truth. People on social media use derogatory terms and block people to attempt to prove their point. Just a side note, I hear a lot of people saying that blocking people online is the solution to fix social media. It's not.

I believe this problem is especially bad here in America. It is very plausible that the divisive nature and spreading of fake news within social media directly caused the outcome of the 2016 presidential election, which has hurt our how we look to other countries and has caused the country to make huge mistakes regarding civil rights, government spending, and climate change.

Algerian 5
According to what is happening now in Algeria, I can simply say that social media has improved the ability of civic society to foster productive dialogue. The quality of dialogues depends on the nature of its topics and on the people. Civic societies have the ability to get people to tackle issues of considerable importance, especially with the help of social media. Facebook, Twitter, and Instagram are platforms that enable them to discuss and exchange ideas and opinions.

Untill now in my Algeria, for instance, social media has played a major role in spreading and facilitating the discussion of ideas, the willingness of Algerians to snatch their rights, and to bring the country back to life. Productive dialogues are being built everywhere, especially when it comes to issues that concern everyone. Facebook, Instagram, YouTube, etc. are being used by Algerians for the sake of participating in the peaceful movements; the wind of change is supported by social media that is allowing them to know what is happening and what is supposed to be done.

People take pictures/videos and post them to social media so that everyone will be up-to-date. People discuss new ideas and how to apply them. They talk about what each should do and the appropriate manner to do it. At the very beginning, they agreed that our marches and movements must take a peaceful form, and it is crystal clear that the idea has succeeded. Social media helps Algerians challenge themselves to clean the environment, to paint walls, and much more. Social media is helping most people to be flexible in receiving new ideas and feeling free to build productive public dialogues. Apart from politics, social media can play the role of a facilitating tool for social integration. Any civic society can gain a lot by dialoging. If social media speaks for productive dialogues, it will make a difference. Social media gives people the chance to create and share ideas and solutions. This way, they are paving the way for the world and their worlds, to get interconnected and united with time.

Algerian 2

I guess most of us agreed that social media helps in creating productive dialogues, but we also spoke about the misleading information and people who use social media to guide people to the unknown and spread hatred. I like the discussion about blocking people not being the solution to fix social media. Instead, people should listen to each other. It's alright not to agree on everything. But I also think that there is a certain category of people that we just can't talk to; it is the category of people who produce malicious thoughts. The question is how to stop these people, how to recognize it?

Algerian 6

In response to your question, I think that it's kind of impossible to stop this misleading information as well as it being impossible to stop those people. It's a very large world, and the number of this kind of people is growing day after another. What we can do, in my opinion, is to stop supporting them, don't share false information, don't help them in continuing to do what they're doing, and help make people aware of how dangerous the matter is. In other words, just try to be the anti-power that will fight them.

Algerian 5
How could you tell whether the information is true or not?

Algerian 6
It's kind of another hard thing to deal with, but I can give you a simple example from what we are living through now. For instance, as an Algerian citizen interested in what's happening in Algeria, what I saw through social media was a big, misleading flow of information. The problem was that most of the people were just following what's said. What we can do in these cases is to build our own knowledge based on laws and logic. I've read the Algerian Constitution several times in order to know what's right and what's wrong. It may help a bit. I'm not saying that it would be that simple in other cases, but in a situation where you can be the anti-force, just try to be.

Algerian 2
Please allow me to say that it is true that if people read their laws and think logically, they would recognize this and that, but not everyone can do that. You know in our case, in Algeria, many people really have no political awareness. They know nothing about the political field, yet they get into conversations and suggest some illogical things to be done. My point is, the educated class is the one responsible for being objective and leading its people to think properly.

Algerian 5
Do not expect people who cannot distinguish between their dreams and their rights to be ready and aware enough to know and discuss things that really matter.

Algerian 2
I believe some people were just not given the chance to really express themselves. We've always been thinking that our people cannot think right or discuss things that matter. But the protests' example is kind of a good example to prove that our generation is aware of what's going on and can lead the public opinion.

Algerian 5

Please do not forget that it is a national protest. Do not forget the regime. Everything is social media, and, in real life, everything is under observation. I do not mean that we are naive or apathetic, but it is hard and too early to say that. Give it some time! The problem is that even with those who are expressing themselves, most of them suffer from lack of confidence or knowledge. We tend to believe that what is said by someone with power or even posted/written on a picture is a fact. It is hard to specially decide that we are witnessing a large variety of ideologies; each one wants to be on the top.

Algerian 2

Of course, everything is on probation. Most of those expressing themselves are from the general public, and as I said before, not everyone has political awareness. Students and those intellectuals that have that kind of awareness is who we need. There was a noticeable difference between now and then. Some efforts should be appreciated. That is why I said people can rely on these educated people to deliver their messages and speak on behalf of them. And I did not mean any political party or the opposition because they obviously cannot be trusted.

Algerian 5

Yes indeed, good things must be appreciated and complimented. You rely on someone and allow her/him to talk on behalf of you when things are clear. The thing is that we are being showed the things they want us to see. So, it is not the same. Talking about intellectuals, there is no guarantee that they would do the right thing. On social media, you do not know who is spreading the misleading ideas; it may be an intellectual doing so, who knows?!

It is not that easy to teach people how to deal with social media. However, if they are taught or are used to thinking critically, if they reflect and not just accept blindly, nothing will easily trick them. No matter how bad it is, how misleading it is, and how destructive it is, people who can think and differentiate between the right and the wrong. They will not be deceived.

Algerian 6
That is why, in my opinion, we must teach critical and analytical thinking in schools and how to duplicate that thinking in real life because, honestly speaking, I don't think that teaching math is more important than this.

Further Engagement

Ally Masterson

> I pulled up the familiar blue bird logo on my phone
> Hopefully getting a bit of humor in a boring ride.
>
> I got more than I asked for.
>
> I scrolled through the news alerts and ads to
> Something I had never seen before.
>
> I saw the username of a good friend of mine
> One I had saw in school just the other day.
>
> I saw a set of pictures which showed a Ziploc baggie
> Containing a lollipop and an ad for joining the KKK.
>
> I saw a baggie left on the doorstep of a good friend
> Who's family happened to be mixed.
>
> I read her tweet saying that she woke up to many
> Baggies like that laying on her porch.
>
> I read her tweet saying this was not just at her house,
> But her neighbors houses as well.

I felt a sense of confusion considering this was 2018,
The future everyone claimed was more progressive than this.

I felt a sense of terror run through my blood
For not only my friend but her neighbors as well.

I felt a sense of shame that I was not aware that
The KKK was still on the prowl for new members.

I asked myself how could I not have known since
Every year we learn about them and their horrible deeds.

I thought that we as the USA, the country that prides
Itself on being the mixing pot, were different now.

I was ashamed to see that disgusting groups like them
Still existed and are shamelessly promoting themselves.

I took myself to Instagram and released my disappointment
And rage into an Instagram post.

Isabelle Ezratty

The following is an account of events that took place in the life of my grandfather, Sam Ezratty, as described to my father, Ari Ezratty, and my family. The events occurred during the years 1942-1945 when my grandfather was approximately 16-19 years old. He has since passed away, but the memory of his experience during this time has not been forgotten and is clearly described to me now by my father.

He remembered the train ride. It was long, very crowded, dirty, and cold. The windows were open. It was winter. Everyone was huddled together, mostly in fear of the unknown destination. Many families, like my grandfather's, were separated before boarding the train. In my grandfather's case, he was with his father and his younger sister. His mother and brothers were not on the train, as they had been killed in their town in Greece.

The train finally arrived at their destination: Auschwitz. The passengers nervously gathered whatever belongings they had and exited the train cars. They were sorted by the Nazi soldiers. The herd of Jewish passengers were formed into seemingly endless lines for a purpose only revealed at the front of the line. After countless hours, my grandfather got to the front of the line. The Nazi commander asked him and his father a few questions. He then asked his father to choose between staying with his daughter or his son. If he chose his daughter, he would be sent to the left: the gas chamber and crematorium. If he chose his son, he would be sent to the right: the labor camps. This most horrific, haunting, and painful choice for any parent was forced upon many families upon their arrival at Auschwitz. My great-grandfather and my grandfather's sister went to the gas chamber. At the young age of 16, my grandfather had to learn how to survive alone.

Throughout his time in Auschwitz, my grandfather worked hard labor in the cold of winter, often without shoes. He quickly learned that the prisoners that were thrown into the gas chamber were those that looked ill, weak, or unhealthy. The lineups were assessments. If you passed, you lived. On one lucky occasion my grandfather found a gold coin in the snow and used it to get a new uniform of striped pajamas and to shave to make him look healthier than the prisoner next to him.

At one line up, an officer asked the prisoner next to my grandfather to name the chemical formula of water. It was a seemingly simple question, but the man next to my grandfather had spent two full years in the concentration camp already. Though a pharmacist before enslavement at Auschwitz, the man could not recall the formula. My grandfather, on the other hand, answered the question for the prisoner, saving the man from going into the gas chamber but putting his own life at risk...

As I press my hands on the quilted train seats on my way back to my hometown in Connecticut, I think of the stories of my grandfather's past, recounts that seem like distant scenes from a horror film. My fingers pull aimlessly at the loose threads of the cushion, and my mind wanders. I can almost feel the loneliness and fear that must have consumed his body and kept him awake every night, sense the aching hunger that weakened his bones. Almost.

When asked the question, "who do you write for?" my mind immediately went to my grandfather. I write for the tears that he forced himself to hold back. I write for the sweat that he put into every forward step he willed himself to take. I write for the love and compassion that he felt for every life around him. I write for the strength he had, even when he felt so weak. While I am writing for my grandfather, I am writing to my peers and colleagues across the country. I am pleading with them to understand my grandfather's story and consider the impact of their hateful words and anti-Semitism.

Hearing of my grandfather's strength gives me the power and drive to use my own words to take a stance against the rising attacks on Jewish populations, particularly on college campuses. Knowing even just some of the pain, blood, sweat, and tears that were shed during my grandfather's time motivates me to write about the issues of anti-Semitism in today's society. Today's sociopolitical climate is a breeding ground for hate groups, and anti-Semitism is on the rise. In particular, college campuses have been horrifically vandalized by students painting swastikas in public areas. At best, these students are tragically ignorant of history; at worst, they are actively and brazenly expressing hatred and discrimination. Students at Duke University, where a swastika was spray painted over a tribute to Jews killed in the Pittsburgh mass shooting, stated that "it feels like there is no safe space from anti-Semitism" (https://www.newsobserver.com/news/local/article221897470.html).

Sadly, anti-Semitic crimes have taken place in many shapes and forms, ranging from direct physical confrontation to verbal abuse to property vandalism. Since the early 2000's at UC Irvine, Jewish students have been verbally ridiculed by neo-Nazi slurs, confronted with threats of physical violence if they did not remove their Star of David necklaces, and a Holocaust Memorial was vandalized with a spray-painted swastika. At UC Berkeley, student Jessica Felber was participating in a counter-protest to an anti-Israel demonstration when she was rammed into by a shopping cart by one of the anti-Israel protesters. These incidents are merely a few examples of anti-Semitic acts that occur on college campuses—institutions that promote education, tolerance, acceptance, and diversity. Other forms of hatred and intolerance—including white supremacy, homophobia and Islamophobia—are also being seen around campuses.

Many university administrations do not respond to anti-Semitic incidents in a formal statement, and if they do, it is typically in a vague language that is too general and unhelpful to put a stop to the issues; they normally use their voices in these situations to speak of "diversity" or "tolerance." One byproduct of the growing trend of anti-Semitic incidents on campuses is a wider shield of academic freedom protecting biased professors and scholars. While academics are entitled to their own opinions, there are an increasing number of reports pointing to professors attempting to indoctrinate students in their class. This type of abuse is documented in Columbia Unbecoming, a 2004 film of Columbia University. The film highlights professors using their position to preach their personal biases.

En route back to the white picket-fenced households of Greenwich, Connecticut, I realize the sacrifices my grandfather and others like him made so that I never had to endure the pain he did. I am fortunate to have never really known the real hardships that innumerable people have to face throughout their lives. While I recognize this as privilege, it is not blinding; however, it can distort perspective. In this blissful bubble, the question of "will I be eating tonight?" never crosses the minds of the consumers of thinly sliced sirloin steak of organic grass-fed cattle. The mundane "struggle" of choosing spin class or yoga, kale salad or sushi show how some of us are so far removed from our heritage that, sadly, the struggles of generations ago seem unfathomable, or worse, simply forgotten.

Although I grew up in this "bubble" of a community, my family's lifestyle was a bit different. While of the same class and privilege as those around us, my parents instilled the lesson of working for what you want; the only true failure is to be given a gift that was not rightfully earned, and my parents worked for everything we had. Growing up, they were superheroes: both of my parents would slip on their scrubs—not their designer shoes—and head to the hospital to devote their days to saving lives. I grew up watching their commitment, dedication and compassion. Hearing my grandfather's story helped me realize that such kindness and such drive is a part of my heritage. It's a part of my story as much as it is my grandfather's and father's. While we may be fortunate enough to never experience body-aching hunger or real life-or-death situations firsthand, my grandfather's stories—memories that I have locked within—have fueled my passion and determination to make a difference in other's lives.

I've heard my grandfather's incredible story of survival against all odds once from him, again from my grandmother, and now from my own father. Each time, new details help me create a clearer vision of the man I was lucky enough to know. I transcend time and space in an effort to grasp the true horror of the Holocaust for him and so many others. To say I empathize is naïve; my heart breaks, but I will never truly fathom the depths of such fear and pain. And yet, my grandfather was not hardened or bitter. I am always in awe of the amount of strength and compassion he was said to have displayed in an environment comparable only to Hell. In a situation where his very life was at stake every day, he would still give his piece of bread to another prisoner if it meant saving them; no life was not worth saving, even if it put his own life in danger. He engrained his compassion, humility, tenacity, and courage into his own children, and my father has subsequently told me and my siblings of these stories in order to teach us to appreciate the life that we have been lucky enough to have been given.

And so, I write for my grandfather. I write so that his words can be heard, so that his story can be told, and so that his memory can continue to inspire others as it has inspired me.

Michael Chehade

I woke early that morning.

Soon after, my group and I started the thirty-minute walk to cross the United States/Mexican border. I was fully expecting to go through Mexican Customs since we were entering their country. We soon arrived at the Kino Border Initiative (KBI), which was where I would be working for the week. Lined up outside the building were about seventy people waiting for the doors to open. We had been told these were all recently deported migrants. I was expecting them to look at us with disgust, given we were Americans and given they had just been kicked out of the country. Many of them stayed quiet, but a good amount of them asked how we were doing and wished us a good morning.

Once we were inside, those who worked at the KBI told us we would be serving breakfast and then washing the dishes. They encouraged us to talk to those who were eating and learn about their backgrounds. I was the "orange juice man," whose job was to ensure that everybody who wanted orange juice got it. I would walk around saying "Jugo, alguien, quieren jugo?" I was wildly popular, well actually the juice was wildly popular. I was not sure if I was going to be able to start conversations with the people eating. Luckily for me, my shirt came to the rescue. I was wearing a Washington Nationals Baseball shirt, and many of the people there had been fans of baseball when they had lived in the United States.

My t-shirt helped me introduce myself and communicate with many of them, but there were two men who I developed a close bond with throughout that week. The first was Jose, a man from Tijuana, Mexico. Jose had lived in the United States for fifteen years before one night being pulled over for being under the influence while driving. The officer recognized that Jose's papers were fake, which almost immediately led to his deportation. His family still lived in North Carolina. He missed them dearly, but he was willing to never see them again if they could continue their lives in the United States. He then spoke about how he worked mainly construction during his time in North Carolina and Florida. By no means did he live an extravagant life, but he was able to find work to support himself as well as not while at the same worry about being involved in gang violence. It was all he needed. He told me to remember that a Mexican immigrant was no different than an American. If you stood them together you would find two people willing to work hard to support their families. The only difference is that a Mexican would know how bad it is to live in a country where such an opportunity is not available.

I also developed a close bond with Emmanuel, who had been recently deported through Texas. He was sure of the reason. He was from El Salvador. That was an immediate talking point for the two of us. Much of my mom's family lives in El Salvador. I had visited several times. We talked about places in El Salvador and about Pupusas, which is a traditional El Salvadoran food made up of bread, cheese, and beans. I asked him why he had left the country because he seemed to talk about it with quite a bit of pride. He rolled up a sleeve and showed me a tattoo. I recognized immediately that it was an MS-13 gang tattoo. I was in quite a bit of fear at this point. I think Emmanuel could see that fear. He told me not to worry. He then showed me three other gang tattoos. Now I was not sure whether to be horrified or relieved. He explained how he was not in any gang. He had tattoos for the four major gangs in El Salvador so that when he was threatened by them, he could show them a tattoo. They would think he was one of them. He knew this was risky because if any gang members realized what he was actually doing, he would have been immediately killed. He repeatedly stipulated that, in countries like El Salvador, working hard was not enough to live a good life. The countries simply were not safe to live in.

I learned so much from this trip in terms of values. The most important one to me was that I should never judge a group of people until I fully understand what they go through. It is really easy for us, especially here at UVA, to sit on our high horse and claim it is other people's faults that they are in the situation they are in. My whole life has involved hard work. My life has been set up, however, that if I put the work in, I can reap the benefits of my rewards. People like Jose and Emmanuel are two of the hardest working people I have ever met. Yet they could not catch a break throughout their lives. When I returned back home, I told as many people as I could about my experience. Some agreed with my newfound values and were happy to discuss the trip with me. Others did not agree and stood with their ideals. They had the complete right to do so, but it was a little disheartening since they would not even listen to what I had to say. To be fair, it is likely I have done the same to others in my past.

Personal experience really does change a person's view.

I also began to reconsider the histories of my parents. My dad is from Lebanon; my mother from El Salvador. They certainly had to adjust when coming to the United States. Yet it is quite clear they still kept their identities. Witness the three languages, Arabic, Spanish, and English being spoken in our house. Taste the food served nightly for dinner. When I was younger, I certainly did not appreciate this part of our family. I would complain about having "weird" food in my lunch and beg my parents to only speak English to me in front of my friends. I didn't understand their journey as also being about safety, economic security, and political freedom. Often, we don't think about those whose lives lack these qualities. We do seem to consider allowing more people to partake in such rights by coming to the United States. We limit the "public sphere" to those already in America, already citizens. While it is physically impossible for all people to become citizens, we have to consider the problems of those who lack fundamental rights and freedoms. We have to see that as a reason to join our country.

After my trip to Mexico, I visited a detention center in Northern Virginia and talked to some undocumented migrants being housed there. I made it a point to call my local congressman during the DACA crisis and express my support for Dreamers. I continue to try to involve myself in activities that support undocumented migrants, including going to a protest in front of the capital and speaking with Senator Dick Durbin. I still receive the weekly newsletter from the KBI that details ways that students can help with problems surrounding undocumented migrants. I hope I can continue to be active in the cause.

Looking ahead, I see my future as a writer focused on those who do not have rights, specifically those who are forced to leave their home countries since they do not have rights. Before my trip I had never really thought about these people. I am an American citizen, and my rights are guaranteed. I grew up never having to worry about not having a voice. I felt that if I had something to say, I could say it, and even if others did not agree with me, there would be no serious repercussions for my personal beliefs. I never concerned myself with people who were not blessed with the freedoms I had. The sad part is that two people who grew up in an environment where they were not guaranteed these freedoms, my parents, lived in the same house as me and raised me. It was not till after my trip that I realized what they had been through. Luckily for them, they were able to leave and start new lives and be successful. The problem is that, these days, it rarely is that simple. Most people do not have the opportunity to move and start over. Nowadays, it is a different story, and more and more people outside our country are being pushed out and being thought of less and less. I hope to become a writer that brings these people back into our sphere. They have voices I experienced first-hand, and they deserve to be heard. I hope I can continue to play a small part in that happening.

Equality and Justice

Caroline Campos
On the Importance of Informality

On October 31st of 2018, I received a message in my inbox from a past co-worker at a Latinx community center in Richmond where I had worked the previous summer. She was promoting two volunteering opportunities. One opportunity came from a local community organizer I had met at a radical storytelling workshop over the summer, but with whom I had lost contact. In the message, he spoke of how the White House and the Department of Homeland Security had quietly begun to release thousands of detained migrants in Texas over the last two weeks. Parents, children, families, as well as lone men, women, and minors were being dropped off by the Immigration and Customs Enforcement (ICE) at the Greyhound station in McAllen, Texas. Each had been given a manila folder labeled with sharpie marker noting each migrant's identification number and pathway along the cross-country bus line. Paying around two to three hundred dollars for each ticket, people traveled along the longest Eastern bound bus line from Dallas, Texas to Richmond, Virginia. The stop in Charlottesville, where I go to college, is the second to last stop on an almost 50 hour bus ride.

When myself and other Charlottesville organizers first put out a call for volunteers to assist the individuals, a massive flow of sympathetic efforts came through for everything from cookie baking to card writing and clothes donations. I remember telling one of my friends that I was blown away by the support from the local community, especially from the elderly white population. From group chats to social media pages, through contacting and expanding volunteer efforts across the country, a national band of organizers and everyday people stepped out from their daily responsibilities to aid and support thousands of asylum seekers. And yet, the largest issue the organizers encounter is consistency. An effort that was meant to last two weeks is still going on today, almost ten months later. In the fight for liberating migrants, the initial rush that comes with this kind of community work does not suffice for long term efforts. Today, the same group of ten organizers and volunteers are running the assistance, one that not only defies sustainable community work practices, but one that neglects the fostering of interdependent communities. Activisms must be defined by their plurality. There are an almost infinite amount of ways that we must show up for each other. From offering to come over and do work with someone as they go through difficult times, to paying for a meal, to sitting for coffee, to reading books together—solidarity and acts of communal support do not have to be loud for them to be important. Activism isn't singular. Plurality.

The stories of migrants I have met in my work in Charlottesville and Richmond are mostly documented in my notes app on my iPhone. From the empty look of the feverish babies in crammed leather seats to the five-year-old boy who took it upon himself to bring his other siblings coffee and clothing from our volunteer table, there is not one story that represents the destiny of these asylum seekers existing in the purgatory of our immigration system. This work is not glamorous and not even always rewarding, but is it necessary.

In the United States, legality has always been created to the benefit of some and the detriment of others. Slavery was legal. Segregation was legal. Unethical and violent interference in developing countries was legal. Japanese internment camps were legal. This comparison is not to defy all forms of law and legal structure in this nation, but rather to call attention to the human rights violations that often occur under the guise of legality. The point is rather to understand the practices of informal and non-monetized community organizing that have run through the veins of liberatory work in this nation and the world over. Participatory economics that redistribute wealth on a community-based level or providing aid for undocumented asylum seekers, even when deemed illegal, challenge national systems of legality that inadequately uphold essential human rights. In doing so, we can reimagine socioeconomic, political, and cultural standards in a way that centers communities to build structures and routines of solidarity and support.

Embracing informality undoubtedly brings with it a profound discomfort. Challenging what has been intrinsically conditioned is uncomfortable. Yet discomfort underlies growth, and growth underlies change. In the fight for undocumented or DACAmented students, accepted notions of who deserves or merits an equal opportunity for education in this country reveal themselves as deeply fractured. As student debt skyrockets in hand with the access to information and community-based education, institutions of higher education disclose themselves as elitism-powered businesses. The fight for migrants released from detention centers is one that is inseparable from the fight for access to education for all. It is one that is rooted in the lives and stories of Black, African, and African-descended migrants. It is one that does not exist without the contributions of Trans and Queer migrants leading migratory efforts for survival. It is a fight that relies upon an unwavering understanding of humanity and human rights from our most intrinsic capacity and responsibility to listen, see, and care for one another. Activism is both action and inaction, movement and rest. As a college student, I have not only observed but also partaken in destructive forms of student activism. Forms that lead to unsustainable efforts and overwhelmed students. If I have learned anything from working alongside asylum seekers and Charlottesville community members, it has been to listen to and learn from the preexisting structures of resistance, activism, aid, and solidarity to better understand how I do or do not fit into the community.

Spoken word poem on the transit work:

> I offer him a cup of coffee and a Spiderman coloring book
> He steps onto the big blue bus that's travelled cross country for the past 42 hours
> His father follows right after him heading somewhere along the East Coast
> Asylum seekers almost
> Carlos is five and has been on a Greyhound bus for 42 hours
> They are asylum seekers seeking asylum

Asylum the protection granted by a nation to someone who has left their native country as a political refugee

Carlos and his father were held in a detention center in McAllen, Texas for weeks
They stand in an ice box for days
Holding on to each other for hours
Thinking who knows what every minute
Surviving for a never ending second
La Hielera, a concrete room with ice cold air rushing from the ceiling, cracking skin under aluminum blankets
asylum seekers seeking asylum
They stand in an ice box for days

Carlos is five and he has been on a Greyhound bus for 42 hours
Carlos is five and he has been on a Greyhound bus for 42 hours
Carlos is five and he has been on a Greyhound bus for 42 hours
In the same clothes, and the same shoes, and the same socks, and the same shirt, in the same bus for 42 hours on stolen lands that deem him illegal

Since 1994 10,000 people have died crossing the US Mexico border
A border that is not real
A border that is constructed
A border that is a product of colony
A border the refuses to see itself and that fails to understand that nobody can be illegal on stolen land

Legality has always been created to the benefit of some and the detriment of others
Slavery was legal
Segregation was legal
Jewish genocide was legal
US Imperialism was legal

European colonialism was legal
A japanese internment camp was legal
All of these things were legal and yet it doesn't mean that they were right
There are too many things that demand a continued fight
Concentration camps are legal
Mass incarceration is legal
US Imperialism is legal
European colonialism is legal
Food injustice is legal
Police brutality is legal

My freedom is not freedom if it is dependent on someone else's oppression
We are a country that runs on incarceration of all forms
Carlos is five and has been on a Greyhound bus for 42 hours
There are babies sitting in cages at the Southern border and in Georgia and Nevada and Florida and Virginia and South Carolina and Texas and California and it's becoming harder and harder to concentrate on what's important at hand because everyone seems to be stuck in a never-ending cycle of infinite movement towards a seemingly science fictional future it is so overwhelming, and yet we must not be overwhelmed.

Activisms are defined by their plurality
A plurality of ways we can show up for each other in putting together pieces and parts of a people who's president's politics and policies police people to a purposeless end

Carlos is five and has been on a bus for 42

hours

straight

And he cannot for this wait for this nation to understand the weight of its fate as a country built upon hate and a red white and blood covered plate

and at this rate our hope begins only with a clean slate to translate and circulate knowledge and action and movement and power and people and people and people and people and people and people and people whose purpose must be and be and be and be to liberate

Jonathan Brownlee

The opportunity to write on the topic of activism seems almost heaven sent or like a stiff nudge from the universe. Over the last several days, I have been pondering the death of the rapper Nipsey Hussle, black manhood, entrepreneurship, activism, and how best to impact underserved communities. These things might seem disparate at first glance; however, they are anything but. They are an interconnected web that I been stuck thinking about, and all of these things have made me reevaluate my (approach to) life and my future.

Before the death of Nipsey, I only peripherally knew of him and his work. I had heard a few songs and viewed a few quick interview clips. But through much research, I have come to understand who and what he stood for. To downplay his impact, many have and will say that Nipsey was simply a "gangsta rapper." But despite of, or in unique contrast to the harsh and violent lyrics in many of his songs, his life as a man was about building up his community and the various factions in it. He did this through creating businesses and various corporate partnerships in the harsh community he grew up in, right there on Crenshaw and Slauson. He gave his friends jobs, many of whom were convicted felons. He tried bringing people together. Nipsey put action behind his words.

In various rap circles, Nipsey's death is being compared to the death of Tupac Shakur. While YouTubing old videos of Nipsey talking about his aspirations for his community, videos of Tupac popped up. After a deep dive into his interviews, the connection between the two men became clear. It's about more than rap. It's about growth. Both individuals had a freedom and a fearlessness to speak the truth. The way they spoke was so passionate, so insightful, so pure. Their words always seem to be aimed at the heart of something, the foundational crux of the matter. They often spoke of their past mistakes and their growth. There is a deep connection between honesty, fearlessness, and value. I see myself in these men. But somewhere along the way, I'd exchanged my passion and vigor for privacy and advancement. The realness never left me, but my passion to help others and fearlessness was quieted in exchange for a semi-peaceful respite. These last few days, I have been wondering if this change in my approach to life should be reversed.

I said all that to say that activism is more than marching, shouting, and tweeting. It is more than the ideology you hold. It is more than picking sides. It is about acting to solve real-life problems. The life of Nipsey Hussle is about growth and trying to influence real change in the places where it is needed the most.

Pondering Nipsey's story, and listening to Tupac's unimpeded passion, I feel reinvigorated, reenergized, and less cloistered. I have always wanted to and tried to give back to my community, but now I will do so by tenfold. I will be less reserved, I will speak the facts and the truth much louder, and I will put myself in harm's way to help those who need it the most. From their example, I will grow more courageous.

In one interview, Nipsey said that the highest power is to inspire others. So, yes. Anyone can be an activist. Even a gang-member-turned-community-builder. Anyone who is willing to take real action to honestly better the plight and understanding of others. Anyone who aims to inspire (through action). That is real activism in my view. And I hope to learn from those who inspire even after death.

Friederike Piehler

Overlooked Stories: The Importance of Local Actors for Human Rights Advocacy

In 2019, the United Nations Security Council passed a resolution on sexual violence in conflict. In part, this was a reaction to the increasing use of rape as a means of warfare. When the issue reached the United Nations, it attracted a lot of attention. Newspapers shed light on political quarrels within the Security Council that weakened the resolution and the advocacy of Amal Clooney, George Clooney's wife and human rights lawyer. In contrast, little attention was paid to the people "behind the scenes" who had worked for years to get the issue to the United Nations. To me, their story is the real story. It shows that human rights are just as much about the local actors who fight for what they believe in every day, as about the big picture that we (in the Global North) tend to focus on.

Nadia Murad is one of the people behind the scenes of the resolution. In 2014, her village in Iraq fell victim to a genocide committed by the Islamic State against the Yazidi minority. Thousands of people were killed, and women and children were abducted. Nadia Murad was one among countless women who ISIS held as sex slaves. Since her escape in 2014, she has restlessly been telling her story. With the help of Yazda, a small non-governmental organization consisting of a few people only, she spoke to members of parliaments around the world, talked to news stations, wrote a book and made a documentary. In the documentary, Nadia Murad keeps saying that she never wanted to be an activist. But she kept fighting to protect other people from suffering what she had suffered and to try to get justice. Without her courage and persistence, the Security Council might never have passed the resolution.

Why then is Nadia Murad hardly mentioned in the coverage of the United Nations resolution? I would not know about her story if her movie had not been screened at the University of Virginia, where I got my

Master of Laws. Maybe the reason for this is that Nadia Murad's story is just one of thousands of individual stories relating to human rights. It is impossible to know all of them. But I believe that there is also a structural reason: In the Global North, human rights are talked about in terms of big international actors like the United Nations or Amnesty International. They are talked about in terms of treaties and the best policies to implement them. Often times, it seems to be forgotten that, at their core, human rights are about individuals.

This not only leads to a limited view of human rights, but also undermines their power as a tool for change. If human rights are only thought of and talked about in terms of the big picture, the big international players are the only places for effecting change. But, as Nadia Murad's story shows, it often takes a long time for an issue to reach the big scene. A lot of issues never get there. And even if they do, the remedies the international system offers might not be sufficient or best-suited to resolve the issue. The Security Council resolution condemns the use of sexual violence in conflict. But it does not remedy the genocide that was committed against the Yazidi. A broader approach is necessary. There are calls for a comprehensive peace-building process in the region. Local actors are best suited to administer this because they understand the complexities and challenges of the region. People will more readily talk to them and engage in the process because the local actors are part of the same group. They can relate in ways that are impossible for international actors, and they know what will actually be effective in the specific context.

Things can change with or without international actors, but not without local actors. Without their knowledge and engagement, human rights work cannot be effective. I believe that telling the stories of people like Nadia Murad is crucial for human rights. It shows that every individual can contribute to the advancement of human rights, and that local actors are invaluable to achieving change. Emphasizing this, will strengthen the human rights movement as a whole.

Alex Martinez
Collisions at the immigration office

North and South meet-
at the detention center where I left my identity
glued to the biometrics machine.

My false sense of security was born
in a place like this, where my appetite for light was
satisfied, briefly.

North and South meet-
inside the child of an indigenous worker from Peru
and a Caucasian doctor from the Americas;

his golden skin celebrates
the future of not knowing
green fields full of hard labor and despair.

At the same time,
it resents the privilege
that perpetually lives just beneath his skin.

North and South meet at the waiting room
where documents are only valid if your soul is conceded
to the masters who rule the stolen lands of our parent's
parents.

The center of the universe is not in this dark place
where my broken innocence asks politely
to be pieced back
together.

Love does not live here,
technicality and processes live here,

along with chaos, fear, and citizenship stamps.

Some of us are imprinted with labels
to recognize us as good immigrants,
and some of us are dragged around from mouth of diplomats
to the short fiery fingers of a president.

North and South meet-
at the place where we are called aliens,
where we are treated as If we were beings from another world.

We are second class citizens,
because living undocumented is not real
but feeling undocumented is everything.

Here at this place where my darkest fear come true,
my brother sits,
his legs are shackled;

I found him where North and South met
and I wish to go back to my mother's womb,
with him.

I wish to prepare him
for his time in solitude
and the deportation that is to follow.

But there are things I can't do anymore,
because time was stolen from us and
the only clock that is turning back is this country's.

The man sitting next to me is not my brother,
he tries to figure out the foreign language in the contract
where he gives his freedom away,

but his brain can't process it all at a fast,
at least not fast enough
for the ice agents;

he looks at me and his eyes ask for help,
he is somebody's brother, perhaps my own brother,
or somebody's dad

and I help him figure out
that there are not enough letters in the English alphabet
to describe the hopelessness he is feeling.

North and South meet-
at the place where we separate his Salvadoran family,
where we cage them,
because they fled north once we moved south and burned
their village.

North and South meet-
where the pain is caused.

North and South meet-
inside me
and I hope to disrupt the turning of the tide,
to overcome the burning of the sun

and meet myself at the other side.
Behind the invisible borders
that separate us all.

Between the north and the south
and even if we can't see them,
I know they are coming down.

Amithav Reddy

Charismatic and influential leaders fill the histories of social and political change. Think Susan B. Anthony, Martin Luther King Jr., and Nelson Mandela. But now, nearly anyone can support change from behind a computer screen. Facebook and Twitter enable everyone from the President of the United States sitting in the White House to a teacher sitting at home to express their view on issues such as abortion, gun control, and environmental regulations. Young adults have been particularly inspired to make a difference. College campuses are hotspots of activism, with student clubs drawing attention to incidents of famines, corruption, and sexual assaults around the world.

For these young adults, using social media is the most powerful and effective method of activism because it fits perfectly with their skillset. People are quick to join causes they care about, and social media gives them an easy way to contribute. The Black Lives Matter movement is a great example of a movement that started off as social media outrage and transformed into street demonstrations internationally. Activism doesn't require money or exceptional passion anymore. It only needs time and technology. This is why the common man leads the charge for change. There is no need to look outward for the next great leader to strike a movement against injustice anymore. People do not have to sit idly by on the sidelines while individuals with influence decide what rules to which the world will adhere. Today, now, is the reign of the ordinary person.

Simran Kaur

I protest because there is injustice in the world, especially in the justice system of the United States. A lot of people fail to see the injustice, so I protest to bring awareness to a good cause. I protest because I am a minority. I am an Asian-American woman that has had injustice done to my people. I don't want anyone to feel the injustice that I felt. I protest because I want to show the government that people do care about a cause, and we will stand our ground until something is done. I protest because I see injustices on social media while other people are getting away scot-free for the same thing. I protest because I want to see the world come together and be happy. I want to see an optimist world. I protest because I want people to see the world the way I see it, so they can understand me. I protest because I hate it when people get hurt because of the system. I protest because the system could be easily changed, but it isn't. I protest because I see the world as a realist. I know the negative things that are going on, but I feel like pushing change will make them better. I protest because I want to push change even if it means that I am the only one protesting. I protest because I want to bring light to issues that are seen as minor in the world. I protest because black lives matter.

Emma Ashley-Grose
I protest to support community.
I protest to spread love.
I protest to be empowered.
I protest to bring positive change.

Talbi Salima Aya
"People shouldn't be afraid of their government. Governments should be afraid of their people."
Alan Moore

Throughout the world, people suffer from poor political conditions, absence of democracy, corrupt entrenched rulers, and violations of human rights. This is especially the case in the countries of the Middle East and North Africa, and eventually, these conditions led to the emergence of the so-called Arab Spring.

Tunisia was the first African country that started the uprisings, calling them the Jasmine Revolution or Jasmine Spring. The first day of the uprising was on December 17th, 2010. The protestors acted in solidarity with the young Mohammed Bouazouzi, who had committed suicide because of miserable living conditions marked by poverty, social injustice, and unemployment—problems from which all Tunisian people were suffering. The revolution lasted twenty-seven days, a period marked by aggressive and violent reactions from the army, as well as strong resistance from the people in the different regions of Tunisia. During this time, over 219 Tunisians died and many others were wounded. The Jasmine Spring resulted in restrictions on the power of the state as well as the forced resignation of the President Zain El Abidine Ben Ali. It was the first in a series of protests to occur in Arab countries.

Both Egypt and Libya were influenced by the Tunisian Revolution. Inspired by Tunisia, people in both countries fought to reclaim their stolen political and human rights. The Egyptian uprisings began on January 25, 2011. The protests were first organized on social media, spreading beyond that platform, and eventually leading to the Tahrir Square demonstrations with marches, cheers, and strikes. The Egyptian state carried out brutal attempts to suppress this revolution by firing shots and tear gas, but the people showed a strong resistance. The revolution ended eighteen days later with the resignation of the President Hosni Mubarak and a promise of political and economic reforms. Libya's revolution in 2011 took a similar course to Egypt, but was more focused on President Muammar Qaddafi's dictatorship. Here, the state's reaction was crueler. The revolution ended with the death of Qaddafi and a significant number of Libyans. Again, political and economic reforms were promised.

Recently, Algeria has joined this "Arab Spring" after the insistence of the government to nominate President Abdul-Aziz Bouteflika for a fifth term. The Algerians didn't want their protests to be like the other Arab African uprisings, full of violence and death. They were against violence because of what the Algerian people witnessed during the Black Decade. Instead, the protestors chanted, "Peaceful, Peaceful." Indeed, each Friday after prayer, moving directly from mosques to the streets, elders, children, women, and men protested all together: "Peaceful, Peaceful." And they were peacefully protected by the police and army.

They demand the resignation of all members of the government as well as these officials being held accountable for their actions. The goal was (and is) to build a new uncorrupted state.

All these uprisings aimed to lift the people out of the suffering. Perhaps, in some cases, many of the goals were reached, but I believe the casualties were greater than results. Yet, the hope of a better tomorrow still exists.

Hind Benlakhal

A change for the better starts by making a positive difference in your own life. Then, if you are determined enough, this will push you to try sharing and reflecting that difference in your small environment and then perhaps in a bigger community. Being motivated and having the courage to tackle any new experience, then, would make a positive change either for a person's own life or for the society in which they live. Indeed, I am someone who moved from making a change in their own life to trying to make a change in society.

Since my early childhood, I have always been passionate by drawing and everything that is related to the arts. As this passion grew within me, art soon became my only way to overcome and deal with the stress and problems of daily life. Throughout this period, I was also always thinking of a way to share and dedicate my humble talents for the benefits of others. For instance, during the summer holidays, I used to be in charge of some workshops for children focused on reading and drawing. I wanted to help them develop their talents because, in our region, such opportunities for kids are a bit rare. Another moment when I worked with children was when I painted on the walls of a hospital in the pediatrics section. It was once a dream of mine to spread joy and happiness with my modest paintings, and I have had the opportunity to realize it. I am extremely happy and proud of this work. The smiles and laughter of the sick children and adults were definitely priceless. Besides, that fraternity atmosphere, solidarity, and team work makes us extremely motivated to get engaged more in such volunteering works.

More recently, I have become active in the #TrashTagChallenge, an important movement created by Algerian youth during the political events of 2019. The challenge is about cleaning areas that are dirty or decayed then showing before and after pictures. I had the honor to take part in this challenge in my city by cleaning the bus station of the university, painting the walls, and then drawing some meaningful and inspiring pictures on them. It was a great experience to be with young people full of energy and motivated for a better change. Indeed, this challenge was spread to all of the Algerian cities through young citizens who truly gave hope to our country for a brighter future. On the whole, children and youth are the future of any country. And as we see in Algeria, there would be no fear concerning such a wise generation, a generation full of willingness to make positive change.

Hamdi Soufian Abdelkarim
A true injustice is done to students when they are assigned unqualified teachers, those who have studied at university in unconnected fields to teaching, such as the trades, instead of in a Teacher's College. So, this message is an alert to our nation's future: Primary school teachers are responsible for giving future generations the basic skills for building their lives. Importantly, this is an injustice and destruction of the psyche of real teachers who chose to deepen their knowledge in the field of education. It sends a clear message to qualified teachers that "you are not valued."

In response to this situation, as future teachers, my colleagues, and I took part in a three-month strike. The Ministry did not respond to our concerns, however. Instead, they used some tactics like taking students away from the school to finish the strike. In the end, we realized that we were swimming in a river of chaos, that we must leave. Today, we, as Algerians, are trying to change our government by taking part in huge marches every Friday. Our goal is to ensure a new government that is based on democracy and law, a government based on justice that can direct our path towards joining the developed nations.

Alex Martinez
A Dreamer's Demise

I dreamt of you once.
In my dream,
you scolded me
for not growing up fast enough.

In my dream,
I promised you I would try to catch up.
And since then
I've been rushed and hurried to get here.

I missed so much along the way
and I don't blame you mother.
I am a victim of time-
and they call me a dreamer

but sometimes
the dreams
we dream,
can kill us too...

Bouchra Rahmouni
The history has marked so many famous activists that led to important changes in the world, people like Martin Luther King, Nelson Mandela, Mahatma Gandhi, and Malala Yousafzai. These leaders and activists have worked to find solutions to humanitarian and political issues. They have worked to change the whole world for the best, and it can be argued that the world has always seen movements of such resistant activists in the face of all that is against humanity. People have always fought against corruption of all kinds, whether political or social. Yet, today, probably the most important part of activist movements in Algeria are the youth.

Youth activism is the engagement of young people in organizing for change in their societies. They are often called the champions for change because they are full of energy and creative ideas. They are smart enough to mark a mark in the world. In Algeria, we have been watching student movements against corrupt regimes and how they could make a difference in our country. We have witnessed the amazing workshops done by youngsters to raise awareness of the importance of changing their society. We see how successful they have been in these efforts, such as with the recent "trashtag challenge." They also work for instilling new good values and erasing all what is bad for humanity. What makes youth interested in activism is probably because they finally realized how important they are as individuals in society and that their energies should not be wasted. These young people are able to lead for a change for a better world because of their ideas and ways of thinking. They feel concerned about all that happens in their countries and they seek for changing what needs to be changed.

Consider the Algerian movement against the previous President Abdelaziz Bouteflika and his regime. The sad truth is that during the twenty years of Bouteflika's regime, young people were politically disconnected and never got involved politically. Yet on February 22, 2019 when the Algerian people from all the states came out to demand regime change, we witnessed the participation of all segments of society, including young people—university students who made and are still making history with their hands. These students have taken to the streets in demonstrations and marches in response to the demands of people. They have staged national strikes and have chosen Tuesda" to be the National Students' day of marches against the political system. Algerian university students have succeeded in bringing the demands of the people to the government. These students could make the government listen to the people's demands. In fact, the government accepted some of the demands. It can be argued that, without the university students participating in the movement, the people would have succeeded in their demands.

Maybe the surprising aspect of this moment is that although most young people in Algeria are not politically engaged and might not have much knowledge of politics, they are organizing conferences and events where experts in politics come to debate the current situation and offer solutions. They create public opinion polls and listen to each other, and if anyone watches their marches and manifestations, it would be clear how well-organized they were. This generation is trying to prove that students are educated about politics, and that they know what they want, which is a better Algeria full of democracy. And it does not end there. These same Algerian students are trying to cultivate new valuable principles in society by volunteering in several Algerian towns and cities to clean public spaces and paint walls with bright colors and pictures. They are using artwork and sharing everything on social media as a platform to popularize this idea, and it is actually working. Many cities now look different. This makes Algerian youth an example of how to reinvigorate urban spaces.

The current situation and events in Algeria are an answer to the question "Why is activism important?" Young activists want their movement to remain civil, peaceful, and clean. This is a strong message to the current government that these people know where they are heading and that Algeria's future is safe in their hands. Many experts and specialists in politics said that Algeria's future depends on youth activism. They believe that Algeria would be a better place to live in if these young students carry on doing what they do because they play an absolutely important role in making the demonstrations look peaceful and powerful. Because of these student activists, Algeria is going on its way to democracy—if nothing goes wrong of course.

Mohand Chibane

For the first time in the history of Algeria, people unite throughout the country for one purpose: a radical change in government. This event amazed all the world not because the people woke up from a deep sleep, but because the demonstrations by the Algerians that launched the movement are peaceful. The slogans they repeat are one on every Algerian tongue: Peaceful ... Peaceful ...... Army and people are brothers.

Demonstrations have been taking place in Algeria since February 16, 2019 to initially protest Abdelaziz Bouteflika's candidacy for a fifth presidential term, followed by protests against his plan to remain in power to the end of his fourth term. On a scale unprecedented for decades and after the defection of the army, these demonstrations led Bouteflika to resign on April 2, 2019.

Still we continue.

We are fed up with a government that has stolen all the dreams of Algerian citizens.

We hate a government that steals from its people.

We hate a government that causes the mass migration of youth, women, and elders to Europe, especially the educated class who want a better future.

Under this government, Algeria became a country without any principle, spreading a culture of corruption, bribery, and, especially, discrimination among the population.

The rich control the poor.

Truth has become false, and falsehoods become truth.

Everyone came out for these peaceful demonstrations, which denounce such crimes against Algeria and demand restoration of individual and community rights.

Everyone wants change for a better Algeria, for a modern Algeria. We have all the qualifications to be among the best countries in the world. The only obstacle is this flawed regime.

So, the Algerians' demands are serious: the unification of the Algerians; the establishment of a democratic state based on justice and equality. Hand the torch to the young people so they can govern and build democratic Algeria.

Hand in hand, we are united in a goal to overthrow the ruling gang and restore national sovereignty. These protests will continue until the demands are met. We are optimistic that there is a change in the coming days. That we will become an example for the world of our peaceful and courageous character. It will be just a few days until this nightmare will over and the sun of Algeria will rise again and will never be absent.

Never be afraid to raise our voice for honesty, truth, and compassion against injustice, lying, and greed.

If people all over the globe would do this, it would change the world.

Chaima Hachemi

A man, a woman, an old man, a child ... a flag in hands and a smile on faces ... this is how the Algerian people decided to make its voice heard and to demand the end of the president's rule.

"سلمية...سلمية Peaceful.. Peaceful."

This is what the protestors keep saying when they go out to march.

No life was lost. No shot was fired. No fight nor quarrel occurred. No one came to blows. All Algerians protest peacefully as one united and connected body. The people want to snatch back their rights and to map out a clearer, more brilliant future for themselves and for Algeria. Nothing could stop them from looking for ways and methods to create a

New Algeria, a new place for people to think big, dream big, and realize their dreams for the sake of themselves, for their beloved country.

The first demand was no fifth term for the president. Bouteflika had ruled Algeria for 20 years. He is too old. He is physically unable to rule any more. This demand is not impossible. It is just seeking to have a new leader for the country. To be more precise, let us say a younger leader. People are simply against the prolongation of the Bouteflikian rule.

They focused peacefully not only on this one demand, but on others as well. They want the corrupted system to end and the country to witness a radical revolutionary change, and each week there has been a remarkable increase in the number of protests. Everyone throughout the country is feeling connected with this movement. People of different ages, working in different fields, and from different backgrounds took part in the marches, and at each moment, youth were asked and undertook vital leadership roles.

These recent events have demonstrated the courage of Algerians. In the beginning, everything seemed to be risky and scary, especially after suffering and experiencing the Dark Decade. Forget about the past, but do not forget the lesson. Now we can proudly say that Algeria is ready to live and enjoy the Light Decade. Seeing all what has been happing to the neighboring Arab countries, people understood that a gun and a fight for peace will bring about nothing but war and blood. Killing each other, killing people who are our neighbors to create change is not a solution. It is crystal clear how the people are willing to make the radical change real.

They did not just protest holding flags. They cleaned the streets when marching. Indeed, walking all around and gathering the trash has become a common practice in the marches. Some families and restaurant owners prepared food for protestors out in the street. Children, men, and women distributed bottles of water for everyone, including policemen. Some gave flowers to people, and others helped those who passed out from heat, got tired, or fell sick. Oh, lucky Algeria; oh, lucky Algerians.

After many weeks of protesting in the street and on social media, Bouteflika resigned. He sent a letter to Algerians stating that he tackled some important issues, but he also sought forgiveness. He apologized. When that news of his declaration spread, the streets were full of people who went out to celebrate. Their first demand had been heard and realized.

The way Algerians got to speak up and freely express themselves is worth admiring. No one died. No one got injured. Peaceful was the path they decided to walk on. Rare are the people who believe in the power of peaceful methods to fight corruption and, even more rare, are those who do it. Despite the fact that the coming days are vague, and the future of the country is considered to be unpredictable, these marches and protests helped the Algerians to get beautiful things out of them and into society. Our people proved that the good intentions and solidarity are part of us. We are united to the point that we cannot even tell when this sense of unity started to take a shape.

Algerian beauty is being demonstrated in every single state. We did not lose ourselves when protesting. We spread the sense of patriotism with an artistic touch, a loving touch that demonstrated what Algerians are able to do when they join hands and act as one citizen. Fighting and trying to clean the darkest files did not push us away from our daily life. We talk to each other. We help. We laugh, maybe we dance. We spread positivity and hope all around.

Devin Willis

Reflections on student activism at the University of Virginia, 2016-2019

I wish that I had understood the term "student activist" to be an oxymoron sooner. I don't mean to dismiss the value of being a student or of being an activist. In fact, I believe that both education and inspired action together form the primary engines of social change. That being said, student activists who strive to effect a change in their respective space and time should understand the contradictions with which they are operating. Higher education is designed so that our radical politics can only be performed and heard upon an arbitrarily exclusive platform. Understand this contradiction sooner rather than later. Not for the sake of being the most pure or inspiring young activist, but because a firm grasp on yourself and your position will carry your cause so much further against the social structures and institutions that are designed to oppress you.

Both of my parents are first-generation college graduates originally from poor Black neighborhoods in the Midwest. Their image of university will always be that of a Willy Wonka golden ticket to a better life. When I was 17, I became very engrossed in Marx and desired to be the next Che. I had the nerve to tell my mom that I was a proud socialist who thought college was a scam and that I would not be joining her in debt slavery. Looking back, I'm surprised she held back her laughter. She said that it was not up for discussion.

Disrespecting Mom's biggest dream for her only son was out of the plans. I was on my way to Jefferson's university. Ol' Virginia, old money. The central quad was a plantation! My young, black, angsty mind didn't vibe with it. I thought myself an outsider and I failed to see myself as part of the grand institution, for better and for worse.

Trump became president at the end of my first, very depressing semester at school. The political climate's intensity tripled and I fell in love with politics all over again. By the end of that first year I was knee-deep in the student activist scene alongside other marginalized and exasperated young students.

We made our way, as did many before us, to the advocacy and activist student organizations. The NAACP, the Black Student Alliance, the Minority Rights Coalition, the Very Very Angry Club; the list goes on and on. Unfortunately, the ecstasy of finally discovering an outlet for our pain and anger became blinding very quickly. As a green, so-called student activist I could not yet be bothered to notice how my loud voice was only heard because it was the privileged voice of a student, the voice of one who could afford to be a student.

The student activist contradiction is being available to attend a protest or a club because you can afford not to work a job in your spare time. It is the freedom to explore and discuss ideas that do not affect your social and financial future for extended periods of time. This seems obvious to me now, but I remember how hard it was to process such an inconvenient truth in the heat of my early college days. Many other bright-eyed activists and I preferred to believe that we were the vocal champions of social justice, not because we happened to be available, but rather because of our individual merits. I think many of us believed that we possessed some special capacity to get the job done. Maybe it was our passion, our zeal, or our internet presence. Something would give us the ability to navigate exclusionary spaces and to oppose systems of power better than those who came before us. We fell prey to a really good trick; we were convinced of our own exceptionalism, a serious mistake that would cost.

Unite the Right
By the end of my freshman year, I had been appointed to the Black Student Alliance Executive Board. The BSA, although centrist in outlook, was the most dominant Black student organization on grounds. I served as the 2017-18 secretary, but because I was the only BSA officer living in Charlottesville during the summer of 2017, I was quickly promoted to something like a political liaison to the hotbed of community

organizers working in Charlottesville at the time. People had begun to call it "the summer of hate," and there were a million groups to keep track of from Black Lives Matter C-ville to Showing Up for Racial Justice (SURJ). By June 2017, I was drawn into an impressive coalition of UVA-Charlottesville community members organized around the cause of resisting Jason Kessler, the Proud Boys, and other fascist groups whose activity became prolific.

Leaders in the community showed me the ropes. They took me along for nonviolent direct actions and to clandestine meetings in anticipation of Unite the Right. I reported everything back to the Black Student Alliance and a network of other student groups who were horrified at the developments and upset at being away from the city during the crisis. I don't think this sentiment survived the summer, as the stakes elevated so quickly.

I saw members of the Klu Klux Klan for the first time with my own eyes on July 8th when the neo-fascists held a demonstration in downtown Charlottesville at Justice Park (formerly known as Jackson Park). They looked pretty silly out there in those infamous costume robes ... in the middle of a Virginian summer. Nonetheless, a few images from that first encounter stand out to me: I remember there being a surprising amount of women chanting alongside the old Klansmen that you might expect to see; I remember the multiracial police force who stood between us protesters and the Klansmen as if we were the real threat to public safety; and lastly, the image of an older white man standing beside a fellow Klansmen. He was looking at us but gesturing to the pistol on his hip, protected by a wall of police officers. He was actually threatening people. How many unarmed Black men have been killed by the police for so much less?

July 8th was also memorable because it was the first time I personally witnessed that the police prioritize order above justice. The fascists were escorted out of the city by Virginia state police. The day was basically over. My BSA friends and I went to a Mexican restaurant.

Maybe 20 minutes had gone by when we sensed a commotion coming from the direction of the park—of course. The police were attacking the protesters who had not left the area in less than twenty minutes. People were gassed and beaten. Was it just a coincidence that police violence against community members erupted once the student and academic crowd had dispersed? We were confused and disgusted. At that time, I still had excuses for the police. Maybe the crowd was being too rowdy. It was a long, hot, and emotional day.

After that incident, we all knew that a lot of the bigots would be returning to Charlottesville in less than a month. This time, we had the benefit of knowing about whose safety the police would be most concerned. Fortunately, the people of Charlottesville took safety into their own hands. Nonviolent direct-action trainings took place all around the region in the days leading up to Kessler's rally. Without a doubt, these proactive moves saved some lives and prevented violence.

That network of activists, religious leaders, antifa, students, journalists, etc. were thoroughly prepared for round two of July 8th. The People's Action for Racial Justice (PARJ) committee led by Walter Heinecke had the brilliant idea of securing a counter-demonstration permit for Justice Park and McGuffey Park. These two parks were located only several blocks away from the site of Kessler's coming demonstration at Emancipation Park (formerly Lee Park). That foresight accomplished two things. First, it prevented more public space from being utilized by the fascist threat. Second, it provided a safe space for the many brave counter-demonstrators who would show up to oppose Kessler's Nazis in person. I am convinced that even more lives were saved by these preparations, made by ordinary people who just happened to care and who wanted to show up.

We had all been warned that Kessler's Unite the Right demonstration would be larger than the Klu Klux Klown show of July 8th. I thought I was prepared. I was not.

I was not prepared for August 11th, 2017 when my university allowed Richard Spencer and his tiki torch fascists to assault a nonviolent group of students, Antifa, and community members beneath the campus statue of Thomas Jefferson. I still don't know how to describe the fear and stress we experienced beneath that statue. My vision was limited by the torchlight, and I was covering my face to protect my identity. I was scared to death and kept thinking that one of the fascists would start shooting. We took their slurs, their pepper spray, and eventually their fists and elbows as we were forced off of the statue. Only after the fascists had finished their assault did the police then force the protesters out of the plaza. Many of them had been pepper sprayed, maced, or burned by tiki torch-turned-spear. The cops did not care.

I was not prepared for August 12th, 2017 when a sea of neo-Nazis, neo-Confederates, and militarized nationalists swarmed Emancipation park. No one was prepared for how they murdered Heather Heyer and assaulted innocent people, many of whom were my friends.

Who could have prepared us for that kind of trauma? For the coming storm of student protests, the unresponsive administration at UVA, for Trump's "both sides," for predatory media reporters, for the lopsided student response ranging from massive indifference to blind fury, and for the years of legal proceedings that would consume my life for the next year.

A million mistakes were made amongst the well-meaning elements of post-August 2017 Charlottesville-UVA. I prefer to discuss some of the pitfalls experienced by myself and the students who tried to be activists in the aftermath of a national emergency. We had no control over what happened to our community but all of the control over our individual responses. For at least a few weeks, people had to listen to us.

The purpose of this criticism is not to push some revisionist history but to spotlight avoidable mistakes in the praxis of contemporary student activism. Some topics, like my emphasis on the importance of humility, might seem sentimental or trite. I don't apologize for that. Concerns about the personal and interpersonal become extremely consequential when your community faces a crisis and it's time to organize across difference. So, here are some lessons and questions inspired by my time as a student activist at UVA after Unite the Right.

Be Humble
Humility is key because it precedes all the other virtues of organizing (and life, really). Student activists tend to buy into a currency of noise—whoever is the loudest, angriest, and most righteous is praised as a shining example. There's nothing wrong with a firebrand when that fire is grounded in something substantive that can speak for itself. But that combination is very rare. It takes humility to admit that you, an aspiring organizer and agent of change, do not know everything. We can always stand to benefit from more reading (and writing, too). Don't be silly enough to think you are the first person facing whatever challenge is before you. No need to reinvent the wheel. Some previous revolutionary has written about your situation. Read them! Or else succumb to your own ignorance and become a hindrance in the field.

I know that more humility on my part could have been handy during our student organizer coalition meetings. Let me set the stage before I elaborate. Imagine spending three or four hours every Sunday night on the top floor of a coffee shop with over 40 college students trying to orchestrate a unified student response to Unite the Right. Every Sunday for weeks, all of the student activists would descend upon this small attic and argue about organizing strategy to no constructive result. Questions before us often sounded like this: Should we trust this or that administrator? How can we be more inclusive in our movement? How do we frame ourselves to the media? What's at stake if we take the streets?

All of the various factions were at each other's throats. Skepticism emerged from every direction; militants didn't trust radicals, who didn't trust liberals, who didn't trust centrists, who all resented the majority of students who resumed their normal schedules. We became bitter and frequently condescended to the seemingly indifferent student body. Then, we would turn around and plead with that shameful silent majority of students to come and join our marches.

Different individuals and factions tried hard to pull the activist's coalition in different directions. The University of Virginia tried hardest. For example, the Black Student Alliance could get meetings with the deans of UVA, but smaller groups of equal importance could not. BSA was far from the only group suffering with a lot to say. Before we knew it, we had sipped the exceptionalist Kool-Aid again and allowed a hierarchy to divide our coalition.

We were all united by intention, and we wanted to heal our school and our communities. We shared a simple objective: the satisfaction of a published list of student demands. Rapidly, we balkanized and became factional, divided by questions of tactic and strategy. A lot of those questions about organization, structure, and pace could have been resolved if only the clock were on our side. We had limited time with the national public's attention. I like to believe that a more respectful, humble, and less alienating praxis might have kept our team together long enough to effect more change with our moment.

Let's say that you are, in fact, America's Next Top Activist. You already know everything and you've read everyone from bell hooks to Franz Fanon to Huey Newton. You have already earned your activist-organizer stripes, and your authority is unquestioned. Time to take charge and set people straight, right? Not likely. The opposite is true to me—I think you can only benefit from humility, even in that case. True knowledge is not intimidated by the inexperience or ignorance of others. Why should anyone draw pleasure from knowing more about activism or wokeness than the next person? Existing further left of center than the ordinary Joe whom you organize beside is nothing but a circumstance. The revolution cannot simply become the new hierarchy of exclusive consciousness. Be humble and teach others as you were once taught.

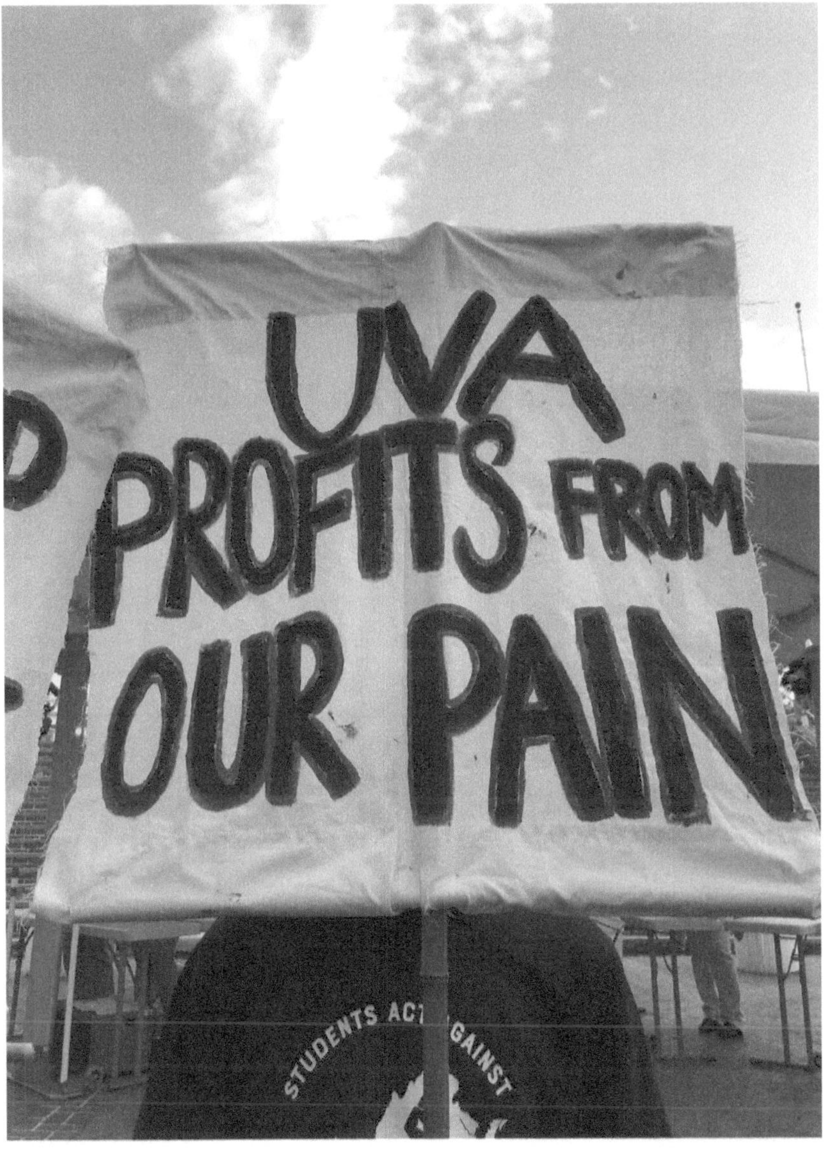
UVA
PROFITS FROM
OUR PAIN
STUDENTS ACT
GAINST

Humility can defeat this new phenomenon where student activists race towards an exclusive social consciousness, better known as "wokeness," like an arms race. If the hard-earned wisdom of so-called wokeness is taken for granted, then we are doomed to repeatedly destroy solidarity with condescending, hierarchical attitudes towards our potential friends and allies. We need people who can put their ego aside in order to deftly navigate between all roles of social change, from educator to leader to listener. We need to pass along wisdom organically, building trust and solidarity in the process. Attitudes of superiority always produce hierarchy, and hierarchy is not compatible with grassroots coalition.

Don't allow social consciousness to become commodified. Unlearning the politics of a status quo under which we were all raised is a process that cannot happen overnight. Anyone who expected us to magically shake off the elitist culture of UVA, the logics of settler-colonialism, and of neoliberalism, was ironically asking us to be exceptional. It's a journey, and everybody has one. If you are further along in the process than your peers, please remember that you accomplish nothing important by hanging your enlightenment over the heads of others who are fundamentally on your side and on their way.

Try Compassion

In 2017, my friend Kendall was a much more wise and kind student activist than most of us. She'd been there for everything from the tiki torches to the student marches. We had our political differences, but she never once shamed me for where I was in my journey of political growth. The mutual respect between us lives on to this day. Whenever I get too upset by how activist types can treat one another, I often think back to Kendall. I recall those dreadful Sunday meetings, and I grin with pleasure when I picture her shouting above the chaos, "Remember to assume best intentions!"

People trip. Immature, naive, and straight up hurtful behaviors jump out. And while ignorance is never acceptable, neither is stagnation. I wish

I had shown and been shown much more compassion. Kendall was correct; we all had amazing intentions. We spent way too much time fighting and undermining each other. Even though few of us became or remained friends, I feel permanently connected to that small minority of students who continued to show up and sacrifice their energy and time for our coalition. Showing up is an accomplishment we can't deny each other.

Proactive Moves
Organizing is much more effective when the infrastructure is in place before the crisis happens. I often think about how so few of the student coalition members really knew each other before that national emergency was thrust into our laps. So many of us could have been good friends. If only we had more time to mingle and unthaw before trying our collective hand at forcing political change. Yes, building durable relationships with people is part of an effective resistance strategy. Being proactive makes that possible. In my third year of college, my roommate taught me that the act of breaking bread or sharing coffee with your peeps can be a profoundly radical one. Creating space to be human with each other in the midst of all the pressure, confusion, and coercion. It heals the soul and will come in handy down the road when shit hits the fan.

Be proactive. How many people understood that, for years, there existed a deep divide between Charlottesville community members and the come-and-go of UVA faculty and students? What if that relationship had been repaired before the chaos of summer '17? We don't get to know because that didn't happen.

I lack the necessary experience to write something that even pretends to be an exhaustive critique of the student activist culture. I can only speak to a limited, albeit chaotic window of time. Also, it's not all failure back there. The university conceded some of the easier coalition demands. They removed the pro-confederate plaques off of the Rotunda. The university acknowledged receiving a donation from the Klu Klux Klan and repaid part of its worth to the medical expenses of those injured by Unite the Right. Buildings named after white supremacists and eugenicists around the grounds have been renamed for leaders of marginalized backgrounds.

More satisfying than the enactment of our lay-up demands is being able to watch the student culture of UVA make progress. The needle should have moved much further after all that happened. Still, I can't help but notice how much has changed in the student body culture over the past two years. We are more engaged, more sharp, and more hungry for change than before. I draw hope from our collective strength and our ability to learn and to adapt. In this very moment, we are reaching out to trade wisdom and experiences horizontally. That is amazing. I'm excited to learn about your stories, and I thank you for listening to mine.

In solidarity,
Devin

Concluding Thoughts

Chiraz Retimi
It is well-known that social media is a powerhouse, whether in a positive way or in a negative one. It is true that it works for increasing the amount of information and news, which means the existence of different perspectives, opinions, and dialogues that may or may not be productive. In my country, Algeria, social media was a turning point in producing a civilized society, through organizing peaceful manifestations and marches. It had a role in spreading awareness and holding our principles together. Also, since we are using social media to participate in such dialogues, it proves nothing but how effective social media is in producing productive dialogues . In contrast, it has a bad side, too; It confuses people with its credibility, whether the shared news is real or misleading. People tend to be only consumers of the news and information (good or bad), and only few can criticize it and have a different opinion. And I think negativity is a kind of contagious experience—once the negative news is out there (true or false), people

share it without bothering to look for its authenticity. As a result, the whole society stops critically engaging and only focuses on the negativity, losing the possibility of productively communicating.

Djoumana Hadil Boiughazi

I guess I agree with what you all said, especially that social media is a powerhouse, whether negative or positive because like I said, it depends on how we use it. In the wrong hands, it can lead to a lot of chaos, and we've seen it many times unfortunately. But I think our generation can make a change in the game, not only by taking an active part in social media, but in educating younger generations on how to use it efficiently and positively.

جيلنا يمكن أن يحدث تغييراً في اللعبة ، ليس فقط من خلال المشاركة الفعالة في وسائل التواصل الاجتماعي ، ولكن من خلال تثقيف الأجيال الشابة حول كيفية استخدامها بكفاءة وإيجابية.

أفتقر إلى الخبرة اللازمة لكتابة شيء يمكن اعتباره نقدا شاملا لثقافة الطلاب النشطاء. لا يمكنني التحدث إلا عن فترة محدودة من الزمن ، كانت فوضوية أيضا ، ليس كل شيء فشل هناك. أقرت الجامعة ببعض مطالب التحالف الأسهل تطبيقا. قاموا بإزالة اللوحات المؤيدة للكونفدرالية من روتوندا. أقرت الجامعة Unite the Right. وسددت جزءًا من قيمته للنفقات الطبية للجرحى من Klu Klux Klan بتلقيها تبرعًا من تم إعادة تسمية المباني التي سميت باسم تفوق البيض وعلماء تحسين النسل من حولهم لقادة المجتمعات ذوي الخلفيات المهمشة.

أكثر إرضاءًا من تلبية مطالبنا الأولية هو القدرة على مشاهدة ثقافة الطلاب في جامعة فرجينيا وهي تنمو. يجب أن نتحرك أبعد من ذلك بكثير بعد كل ما حدث. ومع ذلك ، لا يسعني إلا أن أشير إلى مدى التغير الذي طرأ على ثقافة الكتلة الطلابية خلال العامين الماضيين. نحن أكثر انخراطًا ، وأكثر حدة ، وأكثر رغبة في التغيير من ذي قبل. أستمد الأمل من قوتنا الجماعية وقدرتنا على التعلم والتكيف. في هذه اللحظة بالذات ، نتواصل من أجل تبادل الحكمة والتجارب أفقيا. هذا مدهش. أنا متحمس للتعرف على القصص الأخرى ، وأشكركم على الاستماع إلى قصصي.

تضامنا مع،
ديفين

أفكار ختامية

شيراز رتيمي

من المعروف أن وسائل التواصل الاجتماعي تعد القوة المحركة ، سواء بطريقة إيجابية أو بطريقة سلبية. صحيح أنها تهدف لزيادة كمية المعلومات والأخبار مما يعني وجود وجهات نظر وآراء وحوارات مختلفة قد تكون أو لا تكون مثمرة. في بلدي الجزائر ، كانت وسائل التواصل الاجتماعي نقطة تحول في إنتاج مجتمع متحضر ، من خلال تنظيم مظاهرات ومسيرات سلمية. كان لها دور في نشر الوعي والربط بين مبادئنا. نظرًا لأننا نستخدم وسائل التواصل الاجتماعي في مناقشة مثل هذه الحوارات ، فإنه لا يثبت شيئًا سوى مدى فعالية وسائل التواصل الاجتماعي في إنتاج حوارات مثمرة. في المقابل ، يوجد جانب سيئ أيضًا وهو مسألة المصداقية ، سواء كانت الأخبار المشتركة حقيقية أو مضللة. يميل الناس إلى أن يكونوا مستهلكين فقط للأخبار والمعلومات (سواء جيدها أو سيئها) ، وقلة فقط هم الذين يمكنهم انتقادها ولديهم رأي مختلف. وأعتقد أن السلبية هي نوع من التجربة المعدية ، بمجرد مشاركة الأخبار السلبية (الحقيقية أو الخاطئة) من قبل الناس دون أن يكلفوا أنفسهم عناء البحث عن أصالتها. نتيجة لذلك ، يتوقف المجتمع بأكمله عن الانخراط بشكل حاسم ويركز فقط على السلبية ، ويفقد إمكانية التواصل المنتج.

جمانة هديل بوغازي

أعتقد أني أتفق مع ما قلته جميعًا ، خاصة أن وسائل التواصل الاجتماعي هي مصدر القوة ، سواء أكانت سلبية أم إيجابية ، لأنه كما قلت ، يعتمد الأمر على كيفية استخدامنا لها. إذا وضعت في الأيدي الخطأ ، يمكن أن يؤدي ذلك إلى الكثير من الفوضى و هذا ما رأيناه عدة مرات للأسف. لكني أعتقد أن

لا تسمح بأن يصبح الوعي الاجتماعي سلعة. التخلص من سياسة الوضع الراهن الذي أنشأنا جميعًا هو عملية لا يمكن أن تحدث بين عشية وضحاها. أي شخص توقع منا أن نتخلص بطريقة سحرية من الثقافة النخبوية لجامعة فرجينيا، ومنطق الاستعمار الاستيطاني، والليبرالية الجديدة، كان من المفارقات أن يطلب منا أن نكون استثنائيين. إنها رحلة، ولكل واحد رحلة. إذا كنت في هذه العملية أكثر من نظرائك، فالرجاء تذكر أنك لن تنجز شيئًا مهمًا من خلال تعليق تنويرك على رؤوس الآخرين الموجودين أساسًا في صفك والذين يخطون طريقهم.

جرب الرحمة

في عام 2017، كان صديقي كيندال ناشطةً حكيمةً ولطيفةً أكثر من معظمنا. لقد كانت معنا هناك في كل المراحل بدءا من المشاعل إلى مسيرات الطلاب. كانت لدينا اختلافات سياسية، لكنها لم تجادلني أو تؤنبني حول اتجاهاتي السياسية. الاحترام المتبادل بيننا مازال حتى يومنا هذا. كلما شعرت بالضيق الشديد بسبب كيفية تعامل أنواع الناشطين مع بعضهم البعض، كثيرا ما أفكر في العودة إلى كيندال. أتذكر تلك اجتماعات الأحد المروعة، وأنا ابتسم بكل سرور عندما أتصورها وهي تصرخ فوق الفوضى، "تذكروا أنه ينبغي علينا افتراض النوايا الحسنة!"

الناس يتعثرون. تظهر سلوكيات غير ناضجة وساذجة. وعلى الرغم من أن لا أحد يعذر بجهل، و كذا الركود والاستكانة غير مقبولان. أتمنى لو كنت قد أظهرت وأظهرت المزيد من التعاطف. كانت كيندال على حق. كان لدينا جميعا نوايا مذهلة. قضينا الكثير من الوقت في التعارك وتقويض بعضنا البعض. على الرغم من أن قلة منا أصبحت أو بقيت أصدقاء، إلا أني أشعر بالارتباط الدائم بتلك الأقلية الصغيرة من الطلاب الذين واصلوا الظهور والتضحية ببطاقاتهم ووقتهم من أجل تحالفنا. الحضور الدائم هو إنجاز لا يمكننا إنكاره.

التحركات الاستباقية

التنظيم يكون أكثر فعالية عندما تكون البنية التحتية في مكانها قبل حدوث الأزمة. كثيرًا ما أفكر في كيف أن عددًا قليلًا من أعضاء التحالف الطلابي كانوا يعرفون بعضهم بالفعل قبل أن تقع حالة الطوارئ الوطنية على رؤوسنا. الكثير منا كان يمكن أن يكون أصدقاء حميمين. لو كان لدينا المزيد من الوقت للاختلاط والذوبان قبل محاولة وضع أيدينا مع بعض للعمل على التغيير السياسي.

نعم، بناء علاقات دائمة مع الناس هو جزء من استراتيجية مقاومة فعالة. والعقلية الاستباقية تجعل هذا ممكنا. في السنة الثالثة من دراستي، علمني زميلي في الغرفة أن عمل حفلات طعام أو مشاركة القهوة مع الناس يمكن أن يكون عملاً جذريًا عميقًا. خلق الفضاء لنكون إنسانيين مع بعضنا البعض في خضم كل الضغط، والارتباك، والإكراه، يشفي الروح ويعود لينفعنا عندما تسوء الأمور.

كن سباقا. كم من الناس أدركوا أهمية ذلك، لسنوات كانت هناك فجوة عميقة بين أفراد مجتمع شارلوتسفيل وبين أعضاء هيئة التدريس وطلاب الجامعة الذين كانوا يأتون ويروحون، ماذا لو تم إصلاح هذه العلاقة قبل فوضى الصيف؟ لن نعرف صحة هذا الافتراض لأن هذا لم يحدث.

جميع الفصائل المختلفة كانت غصصا في حلق بعضها البعض. نشأت الشكوك من كل اتجاه. لا يثق المتشددون بالراديكاليين ، الذين لا يثقون بالليبراليين ، الذين لا يثقون بالوسطيين ، الذين استاءوا جميعهم من غالبية الطلاب الذين استأنفوا مواعيدهم العادية. لقد مررنا وتنازلنا مرارًا لرغبة الطلاب غير المبالين على ما يبدو. بعد ذلك ، كنا نلتفت ونطالب بتلك الغالبية الصامتة المخزية من الطلاب ونترجاهم للحضور والانضمام إلى مسيراتنا.

حاول مختلف الأفراد والفصائل جاهدة سحب تحالف النشطاء في اتجاهات مختلفة. حاولت جامعة فرجينيا بشكل أكثر جدية. على سبيل المثال ، يمكن لتحالف الطلاب السود الحصول على اجتماعات مع عمداء جامعة فرجينيا ، ولكن لم تستطع مجموعات أصغر ذات أهمية مساوية. لم يكن تحالف الطلبة السود المجموعة الوحيدة التي تعاني مع الكثير لقوله. قبل أن نعرف ذلك ، كنا قد ابتلعنا الطعم مرة أخرى وسمحنا للتسلسل الهرمي بتقسيم تحالفنا.

لقد اتحدنا جميعًا بالنية الحسنة، وأردنا علاج وضع مدرستنا ومجتمعاتنا. شاركنا هدفًا بسيطًا: تلبية قائمة منشورة من طلبات الطلاب. بسرعة ، وبسرعة تشتتنا وأصبحنا فصائليين ، مقسومين على مسائل التكتيك والاستراتيجية. كان يمكن حل الكثير من تلك الأسئلة حول التنظيم والهيكل والسرعة لو كان الزمن فقط إلى جانبنا. كان لدينا وقت محدود من انتباه الجمهور الوطني. أود أن أصدق أن ممارسة أكثر احترامًا وتواضعًا وأقل استبعادًا قد تكون أبقت فريقنا سويًا لفترة كافية لإحداث مزيد من التغيير.

دعنا نقول أنك ، في الواقع ، ضمن نخبة أميركا الاكثر نشاطا ، وأنك تعرف كل شيء بالفعل وكنت قد قرأت كل المؤلفين المشهورين من بال هوكس إلى فرانز فانون إلى هيوي نيوتن. لقد ريحت كل النياشين الثورية ، ولا شك في أن سلطتك لا جدال فيها. حان الوقت لتولي المسؤولية وتوجيه الناس إلى الوجهة الصحيحة، أليس كذلك؟ غير محتمل البتة. العكس هو الصحيح بالنسبة لي - أعتقد أنه يمكنك الاستفادة فقط من التواضع، حتى في هذه الحالة. المعرفة الحقيقية لاتتأثر بسبب قلة الخبرة أو جهل الآخرين. لماذا يجب على أي شخص أن يكون شغوفا لمعرفة المزيد عن النشاط واليقظة أكثر من أي شخص اخر، وجود في اتجاه اليسار كثر من غير أن لا يعدوا أن يكون ظرف من الظروف. لا يمكن أن تصبح الثورة مجرد تسلسل هرمي جديد للوعي الحصري. كن متواضعًا وعلم الآخرين كما تعلمت ذات يوم.

يمكن للتواضع أن يهزم أن هذه الظاهرة الجديدة حيث يتسابق نشطاء الطلاب نحو الوعي الاجتماعي الحصري، والمعروف باسم "اليقظة" ، مثل سباق للتسلح. إذا كانت الحكمة المكتسبة بشق الأنفس لما يُعرف باليقظة لا يتعامل معها بحذر، فمصير تضامننا محكوم مرارًا وتكرارًا بالدمار من خلال المواقف المتسلسلة الهرمية تجاه أصدقائنا وحلفائنا المحتملين. نحتاج إلى أشخاص يمكنهم وضع الأنا الخاصة بهم جانبًا من أجل التنقل بشكل حاذق بين جميع أدوار التغيير الاجتماعي ، من معلم إلى زعيم إلى مستمع. نحن بحاجة إلى تمرير الحكمة عضويا ، وبناء الثقة والتضامن في هذه العملية. مواقف التفوق تنتج دائمًا تسلسلًا هرميًا ، والتسلسل الهرمي غير متوافق مع تحالف القواعد الشعبية.

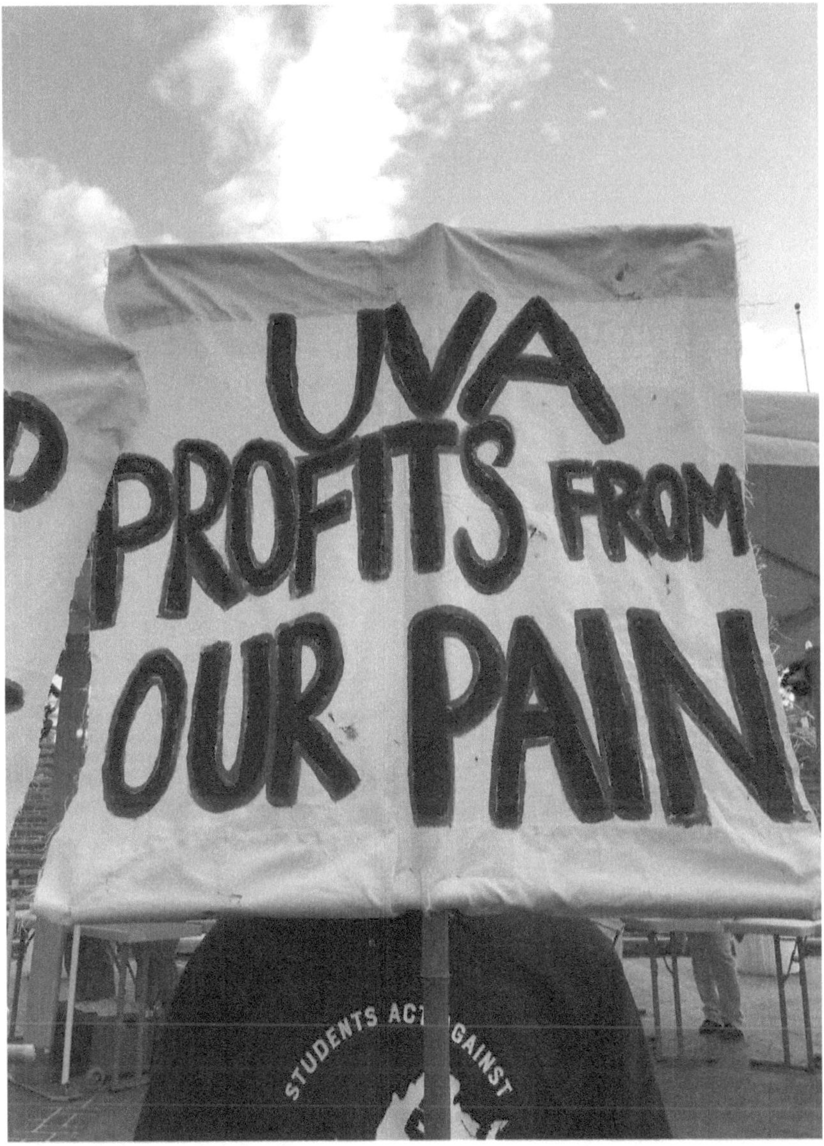
UVA
PROFITS FROM
OUR PAIN
STUDENTS ACT AGAINST

من كان يعدُّنا لهذا النوع من الصدمات؟ بالنسبة للعاصفة القادمة من الاحتجاجات الطلابية ، الإدارة غير المستجيبة في جامعة فرجينيا ، لـ "كلا الجانبين" ، لمراسلي وسائل الإعلام المفترسة ، استجابة الطلاب غير المتوازنة التي تتراوح بين اللامبالاة الهائلة إلى الغضب الأعمى ، وسنوات من الإجراءات القانونية التي تستهلك حياتي في العام الموالي.

ارتكبت ملايين الأخطاء من العناصر ذات النوايا الحسنة لما بعد أغسطس 2017 في جامعة فرجينيا شارلوتسفيل. أفضل مناقشة بعض المآزق التي واجهتني والطلاب الذين حاولوا أن يكونوا ناشطين في أعقاب حالة الطوارئ الوطنية. لم يكن لدينا سيطرة على ما حدث لمجتمعنا ولكن كل السيطرة على ردودنا الفردية. لعدة أسابيع على الأقل ، كان على الناس الاستماع إلينا.

الغرض من هذا النقد ليس دفع بإعادة النظر في الوقائع التاريخية ولكن إلى تسليط الضوء على الأخطاء التي يمكن تجنبها في تطبيق النشاط الطلابي المعاصر. بعض المواضيع ، مثل تشديدي على أهمية التواضع ، قد تبدو عاطفية أو مبتذلة. أنا لا أعتذر عن ذلك. تصبح المخاوف المتعلقة بالشخصية ذات أهمية كبيرة عندما يواجه مجتمعك أزمة وقد حان الوقت للتنظيم رغم الاختلاف. لذلك ، إليك بعض الدروس والأسئلة المستوحاة من وقتي كطالب ناشط في جامعة فرجينيا بعد مظاهرات توحيد اليمين.

كن متواضعا

التواضع هو المفتاح لأنه يسبق كل الفضائل الأخرى للتنظيم (والحياة ، جميعها). يميل النشطاء الطلاب إلى الانزلاق إلى شيء من الضجيج - كل من هو أعلى صوتا وأكثر غضبًا والأكثر استقامةً يستحق الثناء كمثال ساطع. لا حرج في الخطابات المتقدة عندما تكون هذه النار مستندة إلى شيء جوهري يمكن أن يتحدث عن نفسه. ولكن هذا المزيج نادر جدا.

يتطلب الاعتراف أننا لا نعلم شيئا كطلبة وفاعلين الكثير من التواضع، يمكننا دائمًا الاستفادة من المزيد من القراءة (والكتابة أيضًا). لا تكن سخيفا بما يكفي لتظن أنك أول شخص يواجه أي تحد أمامك. لا حاجة إلى إعادة اختراع العجلة. وقد كتب بعض الثوريون السابقون عن وضع عن وضع مشابه لوضعك. اقرأ لهم! أو استسلم لجهلك الذي سيصبح عائقًا في هذا المجال.

أعلم أن المزيد من التواضع من جانبي كان يمكن أن يكون مفيدًا خلال اجتماعات تحالف الفاعلين الطلاب. اسمحوا لي أهيئ المسرح قبل أن أشرح. تخيل أن تقضي ثلاث أو أربع ساعات كل ليلة أحد في الطابق العلوي من المقهى مع أكثر من 40 طالبًا جامعيًا يحاولون تنظيم استجابة موحدة لطلاب توحيد اليمين المتطرفين. كل يوم أحد لأسابيع ، كان جميع الطلاب النشطاء ينحدرون من عليَّة المقهى الصغيرة ويتجادلون حول تنظيم الإستراتيجية دون نتيجة بناءة. غالبًا ما كانت الأسئلة المطروحة أمامنا كما يلي: كيف يمكننا أن نكون أكثر شمولية في حركتنا؟ كيف نؤطر أنفسنا على وسائل الإعلام؟ ما هي الأشياء على المحك إذا خرجنا إلى الشوارع؟

حيرة واشمئزاز. في ذلك الوقت ، كان لا يزال لدي أعذار للشرطة. ربما كان الحشد مشاغبا ، كان يومًا طويلًا ساخنًا مشحونا بالعواطف.

بعد هذا الحادث ، عرفنا جميعًا أن الكثير من المتعصبين سيعودون إلى شارلوتسفيل في أقل من شهر. هذه المرة ، استفدنا من معرفة أن الشرطة تهتم بسلامة المتعصبين بدرجة أكبر. لحسن الحظ ، تولى شعب شارلوتسفيل تأمين المكان بأنفسهم. تم إجراء تدريبات مباشرة غير عنيفة في جميع أنحاء المنطقة في الأيام التي سبقت مسيرة كيسلر. لا شك أن هذه التحركات الاستباقية أنقذت بعض الأرواح ومنعت العنف.

والطلاب والصحفيين ، وما إلى ذلك تم ANTIFA هذه الشبكة من الناشطين والزعماء الدينيين و جماعة إعدادها بالكامل للجولة الثانية من 8 يوليو. كانت لدى لجنة العمل الشعبي من أجل العدالة العنصرية التي يرأسها والتر هاينيكي الفكرة الرائعة المتمثلة في الحصول على تصريح مضاد لمظاهرة العدل (PARJ) بارك ومتنزه ماكجوفي. يقع هذان المتنزهان على بعد عدة مبان فقط من موقع مظاهرة كيسلر القادمة إلى حديقة التحرير (المعروفة سابقًا باسم لي بارك). أن البصيرة أنجزت شيئين. أولاً ، منع هذا التهديد من استخدام مساحة أكبر من الأماكن العامة. ثانياً ، وفرت مكانًا آمنًا للعديد من المتظاهرين المعارضين الشجعان الذين سيظهرون لمعارضة نازي كيسلر. أنا مقتنع بأن المزيد من الأرواح أنقذت من خلال هذه الاستعدادات ، التي قام بها أشخاص عاديون، الذين كانوا يهتمون وتولوا زمام الأمور.

لقد تم تحذيرنا جميعًا من أن مظاهرات توحيد اليمين لكسلر ، ستكون أكبر من مظاهرات Klu Klux Klan في الثامن من يوليو. اعتقدت أنني كنت على استعداد. ولكني لم أكن.

لم أكن مستعدًا في 11 أغسطس 2017 عندما سمحت جامعتي لريتشارد سبنسر وفاشييه مع مجموعة تحمل المشاعل بالاعتداء على مجموعة من الطلاب السلميين ، ومجموعة أنتيفا ، وأفراد المجتمع تحت تمثال الحرم الجامعي لتوماس جيفرسون. ما زلت لا أعرف كيف أصف الخوف والتوتر الذي عانينا منه تحت هذا التمثال. كانت رؤيتي محدودة بسبب المشاعل ، وكنت أغطي وجهي لحماية هويتي. كنت خائفًا حتى الموت وظللت أفكر في أن أحد الفاشيين سيبدأ في إطلاق النار. قاموا بشتمنا، ورشنا برذاذ الفلفل ، وفي نهاية المطاف قاموا بلكمنا قبضاتهم ومرافقهم عندما أجبرنا على الخروج من منطقة التمثال. فقط بعد أن انتهى الفاشيون من هجومهم ، قامت الشرطة بإجبار المتظاهرين على الخروج من الساحة. كثير منا تم رش الفلفل عليه، أو ضرب على رأسه، أو تم حرقه بواسطة شعلة تيكي التي تحولت إلى رمح. رجال الشرطة لم يكترثوا.

لم أكن مستعدًا في 12 أغسطس 2017 عندما اجتاح بحر من النازيين الجدد والقوميين الجدد المجندين حديقة الحرية. لم يكن أحد على استعداد لمأساة قتل هيذر هاير والاعتداء على الأبرياء ، كان الكثير من الضحايا من أصدقائي.

الاستثنائية ومعارضة أنظمة القوة أفضل من أولئك الذين أتوا قبلنا. وقعنا فريسة لخدعة جيدة حقًا ؛ كنا مقتنعين باستثنائيتنا، خطأ خطير من شأنه أن يكلف الكثير.

توحيد اليمين

بحلول نهاية عام دراستي الأول في الجامعة ، تم تعييني في المجلس التنفيذي لتحالف الطلاب السود. أو على الرغم من توجه المجلس الذي يبدو للوهلة الأولى وسطيا، كان منظمة الطلاب ، BSA ما يعرف بـ السود الأكثر هيمنة على الأرض. خدمت كسكرتيراسنة في العام الدراسي 2017-2018 ، ولكن لكوني الوحيد من أعضاء مكتب التحالف الذي يعيش في شارلوتسفيل خلال صيف عام 2017 ، تمت ترقيتي بسرعة إلى منصب مسؤول التنسيق السياسي، وهو منصب سمح لي بأن أكون في خضم الأنظمة الكثيفة للفعاليات المجتمعية في شارلوتسفيل في ذلك الوقت. بدأ الناس يطلقون عليه اسم "صيف الكراهية" إلى منظمة Black Lives Matter C-ville ، وكان هناك ما لا نهاية من المجموعات لتتبعها بدءا من بحلول يونيو 2017 ، انجذبت إلى تحالف مثير للإعجاب بين قيادات (SURJ). العفو عن العدالة العرقية مجتمعية في شارلوتسفيل وجامعة فرجينيا، والذين أنشؤوا الحلف لمجابهة متطرفين مثل جيسون كيسلر ، وبراود بويز، وغيرها من الجماعات الفاشية التي أصبح نشاطها كثيفا.

أظهر لي القادة في التحالف كيفية العمل. شرحوا لي الإجراءات المباشرة اللاعنفية واللقاءات السرية التي تعقد تحسباً لميلاد حركة توحيد اليمين. أبلغت بكل شيء عن "تحالف الطلاب السود" وشبكة من المجموعات الطلابية الأخرى التي شعرت بالرعب من التطورات والتي انزعجت من كونها خارج المدينة خلال الأزمة. لا أعتقد أن هذا الشعور قد كان حبيس الصيف ، لأن المخاطر ما فتأت أن بدأت تتسارع.

لأول مرة بأم عيني في الثامن من يوليو عندما قام الفاشيون الجدد Klu Klux Klan لقد رأيت أعضاء من بمظاهرة في وسط مدينة شارلوتسفيل في حديقة العدل (المعروفة سابقًا باسم جاكسون بارك). بدوا سخيفين إلى حد ما في ملابس الجلباب الشائعة .. في منتصف صيف فرجينيا الحار. ومع ذلك ، بعض الصور من هذا اللقاء الأول بقيت عالقة في ذهني: أتذكر أن هناك عددًا هائلاً من النساء يرددن إلى جانب كلانسمن القدامى الذين قد تتوقعون رؤيتهم ؛ أتذكر قوة الشرطة متعددة الأعراق التي وقفت كما لو كنا التهديد الحقيقي للسلامة العامة ؛ وأخيرا ، صورة رجل أبيض Klansmen بين المحتجين و أكبر سنا يقف بجانب زميله بزي كلانسمن. كان ينظر إلينا ولكنه كان يشير إلى المسدس على وركه ، محميًا بجدار من ضباط الشرطة. كان يهدد الناس. كم عدد الرجال السود العزل الذين قتلوا على يد الشرطة بسبب أعمال أقل من ذلك بكثير؟

كان الثامن من يوليو أيضًا لا يُنسى لأنه كانت المرة الأولى التي شهدت فيها شخصيا أن الشرطة تعطي الأولوية للنظام فوق العدالة. قامت الشرطة باصطحاب الفاشيين خارج المدينة فرجينيا. انتهى اليوم بهذا الشكل أساسا. ذهبت أنا وأصدقائي من تحال الطلبة السود إلى مطعم مكسيكي. ربما مرت 20 دقيقة عندما شعرنا بضجة قادمة من اتجاه الحديقة - بالطبع. كانت الشرطة تهاجم المتظاهرين الذين لم يغادروا المنطقة في أقل من عشرين دقيقة. تعرض الناس للرش بالغاز والضرب. هل كانت مجرد صدفة أن انقضت الشرطة في عنف ضد أفراد المجتمع بمجرد تفريق الطلاب والحشد الأكاديمي؟ لقد كنا في

تمنيت لو فهمت آنفا أن مصطلح "طالب ناشط" على أنه عبارة متناقضة. لا أقصد استبعاد قيمة كونك طالبًا أو ناشطًا. في الواقع ، أعتقد أن كل من التعليم والعمل الملهم يشكلان المحرك الأساسي للتغيير الاجتماعي. ومع ذلك ، يجب أن يفهم الطلاب النشطاء الذين يسعون جاهدين لإحداث تغيير في المكان والزمان الخاصين بهم التناقضات التي يعملون بها. تم تصميم التعليم العالي بحيث أن سياستنا الراديكالية لا يمكن إلا أن تؤدى أوتسمع على منصة حصرية تعسفية. يجب فهم هذا التناقض عاجلاً وليس آجلاً. ليس من أجل أن تكون ناشطًا شابًا أكثر نقاءً أو إلهامًا ، ولكن لأن إدراكك القوي لنفسك وموقفك سيحملان قضيتك إلى أبعد من ذلك بكثير ضد الهياكل المؤسسات الاجتماعية المصممة لقمعك.

كلا والديّ من خريجي الجامعات من الجيل الأول نشئا في الأحياء الفقيرة في الغرب الأوسط من أمريكا. لطالما كانت صورة الجامعة لديهم صورة ذهبية وتذكرة لحياة أفضل. عندما كان عمري 17 عامًا ، أصبحت منغمسًا جدًا في فكر ماركس وتمنيت أن أكون شيغيفارا التالي. كان لدي الجرأة لأخبر والدتي أني كنت اشتراكيًا فخورًا يعتقد أن الجامعة أكبر عملية احتيال وأنني لن أكون مثلها عبدا للديون. بتذكري لذلك الموقف، أتذكر أني فوجئت بأنها كبحت ضحكتها. قالت إن الأمر لم يكن مطروحا للمناقشة. لم أكن أنوي أن أفسد أكبر أحلام أمي لابنها الوحيد. كنت في طريقي إلى جامعة جيفرسون بفرجينيا ، وهي من مدارس الأثرياء التقليديين. الساحة المركزية للكلية كانت تاريخيا مزرعة لاستعباد السود، عقلي الأسود الغاضب لم يستصغ ذلك. اعتقدت نفسي غريبًا وفشلت في رؤية نفسي كجزء من هذه المؤسسة، للأفضل وللأسوأ. أصبح ترامب رئيسًا في نهاية الفصل الدراسي الأول المحبط للغاية في المدرسة. تضاعفت كثافة المناخ السياسي ثلاثة أضعاف ووقعت في حب السياسة من جديد. بحلول نهاية تلك السنة الأولى ، أصبحت منغمسا كليا في الساحة الطلابية الناشطة إلى جانب الطلاب الشباب المهمشين و المستائين.

لقد قطعنا طريقنا ، كما فعل الكثيرون أمامنا ، للانضمام في منظمات المناصرة والجمعيات الطلابية تحالف الطلاب السود ، تحالف حقوق الأقليات ، نادي الغضب الشديد ؛ والقائمة ، NAACP: النشطة تطول وتطول. لسوء الحظ ، فإن النشوة في اكتشافنا أخيرًا لمنفذ لألمنا وغضبنا أصبحت نقمة بسرعة كبيرة. بصفتي ناشطا في جماعة الخضر ، لم أكن منزعجا حتى الآن أن ألاحظ كيف كان صوتي المرتفع يسمع فقط لأنه كان الصوت الطالب ذو الامتياز ، صوت الشخص الذي يمكنه تحمل تكاليف أن يكون طالبًا في ذلك المكان الباهض.

التناقض في مفهوم الطالب الناشط يتجسد أيضا في كونك لا تحتاج أن تعمل عملا إضافيا، وتملك الوقت للمشاركة في احتجاج، إنها الحرية في استكشاف ومناقشة الأفكار التي لا تؤثر على مستقبلك الاجتماعي والمالي لفترات طويلة من الزمن. هذا يبدو واضحًا لي الآن ، لكنني أتذكر مدى صعوبة معالجة مثل هذه الحقيقة المزعجة في حرارة أيام دراستي الأولى. فضلت أن أعتبر نفسي والعديد من الناشطين الآخرين أن أؤمن أننا كنا الأبطال الصرحاء للعدالة الاجتماعية ، ليس لأننا صادفنا أن نكون متاحين ، بل بسبب مزايانا الفردية. أعتقد أن الكثير منا يعتقد أن لدينا بعض القدرات الخاصة لإنجاز المهمة. ربما كان شغفنا ، حماستنا ، أو وجودنا على الإنترنت يمنحنا شيء ما القدرة على التنقل في المساحات

في كل أنحاء البلاد يشعرون بأنهم مرتبطون بهذه الحركة. شارك أناس من مختلف الأعمار ، يعملون في مجالات مختلفة ، من خلفيات متعددة في المسيرات.

لقد أظهرت هذه الأحداث الأخيرة شجاعة الجزائريين. في البداية ، بدا أن كل شيء محفوف بالمخاطر ومخيف ، خاصة بعد المعاناة وتجربة العشرية المظلمة. إنس الماضي ولكن لا تنسى الدرس. الآن يمكننا أن نقول بكل فخر أن الجزائر مستعدة للعيش والاستمتاع بالعشرية النيرة. عند رؤية كل ما يحدث في الدول العربية المجاورة ، أدرك الناس أن السلاح والكفاح من أجل السلام لن يجلب سوى الحرب والدم. قتل بعضنا البعض ، وقتل الناس من جيراننا لاجل التغيير. من الواضح تمامًا كيف يكون الناس على استعداد لجعل التغيير الجذري حقيقيًّا.

لم يحتجوا فقط على حمل الأعلام. قاموا بتنظيف الشوارع عند السير. في الواقع ، أصبح المشي في كل مكان لجمع القمامة من الممارسات الشائعة في المسيرات. أعد بعض العائلات وأصحاب المطاعم الطعام للمتظاهرين في الشارع. قام الأطفال والرجال والنساء بتوزيع زجاجات المياه على الجميع ، بمن فيهم رجال الشرطة. أعطى البعض الزهور للآخرين وساعد آخرون أولئك الذين خرجوا من الحر ، أو تعبوا أو مرضوا. يا لسعادة الجزائر بأبنائها.

بعد عدة أسابيع من الاحتجاج في الشارع وعلى وسائل التواصل الاجتماعي ، استقال بوتفليقة. بعث برسالة إلى الجزائريين مفادها أنه تعامل مع بعض القضايا المهمة ، لكنه طلب أيضًا الغفران. اعتذر. عندما انتشر خبر إعلانه ، كانت الشوارع مليئة بالأشخاص الذين خرجوا للاحتفال. وكان الطلب الأول قد سمع وتحقق.

الطريقة التي تمكن بها الجزائريون من التحدث والتعبير عن أنفسهم بحرية تستحق الإعجاب. لا أحد مات. لا أحد أصيب. كان السلام هو المسار الذي قرروا السير فيه. نادرًا ما يكون الأشخاص الذين يؤمنون بقوة الأساليب السلمية لمحاربة الفساد ، بل والأكثر ندرة من يفعلون ذلك. على الرغم من حقيقة أن الأيام المقبلة غامضة وأن مستقبل البلاد يعتبر غير متوقع ، فإن هذه المسيرات والاحتجاجات ساعدت الجزائريين على إخراج الأشياء الجميلة منهم. لقد أثبت شعبنا أن النوايا الحسنة والتضامن جزء منا. نحن متحدون لدرجة أننا لا نستطيع حتى أن نحدد متى بدأ شعورنا بالوحدة يتشكل.

يتم إظهار الإعجاب بالنموذج الجزائري في كل دولة. لم نفقد أنفسنا عند الاحتجاج. لقد نشرنا الشعور بالوطنية بلمسة فنية ، لمسة محبة أظهرت ما يستطيع الجزائريون فعله عندما يتكاتفون ويتصرفون كمواطن واحد: نتكلم مع بعضنا. نساعد. نضحك ، ربما نرقص. نشرنا الإيجابية والأمل في كل مكان.

ديفين ويليس
حوار وسائل التواصل الاجتماعي والنشاط

تأملات حول نشاط الطلاب في جامعة فرجينيا ، 2019-2016.

والمساواة
تسليم الشعلة إلى الشباب حتى يتمكنوا من الحكم وبناء جزائر ديمقراطية.

يداً بيد ، نحن متحدون بهدف الإطاحة بالعصابة الحاكمة واستعادة السيادة الوطنية. سوف تستمر هذه الاحتجاجات حتى يتم تلبية المطالب.

نحن متفائلون بوجود تغيير في الأيام المقبلة. أن نصبح مثالاً للعالم من شخصيتنا المسالمة والشجاعة. سوف تمر أيام حتى ينتهي هذا الكابوس وستشرق شمس الجزائر مرة أخرى ولن تغيب أبدًا.

لا تخف أبدًا من رفع صوتك من أجل الصدق والحقيقة والرحمة ، من رفع صوتك ضد الظلم والكذب والجشع.

إذا فعل الناس في جميع أنحاء العالم هذا ، فسيتغير كل العالم.

شيماء هاشمي

رجال ونساء، عجائز وأطفال ... علم في الأيدي و ابتسامة على الوجوه .. هكذا قرر الشعب الجزائري إسماع
صوته والمطالبة بنهاية حكم الرئيس بوتفليقة، منشدين:

"سلمية ... سلمية سلمية .. سلمية."

هذا ماكان يردده المتظاهرون في كل مسيرة.

لم تزهق روح. لم تطلق رصاصة. لا قتال ولا شجار. لا أحد تضرر. جميع الجزائريين يحتجون بسلام كهيئة واحدة مترابطة ومتصلة. يريد الناس انتزاع حقوقهم ووضع مستقبل باهر أكثر وضوحًا لهم وللجزائر. لا شيء يمكن أن يمنعهم من البحث عن طرق وأساليب لإنشاء جزائر جديدة ، مكان جديد للناس يفكرون فيه ويحلمون به ويحققون أحلامهم من أجل أنفسهم ، لبلدهم الحبيب.

كان المطلب الأول هو أن لا للعهدة الخامسة. لقد حكم بوتفليقة الجزائر لمدة قاربت العشرون سنة. حكمنا الى غاية تقدمه في السن، إلى أن أضحى غير قادر جسديًّا على الحكم. في نظرنا ، هذا المطلب كان منطقيا. إننا نسعى فقط للحصول على قائد جديد للبلاد. لنكون أكثر دقة ، قائدا أصغر سنا. الناس ببساطة يعارضون إطالة حكم بوتفليقة.

لقد ركزوا بسلمية على هذا المطلب ، و على مطالب أخرى أيضًا. إنهم يريدون أن ينتهي النظام الفاسد وأن تشهد البلاد تغييرا ثوريا جذريا. وكل أسبوع كانت هناك زيادة ملحوظة في عدد الاحتجاجات. الجميع

محند شيبان

لأول مرة في تاريخ الجزائر ، يتحد الناس في جميع أنحاء البلاد لغرض واحد: تغيير جذري للحكومة. أدهش هذا الحدث العالم بأسره ، ليس لأن الناس استيقظوا من نوم عميق ، لكن المظاهرات التي قام بها الجزائريون كانت حركة سلمية. الشعارات التي يكررونها كانت نفسها على كل لسان: سلمية ... سلمية ...... الجيش والشعب إخوة.

تجري مظاهرات في الجزائر منذ 16 فبراير 2019 للاحتجاج مبدئيًا على ترشح عبد العزيز بوتفليقة لفترة رئاسية خامسة ، تلتها احتجاجات ضد خطته للبقاء في السلطة حتى نهاية ولايته الرابعة وتمديدها. على نطاق غير مسبوق على مدى عقود وبعد انحياز الجيش لجهة الشعب ، أدت هذه المظاهرات إلى استقالة بوتفليقة في 2 أبريل 2019.

ما زلنا نواصل.

لقد سئمنا حكومة سرقت كل أحلام المواطنين الجزائريين.

نحن نكره حكومة تسرق من شعبها.

نحن نكره الحكومة التي تسبب الهجرة الجماعية للشباب والنساء والشيوخ إلى أوروبا ، وخاصة الطبقة المتعلمة التي ترغب في مستقبل أفضل.

، في ظل هذه الحكومة ، أصبحت الحكومة الجزائرية دولة بلا أي مبدأ ، تنشر ثقافة الفساد والرشوة وخاصة التمييز بين السكان.

الأغنياء يسيطرون على الفقراء.

أصبحت الحقيقة كذبة، وأصبح الباطل حقيقة.

خرج الجميع لهذه المظاهرات السلمية التي تدين مثل هذه الجرائم ضد الجزائر وتطالب باستعادة الحقوق الفردية والمجتمعية.

الكل يريد التغيير من أجل جزائر أفضل، جزائر حديثة. لدينا جميع المؤهلات لنكون من بين أفضل البلدان في العالم. العقبة الوحيدة هي هذا النظام المعيب.

لذا ، فإن مطالب الجزائريين جادة: توحيد الجزائريين. إقامة دولة ديمقراطية تقوم على العدل.

مدى نجاحهم في هذه الجهود، كما هو الحال مع "تحدي النفايات" مؤخراً. كما أنهم يعملون على غرس قيم جيدة جديدة ومحو كل ما هو سيء للبشرية. وما يجعل الشباب مهتمين بالنشاط هو على الأرجح لأنهم أدركوا أخيراً مدى أهميتهم كأفراد في المجتمع وأنه لا ينبغي إهدار طاقاتهم. وهؤلاء الشباب قادرون على أن يقودوا إلى تغيير من أجل عالم أفضل بسبب أفكارهم وطرق تفكيرهم. وهم يشعرون بالقلق إزاء كل ما يحدث في بلدانهم، وهم يسعون إلى تغيير ما يلزم تغييره.

بالنظر إلى الحركة الجزائرية ضد الرئيس السابق عبد العزيز بوتفليقة ونظامه، الحقيقة المحزنة هي أنه خلال السنوات العشرين من نظام بوتفليقة، كان الشباب منفصلين عن السياسة و لم يشاركوا فيها قط. لكن في 22 فبراير/شباط 2019، عندما خرج الشعب الجزائري من جميع الولايات للمطالبة بتغيير النظام، شهدنا مشاركة جميع شرائح المجتمع، بما في ذلك الشباب - طلاب الجامعات الذين صنعوا ولا يزالون يصنعون التاريخ بأيديهم. وقد خرج هؤلاء الطلاب إلى الشوارع في مظاهرات ومسيرات استجابة لمطالب الناس. وقد نظموا إضرابات وطنية واختاروا الثلاثاء ليكون "يوم المسيرات الوطنية للطلاب ضد النظام السياسي". نجح طلاب الجامعات الجزائرية في إيصال مطالب الشعب إلى الحكومة. وتمكن هؤلاء الطلاب في أن يجعلوا الحكومة تستمع إلى مطالب الشعب. وفي الواقع، قبلت الحكومة بعض المطالب. ويمكن القول أنه لولا مشاركة طلاب الجامعات في الحركة لما نجح الشعب في مطالبه.

ولعل الجانب المدهش في هذه اللحظة هو على الرغم من أن معظم الشباب في الجزائر لا يشاركون سياسياً وقد لا يكون لديهم الكثير من المعرفة بالسياسة، إلا أنهم ينظمون مؤتمرات وأحداثاً يأتي فيها خبراء في السياسة لمناقشة الوضع الحالي وتقديم الحلول. مع خلق استطلاعات الرأي العام والاستماع إلى بعضهم البعض، وإذا شاهد أي شخص مسيراتهم ومظاهراتهم، سيكون من الواضح مدى حسن تنظيمها. هذا الجيل يحاول أن يثبت أن الطلاب لهم معرفة عن السياسة، وأنهم يعرفون ما يريدون، جزائر أفضل مليئة بالديمقراطية. ولا ينتهي الأمر هناك. هؤلاء الطلاب الجزائريون أنفسهم يحاولون غرس مبادئ قيمة جديدة في المجتمع من خلال التطوع في العديد من المدن والبلدات الجزائرية لتنظيف الأماكن العامة وطلاء الجدران بألوان وصور زاهية. إنهم يستخدمون الأعمال الفنية ويشاركون كل شيء على وسائل التواصل الاجتماعي آخذينها كمنصة لتعميم هذه الفكرة، وهي تجدي بثمارها في الواقع فالعديد من المدن تبدو الآن بشكل مختلفة. وهذا يجعل من الشباب الجزائري مثالاً على كيفية إعادة تنشيط المساحات الحضرية.

إن الوضع والأحداث الراهنة في الجزائر هي إجابة على سؤال "لماذا النشاط مهم؟" يريد الناشطون الشباب أن تظل حركتهم مدنية وسلمية ونظيفة. هذه رسالة قوية للحكومة الحالية بأن هؤلاء الناس يعرفون إلى أين يتجهون وأن مستقبل الجزائر آمن في أيديهم. قال العديد من الخبراء والمتخصصين في السياسة أن مستقبل الجزائر يعتمد على نشاط الشباب. إنهم يعتقدون أن الجزائر ستكون مكاناً أفضل للعيش فيه إذا واصل هؤلاء الطلاب الشباب القيام بما يقومون به لأنهم يلعبون دوراً هاماً للغاية في جعل المظاهرات تبدو سلمية وقوية. وبسبب هؤلاء الطلاب الناشطين، تسير الجزائر في طريقها إلى الديمقراطية - إذا لم يحدث أي خلل بالتأكيد.

اليكس مارتينيز
نهاية حالم

حلمت بك مرة واحدة.
في حلمي ،
وبختني
لأني لم أنمو بالسرعة كافية.

في حلمي ،
لقد وعدتك بأني سأحاول اللحاق بالركب.
ومنذ ذلك الحين
هرعت وأسرعت للوصول إلى هنا.

فاتني الكثير على طول الطريق
أنا لا ألومك أمي.
أنا ضحية للوقت
"ويطلقون عليّ إسمُ "حالم

ولكن احيانا
الاحلام نحلم بها ،
يمكن أن تقتلنا أيضا ...

بشرى رحموني

شهد التاريخ الكثير من الناشطين المشهورين الذين أدوا إلى تغييرات هامة في العالم، مثل مارتن لوثر كينغ، نيلسون مانديلا، مهاتما غاندي، وملالا يوسفزاي. وقد عمل هؤلاء القادة والناشطون على إيجاد حلول للقضايا الإنسانية والسياسية. لقد عملوا على تغيير العالم كله إلى الأفضل، ويمكن القول أن العالم شهد دائما تحركات لهؤلاء الناشطين المقاومين في مواجهة كل ما هو ضد الإنسانية. لقد حارب الناس دائما الفساد بجميع أنواعه، سواء كان سياسيا أو اجتماعيا. ومع ذلك، فإن أهم جزء من الحركات الناشطة في الجزائر اليوم هو الشباب.

النشاط الشبابي هو إشراك الشباب في التنظيم من أجل التغيير في مجتمعاتهم. وغالبا ما يطلق عليهم أبطال التغيير لأنهم مليئون بالطاقة والأفكار الإبداعية. فهم أذكياء بما فيه الكفاية لوضع علامة في العالم.

في الجزائر، كنا نراقب الحركات الطلابية ضد الأنظمة الفاسدة وكيف يمكن أن تحدث فرقاً في بلدنا. لقد شهدنا ورشات العمل المذهلة التي قام بها الشباب لزيادة الوعي بأهمية تغيير مجتمعهم. ونحن نرى

بدلاً من ذلك ، هتف المتظاهرون "سلمية ، سلمية". و في كل يوم جمعة بعد الصلاة ،ينتقلون مباشرة من المساجد إلى الشوارع حيث شملت المسيرات كبار السن والأطفال والنساء والرجال جميعًا. وقد حظوا بالحماية من قبل الشرطة والجيش. يطالبون باستقالة جميع أعضاء الحكومة وكذلك المسؤولين. كان الهدف (ولا يزال) هو بناء دولة جديدة غير فاسدة.

كل هذه الانتفاضات تهدف إلى إخراج الناس من المعاناة. و رغم انه تم تحقيق العديد من الأهداف، الا أن الخسائر كانت أكبر من الغنائم. ومع ذلك ، لا يزال الأمل بغد أفضل قائما.

هند بن لكحل

التغيير للأفضل يبدأ بإحداث تغيير إيجابي في حياتك الخاصة. إذا كنت مصمماً بما يكفي ، سيدفعك ذلك لمشاركة هذا التغيير ومحاولة نشره في بيئتك الصغيرة ، وربما في مجتمع أكبر. إن التحفيز الكافي والشجاعة للتعامل مع أي تجربة جديدة ، من شأنه أن يحدث تغييراً إيجابياً سواء لحياة الأشخاص أو للمجتمع الذي يعيشون فيه. في الحقيقة ، أنا من الأشخاص الذين حاولوا الانتقال من إحداث تغيير إيجابي في حياتهم الخاصة إلى محاولة إحداث تغيير في المجتمع.

منذ طفولتي المبكرة ، كنت دائمًا احب الرسم والألوان وكل ما يتعلق بالفنون. مع نمو هذا الشغف بداخلي ، سرعان ما أصبح الفن طريقي الوحيد للتغلب على ضغوط ومشاكل الحياة اليومية والتعامل معها. طوال هذه الفترة ، كنت أفكر دائمًا في طريقة لمشاركة وتكريس مواهبي المتواضعة لصالح الآخرين. على سبيل المثال ، خلال العطلة الصيفية ، كنت مسؤولة عن بعض ورشات العمل للأطفال التي تركز على القراءة والرسم. أردت مساعدتهم على تطوير مواهبهم لأن مثل هذه الفرص المتاحة للأطفال في منطقتنا نادرة قليلاً. كانت لي فرصة جميلة أخرى عندما رسمت على جدران مستشفى في قسم طب الأطفال حيث كان هذا بمثابة حلم بسيط تحقق ، لأني لطالما أردت نشر الفرح والسعادة برسوماتي المتواضعة ، وقد أتيحت لي الفرصة لتحقيق ذلك.أنا سعيدة للغاية وفخورة بهذا العمل. كانت الابتسامات وضحكات الأطفال المرضى البالغين ، بالتأكيد ، لا تقدر بثمن. علاوة على ذلك ، جو الأخوة والتضامن والعمل الجماعي يجعلنا متحمسين أكثر للمشاركة بشكل أوسع في مثل هذه الأعمال التطوعية.

وهي حركة مهمة أنشأها الشباب الجزائري ، #TrashTagChallenge في الآونة الأخيرة ، أصبحت نشطة في خلال الأحداث السياسية لعام 2019. ويتمثل التحدي في تنظيف المناطق المتسخة أو المليئة بالنفايات ، ثم يتم عرضها بصور قبل وبعد . لقد تشرفت بالمشاركة في هذا التحدي في مدينتي بتنظيف محطة الحافلات في الجامعة ، تزيين الجدران ، ثم رسم بعض الصور الجميلة والملهمة عليها. لقد كانت تجربة رائعة مع شباب كلهم حيوية و أمل لتغيير جذري و أفضل. في الواقع ، امتد هذا التحدي إلى جميع المدن الجزائرية من خلال المواطنين الشباب الذين أعطوا الأمل لبلدنا من أجل مستقبل أكثر إشراقاً. بشكل عام ، الأطفال والشباب هم مستقبل أي بلد. وكما نرى في الجزائر ، لن يكون هناك خوف بشأن هذا الجيل الحكيم ،جيل كله إستعداد للقيام بالتغيير الإيجابي.

#whyIprotest

أنا الاحتجاج لدعم المجتمع.
أنا احتج لنشر الحب.
أنا احتج للحصول على التمكين.
أنا احتج لتحقيق تغيير إيجابي.

سليمة طالبي

" يجب ألا يخاف الشعب من حكومته. يجب أن تخاف الحكومة من شعبها."
آلان مور

يعاني الناس في جميع أنحاء العالم من الظروف السياسية السيئة ،غياب الديمقراطية ، فساد الحكام ، وانتهاكات حقوق الإنسان. خاصة في بلدان الشرق الأوسط وشمال إفريقيا ، مما ادى إلى ظهور ما عرف بالربيع العربي.

كانت تونس أول دولة أفريقية بدأت الانتفاضات ، واصفة إياها بثورة الياسمين أو ربيع الياسمين. وكان اليوم الأول للانتفاضة في 17 ديسمبر عشر 2010. حيث بدأت تضامنا مع الشاب محمد بوعزوزي الذي انتحر بسبب الظروف المعيشية البائسة التي تمثلت في الفقر، غياب العدالة الاجتماعية، والبطالة - وهي مشاكل يعاني منها جميع التونسيين. استمرت الثورة سبعة وعشرين يومًا ، وهي فترة تميزت بردود فعل عنيفة من طرف الجيش وكذلك مقاومة قوية من الشعب في مختلف مناطق تونس. خلال هذا الوقت ، مات أكثر من 219 تونسيًا وجرح عدد كبير منهم. أدى ربيع الياسمين إلى فرض قيود على سلطة الدولة وكذلك استقالة الرئيس زين العابدين بن علي القسري. اعتبرت الثورة التونسية انطلاقة لسلسلة من الاحتجاجات التي حدثت في الدول العربية الأخرى.

تأثرت كل من مصر وليبيا بالثورة التونسية. احتج الناس في كلا البلدين لاستعادة حقوقهم السياسية والإنسانية المسروقة. بدأت الانتفاضات المصرية في يناير 25 عشر ، 2011. تم تنظيم الاحتجاجات لأول مرة على مستوى وسائل التواصل الاجتماعي ، ثم انتشرت خارج هذا الإطار ، إلى مظاهرات على مستوى ميدان التحرير، مدعمة بالمسيرات والهتافات والإضرابات. قامت الدولة المصرية بمحاولات وحشية لقمع هذه الثورة بإطلاق أعيرة نارية والغاز المسيل للدموع ، لكن الشعب أظهر مقاومة قوية. انتهت الثورة بعد ثمانية عشر يومًا باستقالة الرئيس حسني مبارك و قيام مشاريع إصلاحية على المستوى السياسي والاقتصادي. اتخذت الثورة الليبية في عام 2011 مسارا مماثلا لمصر، لكنها كانت أكثر رفضا لديكتاتورية الرئيس معمر القذافي. هنا كان رد فعل الدولة أكثر قسوة. انتهت الثورة بوفاة القذافي وعدد كبير من الليبيين. ، والقيام بالإصلاحات السياسية والاقتصادية.

في الآونة الأخيرة ، انضمت الجزائر إلى "الربيع العربي" بعد إصرار الحكومة على ترشيح الرئيس عبد العزيز بوتفليقة للعهدة خامسة. لم يرغب الجزائريون في أن تكون احتجاجاتهم مثل الانتفاضات العربية الإفريقية الأخرى المليئة بالعنف والموت بسبب ما شهده الشعب الجزائري خلال العشرية السوداء .

بين الشمال والجنوب
وحتى لو لم نتمكن من رؤيتهم ،
أعلم أنهم سينزلون.

أميثاف ريدي

يملأ القادة الكارزميون والمؤثرون تاريخ التغيير الاجتماعي والسياسي. فكر مثلا في سوزان ب. أنتوني ، مارتن لوثر كينغ جونيور ، ونيلسون مانديلا. ولكن الآن يمكن لأي شخص تقريبًا دعم التغيير من وراء شاشة الكمبيوتر. يمكّن فيسبوك وتويتر الجميع بدءا من رئيس الولايات المتحدة الذي يجلس في البيت الأبيض إلى مدرس يجلس في المنزل للتعبير عن آرائهم حول قضايا مثل الإجهاض والسيطرة على الأسلحة واللوائح البيئية. لقد تم إلهام الشباب بشكل خاص لإحداث تغيير. تعد الجامعات من النقاط الساخنة للنشاط حيث الأندية الطلابية تثير الانتباه إلى حوادث المجاعات والفساد والاعتداءات الجنسية في جميع أنحاء العالم.

بالنسبة لهؤلاء الشباب ، يعد استخدام وسائل التواصل الاجتماعي من أكثر الوسائل الفعالة للنشاط لأنه يتناسب تمامًا مع مهاراتهم. يسارع الناس إلى الانضمام إلى القضايا التي يهتمون بها وتمنحهم وسائل التواصل الاجتماعي طريقة سهلة للمساهمة. تعد حركة Black Lives Matter مثالًا رائعًا على الحركة التي انطلقت مع غضب وسائل الإعلام الاجتماعية وتحولت إلى مظاهرات في الشوارع في شتى أنحاء العالم. النشاط لم يعد يتطلب المال أو العواطف الاستثنائية بعد الآن. إنه يحتاج فقط للوقت والتكنولوجيا. هذا هو السبب في أن الرجل العادي يمكنه قيادة التغيير. ليست هناك حاجة للبحث عن القائد العظيم التالي لتشكيل حركة ضد الظلم بعد الآن. لا يتعين على الناس أن يقفوا مكتوفي الأيدي على الهامش بينما يقرر الأفراد ذوو النفوذ ما هي القواعد التي ينبغي على العالم أن يلتزم بها. في عالم اليوم، الحكم أضحى للأشخاص العاديين.

سيمران كور

أنا أحتج لأن هناك ظلم في العالم. خاصة في نظام العدالة في الولايات المتحدة. الكثير من الناس يفشلون في رؤية الظلم ، ولذا فإنني أحتج لإثارة الوعي حول قضية خيّرة. أنا أحتج لأنني من ضمن أقلية. أنا امرأة أمريكية آسيوية تعرض شعبي للظلم. لا أريد أن يشعر أي شخص بالظلم الذي شعرت به. أنا أحتج لأنني أريد أن أوضح للحكومة أن الناس تهمهم قضيتهم، ولن نبرح الأرض حتى يتم القيام بشيء ما حيال ذلك. أنا أحتج لأنني أرى ظلمًا على وسائل التواصل الاجتماعي بينما يفلت الآخرون عن فعل نفس الشيء. أنا أحتج لأنني أريد أن أرى العالم يجتمع ويسعد. أريد أن أرى عالما متفائلا. أنا أحتج لأنني أريد أن يرى الناس العالم بالطريقة التي أراها وبذلك يمكنهم فهمي.أنا أحتج لأنني أكره عندما يتأذى الناس بسبب النظام. أنا أحتج لأنه يمكن تغيير النظام بسهولة لكن لا يتغير. أنا أحتج لأنني أرى العالم كواقعية لا كمثالية. أعرف الأشياء السلبية التي تحدث لكني أشعر أن الدفع نحو تغييرها سيجعلها أفضل. أنا أحتج لأنني أريد الدفع نحو التغيير حتى لو كان ذلك يعني أنني المحتج الوحيد. أنا أحتج لأنني أريد أن أسلط الضوء على القضايا التي تعتبر ثانوية في العالم. أنا أحتج لأن حياة السود مهمة.

ولكن هناك أشياء لا يمكنني القيام بها بعد الآن ،
لأن الوقت سرق منا و
الساعة الوحيدة التي تعود إلى الوراء هي هذا البلد.

الرجل الذي يجلس بجواري ليس أخي ،
يحاول فهم اللغة الأجنبية في الوثيقة
حيث يتنازل عن حريته بعيدا ،

لكن دماغه لا يستطيع معالجة كل شيء بسرعة ،
على الأقل ليس بسرعة كافية
للضباط المتبلدين.

ينظر إليّ وعيناه يطلبان المساعدة ،
إنه شقيق شخص ما ، وربما أخي ،
أو والد شخص ما

وأنا أساعده في معرفة ذلك
أنها لا توجد أحرف كافية في الأبجدية الإنجليزية
لوصف اليأس الذي يشعر به.

الشمال والجنوب يلتقيان
في المكان الذي نفصله فيه عائلته السلفادورية ،
أين نضعهم في أقفاص
لأنهم فروا شمالاً بمجرد انتقالنا إلى الجنوب وأحرقنا قريتهم.

الشمال والجنوب يلتقيان
أين يحدث الألم.

الشمال والجنوب يلتقيان
بداخلي
وآمل أن بوسعي تعطيل انحسار المد،
للتغلب على حرق الشمس

ولقاء نفسي في الجانب الآخر.
وراء الحدود غير المرئية
التي تفصلنا جميعا.

حيث تكون الوثائق صالحة فقط إذا تم التنازل عن روحك
للسادة الذين يحكمون الأراضي المسروقة من الآباء.

مركز الكون ليس في هذا المكان المظلم
حيث تسأل براءتي المكسورة بأدب
بأن يتم تجميع شتاتها مرة أخرى

الحب لا يعيش هنا ،
الإجراءات والشكليات هنا ،
جنبا إلى جنب مع الفوضى والخوف وطوابع الجنسية.

البعض منا مطبوع علينا ملصقات
للتعرف علينا كمهاجرين صالحين ،
والبعض منا يتم جره من فاه الدبلوماسيين
وأصابع الرئيس القصيرة الملتهبة.

الشمال والجنوب يلتقيان
في المكان الذي يطلق فيه علينا إسم الأجانب ،
حيث تعاملنا كما لو كنا كائنات من عوالم أخرى.

نحن مواطنون من الدرجة الثانية ،
لأن العيش بدون وثائق ليس حقيقيا
لكن الشعور بعدم وجود وثائق هو كل شيء.

هنا في هذا المكان الذي أصبح فيه أحلك أنواع الخوف حقيقيًّا ،
أخي يجلس ،
ساقيه مقيدتان.

لقد وجدته حيث التقى الشمال والجنوب
وأتمنى أن أعود إلى رحم أمي ،
معه

أتمنى أن أعدُّه
لوقته في عزلة
والترحيل الذي سيتبع.

من الضروري اتخاذ نهج أوسع. هناك دعوات لعملية بناء سلام شاملة في المنطقة. الجهات الفاعلة المحلية هي الأنسب لإدارة هذا الأمر، لأنهم يفهمون تعقيدات وتحديات المنطقة. سيتحدث الناس معهم بسهولة أكبر ويشاركون في العملية، لأن الممثلين المحليين هم جزء من نسيج المجتمع. يمكن للفاعلين المحليين الاتصال بطرق تكاد تكون مستحيلة بالنسبة للجهات الفاعلة الدولية والمحليون على دراية بأي الأدوات أكثر فعالية ب في ذلك السياق المحدد.

يمكن أن تتغير الأشياء مع أو بدون الجهات الدولية الفاعلة، ولكن لا يمكن أن تتغير بدون الجهات الفاعلة المحلية. بدون معرفتهم ومشاركتهم، لا يمكن أن يكون عمل حقوق الإنسان فعالاً. أعتقد أن سرد قصص أشخاص مثل ناديا مراد أمر أساسي لحقوق الإنسان. إنه يوضح أن لكل فرد يمكنه المساهمة في تقدم حقوق الإنسان وأن الجهات الفاعلة المحلية ضرورية لتحقيق التغيير. التأكيد على ذلك سيعزز حركة حقوق الإنسان ككل.

اليكس مارتينيز
تصادم في مكتب الهجرة

الشمال والجنوب يلتقيان
في مركز الاحتجاز حيث تركت هويتي
ملتصقة على آلة البيانات البيومترية.

ولد شعوري الزائف بالأمان
في مكان مثل هذا، حيث أشبعت شهيتي للضوء
، لفترة وجيزة.

الشمال والجنوب يلتقيان
داخل قلب طفل عامل من بيرو
وطبيب قوقازي من الأمريكتين ؛

بشرته الذهبية تحتفل
بمستقبل عدم المعرفة
الحقول الخضراء مليئة بالعمل الشاق واليأس.

في نفس الوقت ،
يكره امتياز
أن يعيش دائما فقط تحت جلده.

الشمال والجنوب يلتقيان في غرفة الانتظار

فريديريك بيهلر
قصص مهملة: أهمية الجهات الفاعلة المحلية في الدفاع عن حقوق الإنسان

في عام 2019 ، أصدر مجلس الأمن التابع للأمم المتحدة قرارًا بشأن العنف الجنسي في النزاعات. في جزء منه ، كان هذا رد فعل على الاستخدام المتزايد للاغتصاب كوسيلة للحرب. عندما وصلت القضية إلى الأمم المتحدة ، جذبت الكثير من الاهتمام. ألقت الصحف الضوء على المشاحنات السياسية التي أضعفت القرار داخل مجلس الأمن، كما سلط كثير من الضوء على دعوة أمل كلوني ، زوجة جورج كلوني ومحامية حقوق الإنسان الشهيرة. على النقيض من ذلك ، لم يتم إيلاء اهتمام كبير للأشخاص "وراء الكواليس" الذين عملوا لسنوات لإيصال القضية إلى الأمم المتحدة. بالنسبة لي ، قصتهم هي القصة الحقيقية. إنها تدل على أن حقوق الإنسان تتعلق بالفاعلين المحليين الذين يناضلون من أجل ما يؤمنون به كل يوم ، وكذلك حول الصورة الكبيرة التي نميل إلى التركيز عليها (في نصف الكرة الشمالي).

نادية مراد هي واحدة من الأشخاص الذين كانوا وراء الكواليس في القرار. في عام 2014 ، وقعت قريتها في العراق ضحية إبادة جماعية ارتكبتها الدولة الإسلامية ضد الأقلية اليزيدية. قُتل الآلاف ، واختُطف النساء والأطفال. كانت نادية مراد واحدة من بين عدد لا يحصى من النساء اللواتي احتجزهن تنظيم الدولة الإسلامية Yazda كعبيد جنس. منذ هروبها في عام 2014 ، كانت تروي قصتها بلا كلل. بمساعدة وهي منظمة غير حكومية صغيرة تتألف من عدد قليل من الناس فقط ، تحدثت إلى أعضاء البرلمانات في جميع أنحاء العالم ، وتحدثت إلى محطات الأخبار ، وكتبت كتاباً وأعدت فيلما وثائقيا كذلك. في الفيلم الوثائقي ، تواصل نادية مراد قولها إنها لا تريد أن تكون ناشطةً أبدًا. لكنها استمرت في الكفاح لحماية الأخريات مما عانت منه ومحاولة تحقيق العدالة. بدون شجاعتها ومثابرتها، ربما لم يكن مجلس الأمن ليصدر القرار.

لماذا إذن لا تكاد نادية مراد تذكر في التغطية الصحفية لقرار الأمم المتحدة؟ لم أكن لأعرف عن قصتها ، لو لم يتم عرض فيلمها في جامعة فرجينيا ، حيث تحصلت أنا على درجة الماجستير في القانون. ربما يكون السبب في ذلك هو أن قصة ناديا مراد ليست سوى واحدة من آلاف القصص الفردية المتعلقة بحقوق الإنسان. من المستحيل معرفة كل منها. لكني أعتقد أن هناك سببًا هيكليًا أيضًا: في الشمال العالمي ، يتم الحديث عن حقوق الإنسان فيما يتعلق بالجهات الفاعلة الدولية الكبرى مثل الأمم المتحدة أو منظمة العفو الدولية. يتم تناول هذه الجهات من حيث المعاهدات التي تبرم وأفضل السياسات لتنفيذها. في كثير من الأحيان ، يبدو أننا ننسى أن حقوق الإنسان الأساسية تتعلق بالأفراد.

هذا لا يؤدي فقط إلى رؤية محدودة لحقوق الإنسان ولكن يقوض سلطتهم كأداة للتغيير. إذا فكرنا في حقوق الإنسان وتحدثنا عنها من حيث الصورة الكبيرة ، فإن اللاعبين الدوليين الكبار هم المكان الوحيد لإحداث التغيير. ولكن ، كما تظهر قصة نادية مراد ، غالبًا ما يستغرق الأمر وقتًا طويلاً حتى تصل القضية إلى المشهد الكبير. الكثير من القضايا لم تصل إلى هناك. وحتى لو فعلوا ذلك ، فإن سبل العلاج التي يقدمها النظام الدولي قد لا تكون كافية أو مناسبة بشكل أفضل لحل المشكلة. يدين قرار مجلس الأمن استخدام العنف الجنسي في النزاعات. لكنها لا تعالج الإبادة الجماعية التي ارتكبت ضد اليزيديين

وبهذا المعدل ، لا يبدأ أملنا إلا بقائمة نظيفة لترجمة وتعميم المعرفة والعمل والحركة والقوة والناس والناس والناس والناس والناس والناس والناس والناس والأشخاص الذين يجب أن يكون غرضهم ويكون ويكون ويكون التحرر.

جوناثان براون

يبدو أن فرصة الكتابة عن موضوع النضال المجتمعي من قبيل التخاطر السماوي أو مثل دفعة قوية من الكون. خلال الأيام القليلة الماضية ، كنت أفكر في وفاة مغني الراب نيبسي هاسل ، الرجولة السوداء ، وريادة الأعمال ، والنشاط ، وأفضل طريقة للتأثير على المجتمعات المحرومة. قد تبدو هذه الأشياء متباينة للوهلة الأولى. ومع ذلك ، فهي كل شيء وإلا مختلفة. إنها شبكة مترابطة كنت أفكر فيها ، وكل هذه الأشياء جعلتني أعيد تقييم حياتي (ومقاربتها) في الدنيا والمستقبل. قبل وفاة نيبسي ، كنت أعرفه عنه وعن عمله بشكل سطحي. سمعت بعض الأغاني وشاهدت بعض المقابلات السريعة. لكن من خلال الكثير من الأبحاث ، توصلت إلى فهم من هو وما هي مواقفه. للتقليل من تأثيره ، يقول كثيرون إن نيبسي كان ببساطة "مغني راب عصابات". ولكن على الرغم من /أو على النقيض من الكلمات القاسية والعنيفة في العديد من أغانيه ، كانت حياته كرجل تدور حول المجتمع والفصائل المختلفة المكونة له. لقد فعل ذلك من خلال إنشاء شركات وشراكات مختلفة في المجتمع القاسي الذي نشأ فيه ، هناك في Crenshaw و Slauson قدم لأصدقائه وظائف ، وكثير منهم كانوا مدانين كمجرمين. حاول الجمع بين الناس. وضع نبسي العمل وراء كلماته.

في دوائر الراب المختلفة ، تتم مقارنة وفاة نيبسي بوفاة توباك شاكور. بينما يتحدث مقاطع فيديو قديمة على يوتيوب لـنبسي تتحدث عن تطلعاته لمجتمعه ، بعد ذلك ظهرت مقاطع فيديو توباك. بعد الغوص العميق في مقابلاته ، أصبحت العلاقة بين الرجلين واضحة. إنها أكثر من مجرد موسيقى راب. إنها موسيقى تتحدث عن الازدهار. كل منهما كان لديه الحرية والشجاعة لقول الحقيقة. كانت الطريقة التي تحدثوا بها عاطفية للغاية ، وثاقبة جدا ، نقية جدا. يبدو أن كلماتهم تهدف دائمًا إلى صميم شيء ما ، جوهر المسألة. لقد تحدثوا غالبًا عن أخطائهم السابقة ونموهم. هناك علاقة عميقة بين الصدق والخوف والقيم. أرى نفسي في هؤلاء الرجال. لكن في مكان ما على طول الطريق ، قمت بتبديل شغفي وحيويتي بالخصوصية والتقدم. جوهري لم يتركني أبدًا ، لكن شغفي بمساعدة الآخرين هدء في مقابل فترة راحة شبه سلمية. في الأيام القليلة الماضية ، كنت أتساءل ما إذا كان ينبغي علي تغيير نهجي للحياة.

قلت كل هذا لأقول إن النشاط هو أكثر من مجرد السير والصراخ والتغريد. إنها أكثر من أيديولوجية. إنه أكثر من مجرد اختيار أحد الجانبين. إنه يتعلق بالعمل على حل مشاكل الحياة الحقيقية. تدور حياة نيبسي هاسل حول النمو ومحاولة التأثير على التغيير الحقيقي في الأماكن التي تشتد الحاجة إليها. بالتفكير في قصة نيبسي ، والاستماع إلى شغف توباك بلا عوائق ، أشعر بالحيوية والتجدد. لطالما أردت أن أحاول رد الجميل لمجتمعي ، لكنني الآن سأفعل ذلك بعشرة أضعاف. سوف أكون أقل تحفظًا ، وسأتحدث عن الحقائق بصوت أعلى بكثير ، وسأضع نفسي لمساعدة أولئك الذين هم في أمس الحاجة إلي. من قدوتهم، سأزداد شجاعة. في إحدى المقابلات ، قال نيبسي إن أعلى قوة هي إلهام الآخرين.

العبودية كانت قانونية
الفصل كان قانونيا
الإبادة الجماعية اليهودية كانت قانونية
كانت الإمبريالية الأمريكية قانونية
الاستعمار الأوروبي كان قانونيا
كان معسكر الاعتقال الياباني قانونيًّا
كل هذه الأمور كانت قانونية ولكن هذا لا يعني أنها كانت على حق
هناك الكثير من الأشياء التي تتطلب معركة مستمرة
معسكرات الاعتقال قانونية
السجن الجماعي قانوني
الإمبريالية الأمريكية قانونية
الاستعمار الأوروبي قانوني
عدم العدالة في الغذاء قانوني
وحشية الشرطة قانونية

حريتي ليست الحرية إذا كانت تعتمد على اضطهاد شخص آخر
نحن دولة تعمل على حبس الناس بجميع الأشكال
كارلوس ذو الخمس سنوات وكان في حافلة الغرايهاوند لمدة 42 ساعة
هناك أطفال رضع يجلسون في أقفاص على الحدود الجنوبية وفي جورجيا ونيفادا وفلوريدا وفيرجينيا وكارولينا الجنوبية وتكساس وكاليفورنيا ، وأصبح من الصعب التركيز على ما هو مهم في متناول اليد لأن الجميع يبدو عالقًا في نهاية لا تنتهي أبدًا دورة من الحركة اللانهائية نحو مستقبل خيال علمي يبدو أنه حفرة سحيقة للغاية ، ومع ذلك لا يجب أن نغرق.

يتم تعريف العمل التطوعي بتعريفات متعددة
تعدد طرق يمكننا من خلاله إظهارها لبعضنا البعض في تجميع أجزاء وأجزاء من الشعب الذي رئيسه السياسي وسياساته بضبط الناس إلى غايات بلا هدف.

كارلوس ذو الخمسة أعوام كان على متن حافلة لمدة 42

ساعة

مباشرة

وهو لا يستطيع لهذا الانتظار إلى أن تفهم هذه الأمة وزن مصيرها كدولة مبنية على الكراهية وصفيحة حمراء بيضاء ومغطاة بالدماء

المعونة والتضامن الموجودة من
قبل من أجل فهم أفضل لمدى أدائي ومدى ملائمته مع المجتمع من عدمه.

قصيدة ملقاة حول عمل معابر الهجرة:

أقدم له فنجان قهوة وكتاب تلوين سبايدرمان
دخل إلى الحافلة الزرقاء الكبيرة التي سافرت عبر البلاد خلال الـ 42 ساعة الماضية
يتبع والده مباشرة بعد توجهه إلى مكان ما على طول الساحل الشرقي
طالبي اللجوء تقريبا
لكارلوس خمس سنوات وكان في حافلة غرايهاوند لمدة 42 ساعة
إنهم طالبوا لجوء، يطلبون اللجوء
اللجوء، طلب للحماية ممنوح من قبل دولة لشخص ترك وطنه كلاجئ سياسي

تم احتجاز كارلوس ووالده في مركز احتجاز في ماكالين ، تكساس لمدة أسابيع
يقفون في غرف باردة لعدة أيام
يتمسكون ببعضهم البعض لساعات
من يدري فيما كانوا يفكرون به كل دقيقة
البقاء على قيد الحياة لثانية لا تنتهي أبدا
La Hielera ، يشقق الجلد تحت وهي غرفة خرسانية ينبعث خلالها ريح صرصر من السقف
بطانيات الألمنيوم، طالبي اللجوء الذين يلتمسون اللجوء
يقفون في غرف البرد لعدة أيام

كارلوس في الخامسة من عمره وكان في حافلة الغرايهاوند لمدة 42 ساعة
كارلوس في الخامسة من عمره وكان في حافلة الغرايهاوند لمدة 42 ساعة
كارلوس في الخامسة من عمره وكان في حافلة الغرايهاوند لمدة 42 ساعة
في نفس الملابس ونفس الأحذية ونفس الجوارب والقميص نفسه في الحافلة لمدة 42 ساعة
على أراض مسروقة تعتبره غير قانوني

منذ عام 1994 ، مات 10000 شخص أثناء عبورهم الحدود المكسيكية الأمريكية
حدود غير حقيقية
الحدود التي شيدت
الحدود التي هي نتاج مستعمرة
حد يرفض أن يرى نفسه ويفشل في فهم أنه لا يمكن لأحد أن يكون غير قانوني على الأرض المسروقة

لقد تم إنشاء الشرعية دائمًا لصالح البعض وعلى حساب الآخرين

ما يتحدى ممارسات العمل المجتمعي المستدامة، فضلا على أنه يتجاهل تعزيز المجتمعات المترابطة الذي هو أساس استدامة العمل التطوعي. يجب فهم العمل الجموعي كمتعدد. هناك عدد لا حصر له من الطرق التي يجب أن نظهرها لبعضنا البعض. بدءا من العرض للمجيء والعمل مع شخص ما في أوقات صعبة ، إلى دفع ثمن وجبة ، إلى الجلوس لتناول القهوة ، إلى قراءة الكتب معًا - ليس من الضروري أن يكون التضامن وأعمال الدعم المجتمعي صاخبة لتكون مسموعة. العمل الخير يمكن أن يتم بوسائل متعددة.

قمت بتوثيق معظم قصص المهاجرين الذين قابلتهم في عملي في شارلوتسفيل وريتشموند على تطبيق الخاص بي. من النظرات المرتعبة للأطفال المبعدين في المقاعد الجلدية المزدحمة iPhone مذكراتي على إلى الصبي البالغ من العمر خمس سنوات الذي أخذ على عاتقه إحضار قهوة لأخيه وأخواته من مائدة المتطوعين لدينا ، لا توجد قصة واحدة تمثل مصير طالبي اللجوء الموجودة في أماكن الاحتجاز في نظام الهجرة لدينا. هذا النوع من العمل ليس براقًا ولا يدعوا للرضا غالبا، لكن هل هو ضروري.

في الولايات المتحدة ، تم إنشاء الشرعية القانونية دائمًا لصالح البعض على حساب آخرين. العبودية كانت قانونية. الفصل العنصري كان قانونيا. كان التدخل غير الأخلاقي العسكري في البلدان النامية صحيحا من الناحية القانونيّة أيضا. معسكرات الاعتقال اليابانية كانت قانونية. هذه المقارنة لا تحدى كل أشكال القانون والبنية القانونية في أمتنا الأمريكية، بل هي لفت للانتباه إلى انتهاكات حقوق الإنسان التي تحدث غالبًا تحت ستار الشرعية. الهدف من ذلك هو فهم ممارسات العمل التطوعي الغير الرسمي وغير الربحي، والتي يسري في عروق العمل التحرري في هذه الأمة وفي جميع أنحاء العالم. إن الاقتصاد التشاركي الذي يعيد توزيع الثروة على مستوى مجتمعي أو يقدم المساعدة لطالبي اللجوء غير المسجلين ، حتى عندما يعتبر غير قانوني ، يتحدى الأنظمة الوطنية التي لا تدعم حقوق الإنسان الأساسية بشكل كاف. عند القيام بذلك ، يمكننا إعادة تصور المعايير الاجتماعية والاقتصادية والسياسية والثقافية بطريقة تدفع بالمجتمعات إلى التركيز على بناء هياكل وإجراءات تضامن ودعم.

اعتناق العمل ذي الطابع غير الرسمي مما لا شك فيه يجلب معه انزعاج عميق. إن تحدي ما تم تكييفه جوهريًا أمر غير مريح. ومع ذلك ، فإن عدم الراحة هو سر النمو ، والنمو يكمن وراء التغيير. تتكشف أن المفاهيم حول من يستحق DACAmented في الكفاح من أجل الطلاب غير المسجلين أو تكافؤ الفرص في التعليم في هذا البلد أمر يبعث على الانقسام. مع ارتفاع ديون الطلاب وازدياد امكانية الوصول إلى المعلومات والتعليم المجتمعي ، تكشف مؤسسات التعليم العالي عن نفسها كشركات تعمل على أساس النخبوية. الكفاح من أجل المهاجرين المفرج عنهم من مراكز الاحتجاز هو معركة لا تنفصل عن الكفاح من أجل الحصول على التعليم للجميع. إنها جذور متجذرة في حياة وقصص المهاجرين السود والمهاجرون من أصول إفريقية. إنها معركة تعتمد على فهم لا يتزعزع حول كون البشرية وحقوق الإنسان من قدرتنا ومسؤوليتنا الجوهرية على الاستماع ورؤية ورعاية بعضنا البعض. الكفاح هو كل مزيج من النضال والتراخي، الحركة والراحة. كطالبة جامعية ، لاحظت أشكالًا مدمرة من النشاط الطلابي. النماذج التي تؤدي إلى جهود غير مستدامة والتي تجهد الطلاب. إذا تعلمت أي شيء من العمل إلى جانب طالبي اللجوء وأفراد مجتمع شارلوتسفيل، فقد كان الاستماع والتعلم من أشكال

وجود صوت لي. شعرت أنه إذا كان لديّ ما أقوله ، يمكنني أن أقول ذلك بكل حرية ، وحتى إذا لم يتفق الآخرون معي ، فلن يكون هناك تداعيات خطيرة على معتقداتي الشخصية. أنا لم أهتم أبداً بأشخاص لم ينعموا بالحريات التي كانت لدي. الجزء المحزن هو أن شخصين نشأا في بيئة لم يتحصلا فيها على هذه الحريات ، والداي ، كانا يعيشان في نفس المنزل الذي أقيم فيه وتربيت فيه. لم أدرك حتى بعد رحلتي ما مروا به. لحسن الحظ بالنسبة لهم ، كانوا قادرين على مغادرة بلدانهم وبدء حياة جديدة ناجحة. المشكلة هي أنه في هذه الأيام لم تعد الهجرة بهذه البساطة. معظم الناس ليس لديهم الفرصة للتحرك والبدء من جديد. في الوقت الحاضر ، يتم طرد المزيد والمزيد من الأشخاص خارج بلدنا وتفكيرنا في معاناتهم يقل أكثر فأكثر. آمل أن أصبح كاتباً يعيد هؤلاء الأشخاص إلينا. لديهم أصوات خبرتها مباشرة ويستحقون أن يُسمعوا. آمل أن أتمكن من الاستمرار في لعب دور صغير في ذلك على الاقل.

كارولين كامبوس
حول أهمية الطابع الغير رسمي

في 31 تشرين الأول (أكتوبر) 2018 ، تلقيت رسالة في صندوق الوارد الخاص بي من زميل سابق في العمل في ريتشموند حيث عملت في الصيف السابق. كانت تروج لفرصتي تطوع. LatinX في مركز المجتمع جاءت إحدى الفرص من أحد منظمي المجتمع المحلي الذين قابلتهم في ورشة تعلم الرواية السردية خلال فصل الصيف ، لكني فقدت الاتصال بهم. وتحدثت الرسالة عن كيف أن البيت الأبيض ووزارة الأمن الداخلي قد بدءا في إطلاق سراح الآلاف من المهاجرين المحتجزين في تكساس خلال الأسبوعين الماضيين. الآباء والأمهات والأطفال والأسر ، فضلاً عن الرجال والنساء والقصر الوحيدين ، تم إنزالهم تكساس. تم إعطاء كل ، McAllen في Greyhound في محطة (ICE) من قبل هيئة الهجرة والجمارك مع الإشارة إلى رقم هوية كل مهاجر ومساره على طول خط الحافلات sharpie مجلد يحمل علامة عبر البلاد. تم دفع حوالي مائتين إلى ثلاثمئة دولار عن كل تذكرة ، سافر الناس على أطول خطوط الحافلات من الشرق من دالاس ، تكساس إلى ريتشموند ، فرجينيا. إلى محطة شارلوتسفيل ، حيث جامعتي ، وهي المحطة ما قبل الأخيرة في رحلة تستغرق حوالي 50 ساعة بالحافلة.

عندما وجهت أنا ونشطاء آخرون من شارلوتسفيل دعوة للمتطوعين لأول مرة لمساعدة هؤلاء الأفراد ، جاء تدفق هائل من الجهود المتعاطفة التي تضمنت كل شيء ، بدءًا من تحضير الكعك وحتى كتابة البطاقات وتبرعات الملابس. أتذكر أنني أخبرت أحد أصدقائي بأنني منبهر من دعم المجتمع المحلي ، وخاصة من كبار السن من البيض. بدأت الجهود من الدردشات الجماعية إلى صفحات وسائل التواصل الاجتماعي ، نهاية بالاتصال وتوسيع جهود المتطوعين في جميع أنحاء البلاد ، خرجت مجموعة وطنية من المنظمين والأشخاص العاديين منشغلين عن مسؤولياتهم اليومية لمساعدة ودعم الآلاف من طالبي اللجوء. ومع ذلك ، فإن أكبر مشكلة يواجهها المنظمون هي الاتساق. إن الجهد الذي كان من المفترض أن يستمر لمدة أسبوعين لا يزال مستمراً حتى اليوم ، بعد حوالي عشرة أشهر من الكفاح من أجل تحرير المهاجرين ، الدعم الأولي الذي يأتي مع هذا النوع من العمل المجتمعي لا يكفي لجهود طويلة الأجل. اليوم ، تقوم نفس المجموعة المكونة من عشرة من المنظمين والمتطوعين بتقديم المساعدة ، وهذا

لقد تعلمت الكثير من هذه الرحلة من حيث القيم. كان أهم شيء بالنسبة لي هو أنني يجب ألا أحكم على مجموعة من الناس حتى أفهم تمامًا ما يمرون به. من السهل حقًا بالنسبة لنا ، خاصة هنا في جامعة فرجينيا، أن نجلس في أبراجنا العاجية ونزعم أنه من مسؤولية الآخرين أنهم في وضعهم الذي هم عليه. لقد كانت حياتي كلها كد وتعب. لكن كانت حياتي كالتالي: إذا قمت بالجهد، فيمكنني جني ثمار مكافأتي. الناس مثل خوسيه وإيمانويل هما أكثر الناس الذين قابلتهم جدا وكدا في العمل. ومع ذلك ، لم يتمكنوا من الاستراحة طوال حياتهم. عندما عدت إلى أميركا، أخبرت أكبر عدد ممكن من الناس عن تجربتي. اتفق البعض مع الدروس التي استخلصتها وكانوا سعداء لمناقشة تفاصيل رحلتي. آخرون لم يتفقوا وأصروا على اعتقادهم بالمثل العليا.كان لهم الحق الكامل في القيام بذلك ولكنهم كانوا مُحبطين بعض الشيء لأنهم لم يستمعوا حتى إلى ما كان يجب أن أقوله. لكي نكون منصفين ، من المحتمل أن يكون أي شخص منا قد فعل نفس الشيء مع آخرين في الماضي.

التجارب الشخصية تغير حقا وجهات نظر الناس.

بدأت أيضًا في إعادة النظر في تاريخ والديّ. والدي من لبنان ووالدتي من السلفادور. من المؤكد أنهم اضطروا إلى التكيف عند القدوم إلى الولايات المتحدة. ومع ذلك فمن الواضح تماما أنهم ما زالوا يحتفظون بهوياتهم. خبرتُ اللغات الثلاث ، العربية والإسبانية والإنجليزية ، والتي يتم التحدث بجميعها في منزلنا. تذوقت الطعام الذي يقدم ليلا في العشاء. عندما كنت أصغر سناً ، بالتأكيد لم أقدر هذا الثراء الموجود بمنزلنا. كنت أشتكي من تناول الطعام "الغريب" في غدائي وكم ترجيت والدي أن يتحدث باللغة الإنجليزية أمام أصدقائي. لم أفهم أن رحلتهم تتعلق أيضًا بالسلامة والأمن الاقتصادي والحرية السياسية. في كثير من الأحيان ، لا نفكر في أولئك الذين تفتقر حياتهم إلى هذه الصفات. يبدو أننا نفكر في السماح لمزيد من الأشخاص بالمشاركة في هذه الحقوق من خلال القدوم إلى الولايات المتحدة.نحن نقصر "المجال العام" على الموجودين بالفعل في أمريكا ، وهم مواطنون بالفعل. في حين أنه من المستحيل ماديًا لجميع الناس أن يصبحوا مواطنين ، يتعين علينا النظر في مشاكل أولئك الذين يفتقرون إلى الحقوق والحريات الأساسية. علينا أن نرى ذلك كسبب للانضمام إلى بلدنا.

بعد رحلتي إلى المكسيك ، زرت مركز احتجاز في ولاية فرجينيا الشمالية وتحدثت إلى بعض المهاجرين غير الشرعيين الذين كانوا يعيشون هناك. لقد أشرت إلى دعوة عضو الكونغرس المحلي خلال أزمة DACA والتعبير عن دعمي للحالمين. ما زلت أحاول إشراك نفسي في الأنشطة التي تدعم المهاجرين غير الشرعيين ، بما في ذلك الذهاب إلى احتجاج أمام العاصمة والتحدث مع السناتور ديك دوربين. ما زلت والدتي تتضمن طرقًا يمكن للطلاب من خلالها المساعدة في حل KBI أتلقى الرسالة الإخبارية الأسبوعية من مشاكل المهاجرين غير الشرعيين. آمل أن أتمكن من مواصلة نشاطي في القضية.

بالنظر إلى المستقبل ، أرى مستقبلي ككاتب يركز على أولئك الذين ليس لديهم حقوق ، وخاصة أولئك الذين يضطرون إلى مغادرة بلدانهم الأصلية لأنهم لا يتمتعون بحقوق. قبل رحلتي لم أفكر مطلقًا في هؤلاء الأشخاص. أنا مواطن أمريكي وحقوقي مضمونة. لقد نشأت دون الحاجة إلى القلق بشأن عدم

سبعين شخصًا ينتظرون فتح الأبواب. قيل لنا إن هؤلاء جميعهم تم ترحيلهم مؤخرًا. كنت أتوقع منهم أن ينظروا إلينا بالاشمئزاز ، بالنظر إلى أننا كنا أميركيين وبالنظر إلى أنهم طردوا للتو من البلاد. بقي الكثير منهم هادئين ، لكن عددًا كبيرًا منهم سألوا عن حالنا وقاموا بتحيتنا.

أنا سنقدم وجبة الإفطار ثم نغسل الأطباق. KBI بمجرد أن دخلنا، أخبرنا أولئك الذين يعملون في شجعونا على التحدث مع أولئك الذين كانوا يتناولون الطعام وأن نتعلم عن خلفياتهم. كنت "رجل عصير البرتقال" ، وكانت وظيفتي التأكد من حصول كل من أراد على عصير البرتقال. كنت أتجول قائلا "؟ quieren jugo مع محادثات بدء سأتمكن كنت إذا مما متأكدة أكن لم Jugo ، alguien ، الأشخاص كان الناس يطلبون عصير البرتقال بشدة. كنت أرتدي قميص بيسبول من واشنطن ، وكان كثير من الناس هناك من عشاق لعبة البيسبول عندما عاشوا في الولايات المتحدة.

ساعدني قميصي في التعريف عن نفسي والتواصل مع العديد منهم ، ولكن كان هناك رجلان طورت علاقة وثيقة معهما طوال ذلك الأسبوع. الأول كان خوسيه ، رجل من تيخوانا, المكسيك. كان خوسيه قد عاش في الولايات المتحدة لمدة خمسة عشر عامًا قبل أن يتم توقيفه في إحدى الليالي لكونه تحت تأثير أثناء القيادة. أدرك الضابط أن أوراق خوسيه كانت مزيفة ، مما أدى على الفور إلى ترحيله. عائلته لا تزال تعيش في ولاية كارولينا الشمالية. كان يفتقدهم كثيرا، لكنه كان على استعداد لعدم رؤيتهم مرة أخرى إذا كان بإمكانهم مواصلة حياتهم في الولايات المتحدة. ثم تحدث عن كيفية عمله بشكل رئيسي في البناء خلال فترة وجوده في ولاية كارولينا الشمالية وفلوريدا. بأي حال من الأحوال لم يكن يستطيع تأمين حياة فارهة ،لكنه كان قادرًا على إيجاد عمل لدعم نفسه، وأن يجعل نفسه في منأى عن التورط في عنف العصابات. كان ذلك كل ما يحتاجه. أخبرني أن أتذكر أن المهاجر المكسيكي لا يختلف عن الأمريكي. إذا وضعتهم جنبا إلى جنب، ستجد شخصين على استعداد للعمل بجد لدعم أسرهم. الاختلاف الوحيد هو أن المكسيكي سيعرف مدى سوء العيش في بلد لا تتاح فيه هذه الفرصة.

كما طورت علاقة وثيقة مع إمانويل الذي تم ترحيله مؤخراً عبر تكساس. كان متأكدا من السبب. كان من السلفادور. كانت تلك نقطة نقاش فورية لكلينا. يعيش الكثير من عائلة أمي في السلفادور. لقد زرتهم وهو الطعام السلفادوري التقليدي يتكون ، Pupusas عدة مرات. تحدثنا عن أماكن في السلفادور وعن من الخبز والجبن والفاصوليا. سألته لماذا غادر البلاد لأنه بدا أنه يتحدث عن ذلك بفخر كبير. طوى كمه كنت في خوف شديد في هذه المرحلة. MS-13. وأظهر لي وشم. أدركت على الفور أنه كان وشم عصابة أعتقد أن إيمانويل تمكن من رؤية ذلك الخوف. قال لي لا داعي للقلق. ثم أطلعني على ثلاث مجموعات أخرى من الوشم. الآن لم أكن متأكدا مما إذا كنت اشعر بالرعب أم بالارتياح. وأوضح كيف أنه لم يكن في أي عصابة. كان لديه وشم للعصابات الأربع الرئيسية في السلفادور ، حتى أنه عندما تعرض للتهديد من قبلهم ، كان بإمكانه أن يظهر لهم وشمًّا. كانوا يعتقدون أنه كان واحد منهم. كان يعلم أن هذا أمر محفوف بالمخاطر لأنه إذا أدرك أي من أفراد العصابة خداعه لهم ، لكان قد قُتل على الفور. لقد أكد مرارًا وتكرارًا أن العمل الجاد في بلدان مثل السلفادور لم يكن كافياً للعيش حياة جيدة. البلد ببساطة لم تكن آمنة للعيش فيها.

أني أدرك ذلك كامتياز، ومع ذلك ، يمكن أن يتشوه المنظور. في هذه الفقاعة المبهرة ، لا يعبر سؤال "هل سآكل هذه الليلة؟" أبداً عن أذهان مستهلكي شرائح لحم الخاصرة الرفيعة من الماشية العشبية العضوية. إن "الكفاح" الدنيوي المتمثل في اختيار دروس رياضة الدوران أو اليوغا أو سلطة اللفت أو السوشي يدل على مدى إبتعاد البعض منا عن تراثنا الذي يبدو للأسف أن نضالات الأجيال السابقة لا يمكن فهمها ، أو ما هو أسوأ من ذلك ، نسيانها ببساطة.

رغم أنني نشأت في هذه "الفقاعة" في مجتمع ما ، إلا أن أسلوب حياة عائلتي كان مختلفًا بعض الشيء. بينما من نفس الطبقة والامتياز من حولنا ، غرس والدي فكرة العمل من أجل ما تريد ؛ الفشل الحقيقي الوحيد هو منح هدية لم يتم كسبها عن حق. وعمل والداي لاجل الحصول على كل ما لدينا. كبروا ، كانوا أبطال خارقين: كان والداي يرتديان نعلي المستشفى - وليس أحذية فاخرة - ويتوجهان إلى المستشفى لتكريس أيامهما لإنقاذ الأرواح. لقد نشأت وأنا أشاهد التزامهم وتفانيهم وعطفهم. ساعداني على سماع قصة جدي في إدراك أن هذا اللطف ومثل هذا الدافع جزء من تراثي. إنها جزء من قصتي ، بقدر ما هو جدي وأبي. بينما قد نكون محظوظين بما يكفي لعدم تجربة الجوع المؤلم أو المواجهة الحقيقية للحياة أو الموت بشكل مباشر ، إلا أن قصص جدي - الذكريات التي خبأتها في صدري - غذت شغفي وعزمي على إحداث تغيير في حياة الآخرين.

لقد سمعت قصة جدي المدهشة للبقاء على قيد الحياة، ضد كل الصعاب مرة واحدة منه ، ومرة أخرى من جدتي ، والآن من والدي. في كل مرة ، تساعدني التفاصيل الجديدة في تكوين رؤية أوضح للرجل الذي كنت محظوظة بما يكفي لمعرفته. أتجاوز الزمان والمكان في محاولة لفهم الرعب الحقيقي للهولوكوست بالنسبة له وللعديد من الآخرين. القول بأنني أتعاطف هو عين السذاجة ؛ قلبي ينهار ، لكني لن أستوعب أبداً أعماق هذا الخوف والألم. ومع ذلك ، لم يكن جدي متصلبا أوحقودا. أنا دائمًا في حالة رعب من مقدار القوة والرحمة الذي قيل إنه أظهره في بيئة لا تضاهى إلا الجحيم. في حالة تعرض حياته للخطر كل يوم ، كان لا يزال يقدم قطعة خبزه إلى سجين آخر إذا كان ذلك يعني إنقاذهم ؛ لم تكن هناك روح لا تستحق الانقاذ ،حتى لو وضع حياته في خطر. لقد جسد تعاطفه وتواضعه ومثابرته وشجاعته في أطفاله ، وأخبرني والدي فيما بعد وأشقائي بهذه القصص من أجل تعليمنا أن نقدر الحياة التي كنا محظوظين بها بما يكفي.

وهكذا ، أكتب عن جدي. أكتب حتى يمكن سماع كلماته ، حتى يمكن سرد قصته ، وبحيث يمكن أن تستمر ذاكرته في إلهام الآخرين كما ألهمتني.

مايكل شحادة
استيقظت في وقت مبكر من صباح ذلك اليوم.

بعد فترة وجيزة ، بدأت أنا ومجموعتي المشي لمدة ثلاثين دقيقة لعبور الحدود بين الولايات المتحدة Kino والمكسيك. كنت أتوقع تماما أن تمر الجمارك المكسيكية منذ أن دخلنا بلدهم. وصلنا قريبًا إلى التي كنت سأعمل معهم خلال ذلك الأسبوع. كان يصطف خارج المبنى حوالي ، Border Initiative (KBI)

عندما سُئل السؤال "لمن تكتبين؟" ذهب عقلي مباشرة إلى جدي. أكتب عن البكاء الذي أجبر نفسه على كبحه. أكتب عن العرق الذي وضعه في كل خطوة إلى الأمام أراد لنفسه أن يتخذها. أكتب عن الحب والرحمة التي شعر بها في كل حياة من حوله. أنا أكتب للقوة التي كان يتمتع بها، حتى عندما شعر بالضعف الشديد. أثناء الكتابة لجدي، أكتب إلى زملائي وزميلاتي في جميع أنحاء البلاد. أناشدهم أن تفهموا قصة جدي وأن تنظروا إلى تأثير كلماتهم البغيضة ومعاداة السامية.

إن سماع قوة جدي يعطيني القوة والدافع لاستخدام كلماتي الخاصة لاتخاذ موقف ضد الهجمات المتزايدة على السكان اليهود - وخاصة في حرم الجامعات. إن معرفة بعض الألم والدم والعرق والدموع التي أريقت خلال عهد جدي، كان يدفعني للكتابة عن قضايا معاداة السامية في مجتمع اليوم. المناخ الاجتماعي السياسي اليوم هو أرض خصبة لمجموعات الكراهية، ومعاداة السامية آخذة في الارتفاع. على وجه الخصوص، يتعرض الحرم الجامعي للتخريب بشكل رهيب من قبل الطلاب الذين رسموا الصليب المعقوف في المناطق العامة. في أحسن الأحوال، هؤلاء الطلاب يجهلون التاريخ بشكل مأساوي. في أسوأ الأحوال، يعبرون بنشاط وبصراحة عن الكراهية والتمييز. الطلاب في جامعة ديوك، حيث تم رش الصليب المعقوف على نصب لليهود الذين قتلوا في إطلاق النار الجماعي في بيتسبيرغ، ذاكرا أنه "يبدو وكأنه لا يوجد مكان آمن من معاداة السامية" (https://www.newsobserver.com/news/local/article221897470.html).

للأسف، ارتكبت جرائم معادية للسامية في العديد من الأشكال، بدءا من المواجهة الجسدية المباشرة إلى الاعتداء اللفظي إلى تخريب الممتلكات. منذ أوائل عام 2000 في جامعة كاليفورنيا في إيرفين، تعرض الطلاب اليهود للسخرية اللفظية والقذف من النازيين الجدد. هذه الحوادث هي مجرد أمثلة قليلة من الأعمال المعادية للسامية التي تحدث في حرم الجامعات - المؤسسات التي تعزز التعليم والتسامح - والقبول والتنوع. أشكال أخرى من الكراهية والتعصب - بما في ذلك التفوق الأبيض، والإسلاموفوبيا يتم رؤيتهم أيضًا حول الجامعات.

لا تستجيب العديد من إدارات الجامعة للحوادث المعادية للسامية في بيان رسمي، وإذا كانت تفعل ذلك، فهي عادة ما تكون بلغة غامضة تكون عامة وغير مفيدة لوضع حد للمشكلات؛ يستخدمون عادة أصواتهم في هذه المواقف للتحدث عن "التنوع" أو "التسامح." أحد النتائج الثانوية للاتجاه المتزايد للحوادث المعادية للسامية في الجامعات هو درع أوسع للحرية الأكاديمية التي تحمي الأساتذة والعلماء المتحيزين. بينما يحق للأكاديميين الحصول على آرائهم الخاصة، إلا أن هناك عددًا متزايدًا من التقارير التي تشير إلى أن الأساتذة يحاولون تلقين الطلاب في صفهم. تم توثيق هذا النوع من الإساءة في فيلم وهو فيلم لجامعة كولومبيا عام 2004. يسلط الفيلم الضوء على استخدام Columbia Unbecoming، الأستاذ لموقعه لنشر تحيزاته الشخصية.

في طريق عودتي إلى بيوتات غرينتيش في كونيتيكت ذات السياج الأبيض، أدركت التضحيات التي قدمها جدي وغيره من أمثاله، حتى أنني لم أضطر أبدًا إلى تحمل الألم الذي تعرض له. أنا محظوظة لأنني لم أعرف حقيقة المصاعب الحقيقية التي يواجهها عدد لا يحصى من الناس طوال حياتهم. على الرغم من

إيزابيل إزراتي

فيما يلي سرد لأحداث وقعت في حياة جدي سام إزراتي ، على النحو الذي وصف لأبي ، آري إزراتي ، وعائلتي. وقعت الأحداث خلال السنوات 1942-1945 ، عندما كان جدي حوالي 16-19 سنة من العمر لقد توفي جدي، لكن ذكريات تجربته خلال هذا الوقت لم تُنسى وقد وصفها لي الآن والدي بوضوح.

لقد تذكر رحلة القطار. كانت طويلة ، مزدحمة للغاية ، وقذرة ، وباردة. النوافذ كانت مفتوحة. كان الوقت لشتاء. كان الجميع متراصين، معظمهم خائفون من الوجهة المجهولة. تم فصل العديد من العائلات ، مثل جدي ، قبل ركوب القطار. في حالة جدي ، كان مع والده وشقيقته الصغرى. لم تكن والدته وإخوته في القطار ، حيث قُتلوا في بلدتهم في اليونان.

وصل القطار أخيرًا إلى وجهتهم: أوشفيتز. تجمع الركاب بعصبية مهما كانت ممتلكاتهم وخرجوا من عربات القطار. تم فرزهم من قبل الجنود النازيين. تشكل قطيع من الركاب اليهود في خطوط لا نهاية لها على ما يبدو، كشفت الغاية ذ فقط للجزء الأمامي من الطابور. بعد ساعات لا تحصى ، وصل جدي إلى مقدمة الطابور. سأله القائد النازي مع والده عن بعض الأسئلة. ثم طلب من والده الاختيار بين البقاء مع ابنته أو ابنه. إذا اختار ابنته ، فسيتم إرساله إلى اليسار: غرفة الغاز ومحارق الجثث. إذا اختار ابنه ، فسيتم إرساله إلى اليمين: معسكرات العمل. تم فرض هذا الاختيار الأكثر بشاعة والمؤلم لأي من الوالدين على العديد من الأسر عند وصولهم إلى أوشفيتز. جدي الاكبر وجدتي ذهبت مع الأخت إلى غرفة الغاز. أما جدي في سن السادسة عشرة ، كان عليه أن يتعلم كيف يعيش بمفرده.

طوال فترة وجوده في أوشفيتز ، كان جدي يعمل بجد ، في الشتاء البارد ، وغالبًا بدون حذاء. سرعان ما علم أن السجناء الذين تم إلقاؤهم في غرفة الغاز هم أولئك الذين بدوا مرضى أو ضعفاء أو غير صحيين. الاصطفافات كانت عمليات لتقييم صحة العمال. إذا مررت ، عشت. في مناسبة كان محظوظا جدا حيث وجد عملة ذهبية في الثلج واستخدمها للحصول على زي بيجاما مخططة وحلاقة جعلته يبدو أكثر صحة من السجين المجاور له.

في صف واحد ، طلب ضابط من السجين المجاور لجدي تسمية الصيغة الكيميائية للمياه. لقد كان سؤالًا بسيطًا على ما يبدو ، لكن الرجل المجاور لجدي قضى عامين كاملين في معسكر الاعتقال بالفعل. على الرغم من أنه كان صيدليا قبل الاستعباد في أوشفيتز ، لم يستطع الرجل تذكر الصيغة. جدي ، من ناحية أخرى ، أجاب على سؤال السجين ، وأنقذ الرجل من الدخول إلى غرفة الغاز ، ولكن عرض حياته للخطر...

بينما أضغط على يدي على مقاعد القطار المبطنة في طريق عودتي إلى مسقط رأسي في ولاية كونيتيكت ، أفكر في قصص ماضي جدي ، روايات تبدو مشاهد بعيدة من فيلم رعب. أصابعي تنسحب بلا هدف على خيوط فضفاضة من وسادة ، ويتجول عقلي. يمكن أن أشعر تقريبًا بالوحدة والخوف اللذين استهلكا جسده وأبقياه مستيقظًا كل ليلة ؛ الشعور بالجوع المؤلم الذي أضعف عظامه. تقريبا.

كل عامٍ نتعلم عنهم وأفعالهم الرهيبة.

اعتقدت أننا نحن الولايات المتحدة الأمريكية ، البلد الذي يفتخر به كونها وعاء مختلط ، أضحت مختلفة الآن.

لقد شعرت بالخزي لرؤية تلك المجموعات المثيرة للاشمئزاز مثلهم لا تزال موجودة وتتباهى بنفسها بلا خجل.

أخذت نفسي إلى انستغرام وأفرجت عن خيبة أملي وصببت جام غضبي على منشور فيه.

مزيد من المشاركة

آلي ماسترسون
نقرت رمز الطير الأزرق المألوف على هاتفي
على أمل الحصول على القليل من الفكاهة في رحلة مملة.

حصلت على أكثر مما طلبت.

انتقلت عبر تنبيهات الأخبار والإعلانات إلى
شيء لم أره من قبل

رأيت اسم مستخدم لصديق جيد رأيته لتوي
في المدرسة في اليوم الماضي.

رأيت مجموعة من الصور التي أظهرت حقيبة Ziploc
يحتوي على مصاصة وإعلان للانضمام إلى KKK.

رأيت حقيبة تركت على عتبة صديق جيد
من أسرة مختلطة الاعراق.

قرأت تغريدة قائلة أنها استيقظت على كثير من هذه الحقائب
وضعت على شرفتها.

قرأت تغريدة قائلة إن هذا لم يكن في منزلها فقط،
لكن جيرانها أيضا.

شعرت بالارتباك لأن هذا كان عام 2018،
المستقبل الذي طالب به الجميع كان أكثر تقدمية من هذا.

شعرت بشعور من الرعب يمر عبر دمي
ليس فقط على صديقتي ولكن جيرانها كذلك.

شعرت بشعور من العار أنني لم أكن أدرك ذلك
لا يزال يجند أعضاء جدد KKK كان.

سألت نفسي كيف لم أكن أعرف منذ ذلك الحين

جزائري 5

من فضلك لا تنسى أنه احتجاج وطني. لا تغفل النظام. كل شيء كان الأمر يبدو مثاليا على وسائل الإعلام الاجتماعية ، وفي الحياة الحقيقية ، كل شيء تحت الملاحظة. لا أقصد أننا ساذجون ولا مبالين ، ولكن من الصعب ومن المبكر جدًّا قول أن الأمور تسير في الاتجاه الصحيح. اعط الامر بعض الوقت! المشكلة هي أنه حتى أولئك الذين يعبرون عن أنفسهم ، معظمهم يعانون من انعدام الثقة أو المعرفة. نحن نميل إلى الاعتقاد بأن ما يقوله شخص لديه سلطة أو حتى ما ينشر ويكتب ع ما هو حقيقة واقعة. ما نشهده هو مجموعة كبيرة ومتنوعة من الإيديولوجيات ، كل واحدة تريد أن تكون في القمة.

جزائري 2

بالطبع ، كل شيء تحت المراقبة. معظم الذين يعبرون عن أنفسهم هم من عامة الناس ، وكما قلت من قبل ، ليس كل شخص لديه وعي سياسي. الطلاب والمثقفين الذين لديهم هذا النوع من الوعي هم النوع الذي نحتاجه. كان هناك فرق ملحوظ بين الحين والآخر. ينبغي تقدير بعض الجهود. لهذا السبب قلت إن الناس يمكنهم الاعتماد على هؤلاء المتعلمين لتوصيل رسائلهم والتحدث نيابة عنهم. ولم أقصد أي حزب سياسي أو معارضة لأنه من الواضح أنه لا يمكن الوثوق بأي منها.

جزائري 5

نعم بالفعل ، يجب تقدير الأشياء الجيدة وإشادتها. يمكنك الاعتماد على شخص ما وتسمح له/ها بالتحدث نيابة عنك عندما تكون الأمور واضحة. الشيء هو أنهم يروننا فقط الأشياء التي يريدون منا رؤيتها. لذلك ، الأمر مختلف عندما نتحدث عن المثقفين ، ليس هناك ما يضمن أنهم سيفعلون الشيء الصحيح. على وسائل التواصل الاجتماعي ، أنت لا تعرف من ينشر الأفكار المضللة ، فقد يكون مثقفًا ، اومن يدري؟

ليس من السهل تعليم الناس كيفية التعامل مع وسائل التواصل الاجتماعي. ومع ذلك ، إذا تم تعليمهم أو اعتادوا على التفكير النقدي ، وإذا كانوا يتأملون ولا يقبلون كل وارد قبولا أعمى ، فلن يخدعهم شيء بسهولة. بغض النظر عن مدى ضررها ومدى تضليلها ومدى تدميرها ، يمكن للأشخاص الذين يفكرون ويفرقون بين الغث والسمين أن يتجاوزا الخداع.

جزائري 6

لهذا السبب ، في رأيي ، يجب علينا تدريس التفكير النقدي والتحليلي في المدارس وكيفية استخدام هذا النمط من التفكير في الحياة الحقيقية ، لأني بصراحة ، لا أعتقد أن تدريس الرياضيات أهم من هذا.

جزائري 6

ردًا على سؤالك ، أعتقد أنه من المستحيل إيقاف هذه المعلومات المضللة بالإضافة إلى أنه من المستحيل إيقاف هؤلاء الأشخاص. إنه عالم كبير للغاية وعدد هؤلاء الناس ينمو يوما بعد آخر. ما يمكننا القيام به في رأيي هو التوقف عن دعمهم ، وعدم مشاركة معلومات خاطئة ، وعدم مساعدتهم في الاستمرار في القيام بما يقومون به. ساعد في جعل الناس يدركون مدى خطورة الأمر. بمعنى آخر ، حاول فقط أن تكون قوة مناهضة لهم.

جزائري 5

كيف يمكنك معرفة ما إذا كانت المعلومات صحيحة أم لا؟

جزائري 6

هذه صعوبة أخرى ينبغي التعامل معها ، لكن يمكنني أن أعطيك مثالًا بسيطًا عما نعيشه الآن. على سبيل المثال ، كمواطن جزائري مهتم بما يحدث في الجزائر ، فإن ما رأيته من خلال وسائل التواصل الاجتماعي كان تدفقًا كبيرًا مضللاً للمعلومات. كانت المشكلة أن معظم الناس كانوا يتابعون ما يقال. ما يمكننا القيام به في هذه الحالات هو بناء معرفتنا الخاصة القائمة على القوانين والمنطق. لقد قرأت الدستور الجزائري عدة مرات لمعرفة ما هو صحيح وما هو مخطئ. هذا الأمر يمكن أن يساعد قليلا. أنا لا أقول أنه سيكون بهذه البساطة في حالات أخرى ، ولكن في موقف يمكنك أن تكون فيه القوة المضادة حاول فقط أن تكون كذلك.

جزائري 2

اسمحوا لي أن أقول أنه من الصحيح أنه إذا قرأ الناس القوانين والتفكير المنطقي ، فسيتعرفون على هذا وذاك ، ولكن لا يمكن للجميع القيام بذلك. أنت تعرف في حالتنا ، في الجزائر. كثير من الناس حقا لا يمتلكون الوعي السياسي الكافي. لا يعرفون شيئا عن المجال السياسي. ومع ذلك ، يدخلون في محادثات ويقترحون القيام ببعض الأشياء غير المنطقية. وجهة نظري هي أن الطبقة المتعلمة هي المسؤولة عن أن تكون موضوعية وتؤدي بأفرادها إلى التفكير بشكل صحيح.

جزائري 5

لا تتوقع من الناس ، الذين لا يستطيعون التمييز بين أحلامهم وحقوقهم ، أن يكونوا مستعدين ومدركين لمعرفة ومناقشة الأشياء المهمة حقًّا.

جزائري 2

أعتقد أن بعض الناس لم يُمنحوا الفرصة للتعبير عن أنفسهم حقًّا. لقد كنا نفكر دائمًا أن مواطنينا لا يمكنهم التفكير بشكل صحيح أو مناقشة الأمور المهمة. لكن مثال الاحتجاجات هو مثال جيد لإثبات أن جيلنا يدرك ما يجري ويمكن أن يقود الرأي العام.

أعتقد أن هذه المشكلة سيئة للغاية هنا في أمريكا. من المعقول جدًّا أن الاخبار المثيرة للاستقطاب ولخلاف ونشر الأخبار المزيفة داخل وسائل التواصل الاجتماعي تسببت بشكل مباشر في نتائج الانتخابات الرئاسية لعام 2016 التي أضرت بكيفية نظرتنا إلى الدول الأخرى وتسببت في ارتكاب أخطاء كبيرة في مجال الحقوق المدنية والإنفاق الحكومي وتغير المناخ.

جزائري 5

وفقًا لما يحدث الآن في الجزائر ، يمكنني ببساطة أن أقول إن وسائل التواصل الاجتماعي حسنت قدرة المجتمع المدني على تعزيز الحوار المثمر. تعتمد جودة الحوارات على طبيعة موضوعاتها وعلى الأشخاص أنفسهم. تتمتع المجتمعات المدنية بالقدرة على حمل الناس على معالجة القضايا ذات الأهمية الكبيرة خاصة بمساعدة وسائل التواصل الاجتماعي. يعد فيسبوك و تويتر وانستاغرام منابر تمكن من مناقشة الأفكار والآراء وتبادلها.

حتى الآن في الجزائر ، على سبيل المثال ، تلعب وسائل التواصل الاجتماعي دورًا رئيسيًا في نشر وتيسير مناقشة الأفكار واستعداد الجزائريين لانتزاع حقوقهم وإعادة البلد إلى الجادة. يتم بناء حوارات مثمرة في كل مكان ، وخاصة عندما يتعلق الأمر بالقضايا التي تهم الجميع. يتم استخدام فيسبوك و انستاغرام ويوتيوب وما إلى ذلك من قبل الجزائريين من أجل المشاركة في الحركات السلمية ؛ وسائل التواصل الاجتماعي تدعم رياح التغيير وتسمح للمستخدمين بمعرفة ما يحدث وما يفترض القيام به.

يلتقط الأشخاص الصور / مقاطع الفيديو ويقومون بنشرها على وسائل التواصل الاجتماعي حتى يكون الجميع على علم. يناقش الناس الأفكار الجديدة وكيفية تطبيقها. يتحدثون عما يجب أن يفعله كل منهم والطريقة المناسبة للقيام بذلك. في البداية ، اتفقوا على أن مسيراتنا وحركاتنا يجب أن تتخذ شكلًا سلميًا ومن الواضح تمامًا أن الفكرة قد نجحت. تساعد وسائل التواصل الاجتماعي الجزائريين على تحدي أنفسهم لتنظيف البيئة ورسم الجدران وغير ذلك كثير. كما تساعد معظم الناس على التحلي بالمرونة في تلقي أفكار جديدة والشعور بالحرية في بناء حوارات عامة مثمرة. بصرف النظر عن السياسة ، يمكن لوسائل الإعلام الاجتماعية أن تلعب دور أداة التسهيل للاندماج الاجتماعي. يمكن لأي مجتمع مدني أن يكسب الكثير من خلال الحوار. إذا حدثت حوارات مثمرة على وسائل التواصل الاجتماعي فسيحدث ذلك فرقًا. موفرة الفرصة لإنشاء الأفكار والحلول ومشاركتها. وبهذه الطريقة يمهدون الطريق للعالم وعوالمهم ، مع مرور الوقت ، للترابط والوحدة.

جزائري 2

أعتقد أن معظمنا موافق على أن وسائل التواصل الاجتماعي تساعد في إنشاء حوارات مثمرة ، لكننا تحدثنا أيضًا عن المعلومات المضللة والأشخاص الذين يستخدمون وسائل التواصل الاجتماعي لتوجيه الناس إلى المجهول ونشر الكراهية. أوافق على النقاش حول أن منع الأشخاص من استخدام وسائل التواصل الاجتماعي لا يمكن أن يكون حلا لاصلاحها. بدلا من ذلك يجب أن يستمع الناس لبعضهم البعض. لا بأس في عدم الاتفاق على كل شيء. لكنني أعتقد أيضًا أن هناك فئة معينة من الأشخاص لا يمكننا التحدث معهم. إنها فئة الأشخاص الذين ينتجون أفكارًا ضارة. والسؤال هو كيفية إيقاف هؤلاء الناس ، وكيفية التعرف عليهم ؟

جزائري 4

كانت وسائل التواصل الاجتماعي مساعدة كبيرة للناس للوصول إلى الحشود وإسماع أصواتهم وأفكارهم، خاصة عندما يتعلق الأمر بتنظيم أنفسهم. لقد رأينا بعضًا من أعظم الأمثلة مؤخرًا في بلدنا الجزائر. ساعد أيضًا الكثير من الأشخاص المهمشين والخائفين، من خلال منحهم الدعم العقلي مثل حركة #MeToo التي ساعدت ليس فقط النساء، ولكن الرجال أيضًا، على التجمع، ودعم بعضهم البعض، وتنظيم اللجان والمسيرات، وحتى التبرعات للآخرين. تلعب وسائل التواصل الاجتماعي دور منصة دولية بلا حدود يمكن أن يسمع فيها الجميع ويمكن مشاركة ومناقشة أي أفكار.

ومع ذلك، يمكن أن تشكل أيضا مشكلة. يسيء كثير من الناس استخدام وسائل التواصل الاجتماعي لنشر الأخبار المزيفة وتخريب الأعمال العظيمة التي ربما أنجزها أشخاص آخرون. قد يستفيد الآخرون من موقف معين ويستخدمون وسائل التواصل الاجتماعي لإضافة الوقود إلى النار، بدلاً من البحث عن حل. يشجعون الآخرين في الاتجاه المعاكس. يمكننا استخدام الوضع في الجزائر كمثال أيضًا. يقوم العديد من الأشخاص بعمل رائع لتنظيم المسيرات، مع أخذ رأي الناس في الاعتبار، وتبادل الأفكار والحلول، بينما يحاول الآخرون، لحسن الحظ، أقلية صغيرة جدًا، تخريب هذه الحركة وخلق أعمال شغب. لذلك، أعتقد أن وسائل التواصل الاجتماعي، هي أداة رائعة، ولكن فقط عندما نعرف كيفية استخدامها. لأنه في الأيدي الخطأ، أو إذا أسيء استخدامها، يمكن أن تكون أداة مدمرة.

الولايات المتحدة الأمريكية 3

أعتقد أن السبب الرئيسي في كون الحجج قوية للغاية من كل جانب يكمن في القوة الكامنة للطبيعة المفتوحة وغير المنظمة لوسائل التواصل الاجتماعي. لم يحدث من قبل في تاريخ البشرية أن كان هناك هذا النوع من الوصول إلى النشر الذاتي. عادة ما يكون هناك فاصل بين. كنا محدودين بقدرات الفضاء الجسدي وكلام الفم. يتيح لنا "التجسيد الهجين" الجديد التحرك بقدر ما نرغب متجاوزين المسافات. النظام الذي يمكّن من ذلك يأتي بإمكانية الفساد والمصادرة، حيث إنه مصمم بحيث لا يكون لديه أي سبل للمراقبة والتحري (مثل محرر للنشر، إلخ). هذا يعني أننا، نحن الجمهور، يجب أن نقوم بالمراقبة بأنفسنا على حركات وأنماط الاستخدام التي نجدها غير مستحبة مثل انتشار الأخبار المزيفة، وغرف الصدى، والفاشية الرقمية، ولكن نفس الأدوات التي يستخدمونها لتقوية أنفسهم، قد استخدمت أيضًا لزعزعة استقرارهم. باختصار، فوائد الاتصال الفوري والاتصال العالمي أكبر من أن يتم تجاهلها، على الرغم من سوء استخدام عناصر معينة من وسائل التواصل الاجتماعي. المعلومات هي القوة، ولا يمكن لأحد أن ينازع فيما فعلته وسائل التواصل الاجتماعي لتزويد الناس بالقوة اللازمة.

الولايات المتحدة الأمريكية 4

لقد أضرت وسائل التواصل الاجتماعي بالقدرة على إجراء حوارات مثمرة في المجتمع المدني. سواء كان يواجه المجتمع مشكلة كبيرة عندما يتعلق الأمر بالفعل بمناقشة Facebook أو Twitter ذلك على القضايا. بدلا من الترويج للحلول أو تسليط الضوء على الحقيقة. يستخدم الأشخاص على وسائل التواصل الاجتماعي مصطلحات مهينة ويمنعون الناس من محاولة إثبات وجهة نظرهم. هذه مجرد ملاحظة جانبية، أسمع الكثير من الناس يقولون إن حظر الأشخاص على الإنترنت هو الحل لإصلاح وسائل التواصل الاجتماعي. وهذا أمر خطأ.

ومع ذلك ، يجب أن ندرك أنه بقدر ما تستطيع وسائل التواصل الاجتماعي بناء مجتمع مدني حقيقي ، يمكنها تدميره. يمكن استخدام وسائل التواصل الاجتماعي بطريقة خاطئة ، من قبل أشخاص خطأ ، لتحقيق غايات خاطئة. ما يتبادر إلى ذهني ، هو الدعوات الاخيرة للمشاركة في العصيان المدني من بعض شرائح المجتمع وكذلك عدم وجود متخصصين لتوعية الناس بجدية الأمر. يمكن أن تؤدي هذه المجازفات بنا إلى بعض المشاكل الخطيرة.

ومع ذلك ، يمكنني أن أؤكد أن وسائل التواصل الاجتماعي هي الطريقة التي ستقودنا إلى التغيير الذي نريده ، طالما واصلنا استخدامه بطريقة الإيجابية.

الولايات المتحدة الأمريكية 1

أوافق على أن هناك جوانب سلبية لوسائل التواصل الاجتماعي ، ولكن من خلال تشجيع الحوار المفتوح ، فإن الإيجابيات تفوق السلبيات. بالتأكيد ، يستخدم بعض الأشخاص وسائل التواصل الاجتماعي لنشر المعلومات الخاطئة أو الأيديولوجيات المتخلفة ، لكن جمال الإنترنت هو القدرة على مناقشة هذه المسائل والتحقق منها في أي وقت.

تبرز وسائل التواصل الاجتماعي أيضًا القضايا التي كان من الممكن أن تظل غالبية الجماهير غير مدركين لها. الإنترنت يتيح لك التفاعل والتعلم من الأشخاص الذين لم تتح لهم الفرصة للتحدث معهم ، مما يساعدك على رؤية العالم من خلال رؤى شخص مختلف. لو لم تكن هنالك وسائل التواصل الاجتماعي Twitter ، فلم نكن لنجري هكذا محادثات. أعرف بالتأكيد أنني تعلمت الكثير من الأشياء التي قرأتها على لقد غيرت هذه المواقع الطريقة التي أرى بها العالم وقدمت لي رؤية أعلم أني لا يمكنني Reddit. أو الحصول عليها بسهولة من أي مكان آخر.

الولايات المتحدة الأمريكية 2

أوافق أيضًا على أن وسائل التواصل الاجتماعي يمكن أن تكون أداة إيجابية حقًا تشجع الحوار المفتوح والمثمر. ولكن الشيء الذي أواجهه في هذه المحادثة هو حقيقة أنه يمكن للمرء بسهولة عزل أنفسهم عبر وسائل التواصل الاجتماعي بحيث يتعرضون فقط للمعلومات ووجهات النظر التي تدعم وجهات نظرهم الموجودة مسبقًا. من السهل التمسك بمصادر مريحة لك. عندما نفعل ذلك ، يمكن جعل آرائنا أكثر تطرفًا أو أحادية الجانب. السلبية الأخرى في وسائل التواصل الاجتماعي هو أنه من الصعب التمييز بين ما هو حقيقة وما هو ليس كذلك.

تنتشر المعلومات المضللة بسرعة ويمكن اعتبارها حقيقة من قبل الجماهير الكبيرة من القراء. إذا كان بإمكانك المشاركة في الحوار على وسائل التواصل الاجتماعي مع الأخذ في الاعتبار في الوقت نفسه أن ليس كل ما تسمعه سيكون صحيحًا وأنه من المهم سماع وجهات نظر بديلة ، فهناك إمكانيات كبيرة لما يمكن أن تسهله وسائل التواصل الاجتماعي.

حوار

كجزء من هذا المشروع ، طلبنا من نشطاء جزائريين وأمريكيين مناقشة دور وسائل التواصل الاجتماعي في النشاط. قررنا إخفاء هويتهم للسماح لهم بالتحدث بحرية عن اللحظة السياسية الحالية دون خوف.

جزائري 1

تلعب وسائل التواصل الاجتماعي دورًا كبيرًا في حياتنا بشكل عام ، ولكنها يمكن أن تحسن أو تؤذي المجتمع وفقًا لطريقة استخدامها. تلعب وسائل التواصل الاجتماعي في بلدي دورًا كبيرًا في توجيه المجتمع ، خاصة الآن ، نظرًا لوجود العديد من الاحتجاجات في جميع أنحاء البلاد لأسباب سياسية

جزائري 2

أعتقد أن وسائل التواصل الاجتماعي تحسن بقدر ما تضر بالمجتمع. إنه سيف ذو حدين. فمن ناحية ، قد يجد أي مواطن عادي أفكاره وآرائه مسموعة ويمكنه التحدث بحرية مع أي شخص وهذا يخلق مناقشات مثمرة تؤدي إلى استجابة مناسبة للقضية التي يناضل من أجلها.

من ناحية أخرى ، فإن وسائل التواصل الاجتماعي لها دور في نشر الأفكار الخاطئة. تؤدي أحيانًا إلى فوضى في المجتمع مثل ما حدث في بعض الدول العربية قبل بضع سنوات. في بلدي ، أعتقد أن وسائل التواصل الاجتماعي ساهمت بشكل إيجابي في الحركة التي بدأت منذ شهر تقريبًا.

لقد توحد الناس في كلماتهم. يسمع رأي الجميع. تم إنشاء العديد من المواقع العامة لإظهار كيفية تنظيم الاحتجاجات والمسيرات. أعتقد أن الفكرة هي أنه يمكن للناس استخدام وسائل التواصل الاجتماعي بالطريقة التي يريدونها ، سواء كانت إيجابية أو سلبية.

جزائري 3

إذا نظرنا إلى الوراء في ما يمكن أن يؤثر على الناس في مجتمعي. منذ بضع سنوات ، يمكننا أن نلاحظ أنه بغض النظر عن كمية ونوعية الخطابات والمناقشات المباشرة ، كانت أكثر تأثيرا. اليوم ، الناس لا يثقون في خطابات الآخرين بنفس القدر. إنهم يثقون ويتأثرون بسهولة بوسائل التواصل الاجتماعي.

هذا التأثير من خلال وسائل التواصل الاجتماعي له آثار إيجابية وسلبية. يمكنني إعطاء مثال على ما يحدث في الجزائر. منذ اليوم الذي بدأت فيه هذه الاحتجاجات منذ شهر وحتى اليوم ، يبلغ عدد سكان الجزائر حوالي 42 مليون نسمة. يمكننا القول إن ما لا يقل عن 20 مليون شخص يحتجون. وهذا يعني أن وسائل التواصل الاجتماعي أثرت على كل هؤلاء السكان! خلال هذه الاحتجاجات ، يلعب الإعلام الاجتماعي أيضًا دورًا مزدوجًا. تعمل كصحافة بديلة ، لأن الصحافة الحقيقية غير موجودة كما هو مفترض. كما أنه يلعب دور إعلام المتظاهرين من خلال شرح المفاهيم السياسية المعقدة وكذلك تقديم مختلف الاحتمالات واقتراح بعض الحلول.

عمل فني أصلي لهند بلكحل

صوفي بيكمان

قصيدة لجريس لي بوجز
لقد حان الوقت لحلم جديد.
استعدادا للتغيير.
يدور
مثل العقارب يدور على مدار الساعة
وضعت معا وجمعت من قبل أيدي أصغر سنا
ليست قديمة بما يكفي لنسميها
من صنع الإنسان.
طار عبر البحر بينما الأرض تدور
يحافظ على الوقت وفقا لنبض مقترح.
تكتكة ليست كنبض قلوبنا
تدق بمثابرة مثل حنان الأم
لينة بما يكفي لحماية جمجمة طفلها الهشة
قوية بما يكفي لهز الأرض التي يمكن للرجال فقط تحويلها لساحة معركة.
قادر ، ثابت ، دائم التغير
كيف تطورت
إنها تحول ساحات القتال إلى حدائق نباتية
كل دائب على فعل المقاومة ، المرونة ، والاستعادة
على الرغم من أن ساعة يدها تدور في دوائر
إنها لا تتناسب مع ثورة روحها
تطور روحنا
التمردات اليومية والكوارث التي تم جمعها.
تدفعنا إلى ساعة جديدة
على مدار الساعة على عكس ساعات المعصم لدينا
"كم هو الوقت الآن بتوقيت العالم؟"

القسم ثلاثة:
وسائل التواصل الاجتماعي والنشاط

تغير، والقيام بعمل جيد لبلدهم. لقد شهدنا في الآونة الأخيرة أن هناك بعض النساء من السلطة لسن جديرات بالثقة. وهذا يجعل الناس يعتقدون أن النساء يجب أن يبقى في المنزل. وما زلت أعتقد أن مثل هذا التغيير في الطوائف لم يقصد أبدا أن يحدث في يوم أو يومين. والأمر يتطلب دائما وقتا وجهودا ولكن يجب أن يستمر هذا الجهد.

وأود أن أقول إن هناك بعض النتائج الإيجابية للكفاح من أجل القيادة النسائية في الجزائر. بدأت العقليات تتغير، وتحاول النساء جاهدة إثبات قدرتهن واستعدادهن لأخذ الشعلة ليكن رائدات سواء في الجامعات عبر الأندية، أو من خلال كونهن وزيرات في الحكومة، أو معلمات في الفصول الدراسية. لا يزال هناك طريق طويل يتعين قطعه، لكنني أعتقد أن بلدي بدأ يتعلم أن كونك قائدا لا علاقة له بنوع جنسك. يتعلق الأمر بقدرتك ومسؤوليتك وشخصيتك ومصداقيتك.

أفكار ختامية

فؤاد شريف بلفرد

في رأي، أعتقد أن أساس المجتمع المدني يجب أن يكون الانفتاح العقلي، مما يعني أنه يجب على الجميع قبول الآخرين وقبول اختلافاتهم من حيث الجنس والعرق والدين والثقافة. على هذا النحو، نحتاج إلى إنشاء قادة في المجتمع يناضلون من أجل حقوق الآخرين، مثل الحق في التعليم وحرية التعبير والدين. أعتقد أن هاتين خطوتين أوليتين في تشكيل مجتمع مدني.

علاوة هشام خليل

دور القادة في الدفاع عن حقوق الإنسان أمر حاسم. شكرا لإظهار هذا الأمر، كنت سألمح لذلك أيضًا.

فؤاد شريف بلفرد

دور تم تركه شاغرا في هذا المجتمع منذ 60 عامًا أو نحو ذلك.

القوى العاملة تتألف من النساء. غير أن النساء يحصلن على تعليم أكثر من 80 في المائة من الرجال. ومرة أخرى، أعتقد أن هذا يتعلق بعدم احترام المرأة كقائدة. وجاء في مقال قرأته أن 47.8 في المائة من السكان الجزائريين يوافقون بشدة على أن الذكور يشكلون قادة سياسيين أفضل من النساء؛ ويعتقد 21 في المائة أن التعليم الجامعي أهم للبنين منه للفتيات. وهذا يدل على أن بعض الناس في الجزائر لا يرحبون بفكرة القيادات النسائية في بلدهم سواء في القوى العاملة أو الحكومة.

شخصيا، خضت تجربة القيادة النسائية و واجهت مواقف سلبية نتيجة ذلك. كنت عضواً في نادي في مدرستي. وعندما تخرّج الرئيس كانوا بحاجة لشخص جديد ليقودهم لذا تم إختياري. بعض الأعضاء القدامى لم تعجبهم هذه الحقيقة و غادروا النادي. و الطلاب الذكور لم يريدوا الإنضمام لأن فتاة كانت تقود ناديهم. وكان جميع الأعضاء من الفتيات. سمعت الكثير من التعليقات السلبية في البداية وكان لا بد لي من إثبات نفسي إلى ما لا نهاية. بدأت العمل وبذل الجهود. و بعدما نظم النادي نشاطات ناجحة، أبدى العديد من الطلاب بمن فيهم الذكور اهتماما بالانضمام. لدينا الآن أكثر من 10 أعضاء ذكور. الفكرة هي أن الطلاب في مدرستي لا يؤمنون بقدرات المرأة حتى يثبت أنهم مخطئون. وهذا مجرد مثال بسيط على العقبات التي تواجهها المرأة في طريقها إلى القيادة.

للوصول إلى المناصب القيادية آنذاك أصبحت "الحركة النسوية الجزائرية" حركة تناضل من أجل المساواة بين الرجل والمرأة. وقد بدأت هذه الحركة مؤخرا العمل على نشر بعض الأفكار التي تدافع عن حقوق المرأة. وهذا جعلهم يتحدثون بحرية أكبر عن مشاغلهم، مثل أن يكونوا متساوين مع الرجال في كل شيء. وتقوم المرأة الآن بتنظيم اجتماعات ومناقشات في الأماكن التي تدافع فيها عن نفسها وعن آرائها. إن الهدف الرئيسي للحركة النسوية الجزائرية هو منح المرأة الحرية في أن تكون وتفعل ما تريد. وهم يريدون أن يروا المزيد من النساء في الأدوار القيادية، وهو التزام جلب دعم المرأة لجهودهم. ورأينا نساء يحتجن إلى جانب جميع الجزائريين ضد النظام السياسي الحالي في ما يعرف بحراك فبراير/شباط، 22 فبراير/شباط. ومن بين الأشياء التي يريدونها رؤية المزيد من القيادات النسائية

وهناك نساء آخريات، مثل نادية أيت زاي، أستاذة قانون الأسرة في جامعة الجزائر العاصمة وخبيرة في مجال السياسة، يتحدثن عن إشراك المرأة في السياسة. وعندما أُعلنت قوانين جديدة في عام 2012 تعزز مشاركة المرأة في السياسة المحلية والوطنية، وصفتها أيت زاي بأنها "شجاعة". وبالإضافة إلى "أيت زاي"، هناك العديد من النساء الأخريات اللواتي يكافحن يومياً بإنشاء جمعيات ونوادي، كما ذكر أعلاه. وهناك نساء يكتبن ليثبتن للمجتمع أن المرأة تستطيع أن تفعل أي شيء، وأنه لا يوجد فرق بين الرجل والمرأة عندما يتعلق الأمر بالقيادة. إنهم يحققون إنجازات ملحوظة لأنه في وقت مضى لم يتمكن أحد من التعبير عن رأيه حتى. الآن يستخدمون وسائل التواصل الاجتماعي ويجتمعون لمناقشة قضاياهم. وفي ظل خسارتها للإنتخابات، لدينا الآن أيضا امرأة تقود حزبا سياسيا، لويزة حنون.

ومع ذلك، هناك اختلافات بين النساء اللواتي يدافعن عن الحقوق السياسية والمدنية. وتختلف الأيديولوجيات وأهداف هذه الحركات. البعض يهدف إلى خلق الفوضى، والبعض الآخر يطمح إلى تغيير مثمر. أعتقد أن النساء اللواتي يجب أن نساندهن هن اللواتي لديهن القدرة على القيادة، وإحداث

بشرى رحموني

يعود تاريخ المرأة الجزائرية في السياسة إلى بدايات تاريخنا كأمة حديثة. والواقع أن القيادة النسائية في الجزائر طويلة منذ الثورة الجزائرية التي بدأت في الأول من تشرين الثاني/نوفمبر 1954. وشهدت الأمة مشاركة ملحوظة للمرأة في الحرب مثل لالا فاطمة نسومر، وحسيبة بن بوعلي، وجميلة بوحيرد، فضلا عن العديد من الآخرين الذين ساهموا والذين كانت لديهم أدوار هامة في الثورة.

بعد الاستقلال، بدأت النساء في التصويت، وفي عام 1984 شهدت الجزائر أول وزيرة لها، زهور أونيسي. ومنذ ذلك الحين، عملت منظمات وجمعيات حقوق المرأة جاهدة لإثبات أن المرأة قادرة على العمل وقادرة على المشاركة في "عالم القيادة مع ذلك، هناك أيضاً حالة لويزة حنون، التي كانت أول إمرأة" جزائرية وعربية ترشح للرئاسة في نيسان/أبريل 2004 ولكنها خسرت أمام بوتفليقة (الرئيس السابق). حاولت مرة أخرى في عامي 2009 و 2014، لكنها فشلت أيضا. كان هدفها الرئيسي فصل الدين عن السياسة وهو أمر رفضه الجزائريون. واجهت انتقادات قاسية بسبب برنامجها وأيديولوجياتها.

رغم ذلك، أعتقد أن (حنون) خسرت لأنها كانت إمرأة.

الجزائر بلد مسلم. كل شخص يمارس الإسلام والدين مرتبط بقوة بالسياسة. لذا، من الصعب مناقشة الحديث عن القيادة النسائية. يدعي المتدينون أن هناك قواعد إسلامية لا تسمح للمرأة بقيادة أمة. ومن وجهة النظر الإسلامية هذه، من الأفضل أن تبقى المرأة في المنزل. وعلاوة على ذلك، ليس على المرأة أن تذهب للعمل لأن ذلك واجب على الرجل. يجب أن يعمل لأسرته ويُنظر إلى ذلك على أنه جزء من جعل الحياة أسهل بالنسبة للمرأة لأن المرأة لا تعتبر قوية مثل الرجل. وهناك أيضا عادات وتقاليد إضافية ليست دينية بحتة، ولكنها تعتبر المرأة أيضا متواضعة وخجولة و رزينة. كما يعتقد هؤلاء الجزائريون أن هذه النساء ضعيفات ولا يستطعن التعامل مع ضغط العمل في الخارج كما يفعل الرجال. وكل هذه المعتقدات، مجتمعة، تدعم فكرة أن البقاء في المنزل يضمن للمرأة حياة كريمة. ولهذا السبب، يعتقد العديد من الجزائريين أنه ينبغي على المرأة البقاء في المنزل لرعاية زوجها وأطفالها. يجب أن تبتعد عن مشاكل الحياة الخارجية التي على الرجل تحملها.

أعتقد أن المشكلة الحقيقية تكمن في كيفية سوء فهم الناس لدين الإسلام. يستخدم بعض المتدينين بعض آيات القرآن الكريم ضد المرأة لمنعهم من تولي مناصب قيادية. أنا لست خبيرة، وقد لا أكون متدينة جداً، ولكن يمكنني أن أرى أن معظم الرجال هنا يسيئون فهم ما يقوله الإسلام حقاً. الإسلام لا يمنع المرأة تماما من الحصول على وظيفة. الإسلام يقتضي بأن المرأة لا ينبغي أن تقود أمة بأكملها، ومع ذلك يمكننا القول إن المرأة قد شغلت أدوارا قيادية في التاريخ الجزائري. والواقع أن الإسلام كرّم النساء وجعلهن دعماً للرجال منذ عهد النبي محمد (صلى الله عليه وسلم) ونشر الرسالة الإسلامية. والأخذ بأدوار قيادية هو شكل من أشكال هذا الدعم. وأخيرا، فإن العديد من هذه التقاليد الثقافية ضد المرأة لم تعد مقدسة كما كانت من قبل، وقد تغيرت بعض العقليات ودافعت المرأة عن حقوقها.

ومع ذلك، من المهم أن نضيف أنه على الرغم من جميع القوانين والحقوق المعلنة حديثا، فإن مشاركة المرأة في القوى العاملة لا تزال ضعيفة. وفي الآونة الأخيرة، أعلن وزير التضامن أن 20 في المائة فقط من

cape-xinjiang-muslim-uighurs-speak-china-persecution-180907125030717.html .

هيومن رايتس ووتش، "أزمة روهينغيا"، www.hrw.org/tag/rohingya-crisis.

Rupa Shenoy، "الإيغور"، "فقدان العائلات لأفرادها في معسكرات إعادة التعليم في الصين"، PRI، الأمريكيون، www.pri.org/stories/2018-12-19/families-are-lost-china-s-re-education- معسكرات-نحن-اليوغور-منقسمون .

الأمم المتحدة، "الأمم المتحدة ، الإعلان العالمي لحقوق الإنسان". www.un.org/en/universal-declaration-human-rights/.

Forbes، والاس، تشارلز. "الحرب التجارية تؤذي الصين بينما يزدهر الاقتصاد الأمريكي". مجلة فوربس يوليو 2018 31 www.forbes.com/sites/charleswallace1/2018/07/31/trade-war-hurts-china-while-us-echem- 383 # / ازدهارlc94275b64.

ويستكوت ، بن. "السفير الصيني يهدد بالانتقام من عقوبات الإيغور المحتملة من الولايات المتحدة." سي إن إن ، شبكة أخبار الكابل ، 28 نوفمبر 2018 www.cnn.com/2018/11/27/politics/us-china-uyghur-cui-tiankai-intl/index .html .

نور الهدى بلخضر

من الصعب للغاية أن تكون نفسك كامرأة في عالم يهيمن عليه السكان الذكور. مهما كنت تعمل بجد أو مدى نواياك الصادقة ، فلن تحصل على ما تصبو إليه مثل الرجال. إنها حقيقة محزنة حقا. أقر بوجود بعض المهام التي لا تستطيع المرأة القيام بها ، لكن ماذا عن تلك التي يمكننا القيام بها؟ في بعض الأحيان نقوم بنفس الوظيفة التي يقوم بها الرجل ، مع نفس العدد من ساعات العمل ، نفس النتيجة ، لكننا لا نزال لا نكافأ أو يشيدون بنا مثل الذكور ، وهو أمر غير عادل. يشعر معظم الرجال بالتفوق على النساء لأنهم يعتبروننا ضعفاء وغير متساوين فكريًا لهم. يقول الرجال إن "الجنس اللطيف ، الجنس اللطيف" كما لو كانوا يلعنوننا ، ويصفوننا بشيء سيء ، إذا نظرنا إلى هذا الأمر من منظور مختلف ، فهو طبيعي. أما المضايقات ،النساء هن دائما من يتحملن المسؤولية عن هذا الفعل. نحن دائمًا الطرف "المذنب". يبدو أنه حتى على المستوى العالمي ، حتى الاغتصاب لا يعتبر اليوم "مهمًا كقضية". أعتقد أن الطريقة الوحيدة لحل كل مشاكل التحيز الجنسي والتحرش هي معاملته كمرض. يحتاج إلى تشخيص ، تشخيص ، ويوصف له علاج. يمكن لبعض الرجال القيام به مع جرعة من الد.

أعلم وقد سمعت عن العديد من الأمثلة على تعرض النساء للاعتداء والمضايقة ، حتى أن بعض النساء تقعن ضحايا للاختطاف من قبل بعض الرجال في الشارع - لحسن الحظ ، تم إنقاذ النساء في كثير من هذه الحالات. قضية مهمة في مثل هذه القصص هي أن النساء المعنيات لم يرفعن شكوى إلى الشرطة. يمكن أن يصف معظمهم المعتدي بشكل مثالي ، لكنهم لا يذهبون إلى الشرطة لأنهن خائفات. إنهن يعلمن أن الرجل المعني يمكنه العودة إليها والقيام بأشياء أسوأ. نحن في بعض الحالات خائفات حقًا من بعض الرجال لأنهم أقوى جسديًا منا. يعرف الرجال ذلك وأحيانًا يستخدمونه ضدنا لأنهم يعلمون في معظم الحالات أننا لا نستطيع الانتقام ، خاصةً عندما يعطونك تلك الابتسامة التي تقول "يمكنني أن أؤذيك بامرأة وأنت تعرفين ذلك. أتحداك أن تتصرف"إنها الحقيقة المرة.

الأخيرة بين الولايات المتحدة والصين أن الرسوم الجمركية ستكون لها عواقب وخيمة على الصين. بدأت الصين بالفعل تشعر بتأثير هذه التعريفات ، قال المكتب الوطني للإحصاء في الصين إن مؤشر مديري المشتريات غير التصنيعية انخفض إلى 54.0 في يوليو من أصل 55.0 في يونيو. يغطي المؤشر أشياء مثل البيع بالتجزئة والطيران والبرامج بالإضافة إلى نشاط العقارات والبناء. وفي الوقت نفسه ، كان مؤشر مديري المشتريات التصنيعية 51.2 ، وهو الأضعف منذ فبراير "(والاس). وفي الوقت نفسه ، فإن اقتصاد الولايات المتحدة لم يشعر بتأثير كبير من الحرب التجارية ، "بلغ نمو الناتج المحلي الإجمالي الأمريكي S&P 4.1 في المائة سنويًا في الربع الثاني ، وهو أسرع نمو في أربع سنوات. وارتفع مؤشر للأسهم بنسبة 14 في المائة تقريبًا في العام الماضي ، بينما يرتفع الدولار الأمريكي مقابل العملات 500 الرئيسية الأخرى "(والاس). تمثل هذه الأرقام دليلًا ملموسًا على أن الولايات المتحدة في وضع قوي لاستخدام التعريفات كوسيلة اقتصادية لإحداث التغيير للأفضل للإيغور. علاوة على ذلك ، فإن فرض هذه التعريفات ، والتي ستكون تصحب بشرط عدم رفعها حتى تقوم الحكومة الصينية بحل معسكرات الاعتقال ، تعزز حملة من التسامح الديني وتقوم بتعويض الإيغور الذين عانوا بقسوة شديدة تحت سيطرة الحكومة الصينية ، ستكون التعريفات طريقة أخرى تحاول الولايات المتحدة بها إحداث تغيير. بمجرد أن تتخذ الولايات المتحدة هذا الموقف الإيجابي ، نأمل أن تتخذ دول العالم الأول مثل إنجلترا وألمانيا واليابان إجراءات مماثلة وتوطد وحدة مفهوم حقوق الإنسان العالمية وخاصة الحرية الدينية.

دون تدخل عاجل من الحكومات القوية ذات النطاق العالمي ، فإن سلامة وحياة الإيغور في خطر. يجب أن يكون للولايات المتحدة على وجه التحديد دور رئيسي في وقف اضطهاد الأويغور. الطريقة التي يمكنهم القيام بها هي من خلال إنشاء تعريفات على أفضل أنواع الواردات من الصين. هذا سيجعل الصين تضرر اقتصاديًا حتى تقوم بتفكيك معسكرات الاعتقال ووقف الهجمات على الإيغور. الحرية الدينية هي حق عالمي ضروري لحياة كل إنسان. من الأهمية بمكان أن تحتفظ دول مثل الولايات المتحدة بموقف قوي في دعم الحقوق الدينية وحقوق الإنسان وكذلك استخدام سلطتها لإنهاء هذه الانتهاكات.

ببليوغرافيا

ألبرت ، اليانور. "ماذا تعرف عن العقوبات المفروضة على كوريا الشمالية". مجلس العلاقات الخارجية ، ، مجلس العلاقات الخارجية www.cfr.org/backgrounder/what-know-about-sanctions-north-korea.

، توثيق أعداد ضحايا المحرقة والاضطهاد النازي." توثيق أعداد ضحايا المحرقة والاضطهاد النازي" www.jewishvirtuallibrary.org/documenting-numbers-of-victims-of-the- Holocaust.

هيوز ، رولاند. "الإيغور الصينيين: كل ما تحتاج إلى معرفته عن" الحملة ضد المسلمين". بي بي سي نيوز ، ، بي بي سي ، 8 نوفمبر 2018 . www.bbc.com/news/world-asia-china-45474279

، ميلوارد ، جيمس. "إعادة تعليم" مسلمي شينجيانغ". مجلة نيويورك للكتب ، يناير 2019 www. nybooks.com/articles/2019/02/07/reeducating-xinjiangs-muslims/ .

ريجنسيا ، تيد. "الهروب من شينجيانغ: المسلمون اليوغور يتحدثون عن اضطهاد الصين لهم.". أخبار الجزيرة | الخليج ، الجزيرة ، 10 سبتمبر 2018 ، www.aljazeera.com/indepth/features/es-

شينجيانغ ، تسجن ما يصل إلى مليون شخص ، بمن فيهم الكازاخستانيون والقرغيز ، وخاصة الإيغور ، الذين يشكلون حوالي 46 في المائة من سكان شينجيانغ "(ميلوارد). في حين أن الجميع يجمع الكل على أن ما تفعله الحكومة الصينية أمر فظيع ، هناك خلاف بين جماعات الناشطين الأويغور حول الإجراءات التي يجب اتخاذها.

وعبر عضو إسمه صالح حدير ، من نشطاء جماعة إيدن أنور عن قلقه حيال الانقسام: "الطريقة الوحيدة التي يمكننا بها ضمان حرياتنا وحقوقنا هي من خلال استعادة استقلالنا وهذه هي الطريقة الوحيدة التي من خلالها ضمان بقائنا الشامل ككل. لكن الدعوة إلى الاستقلال أمر مثير للجدل بين جماعات الإيغور. علق حدير قائلاً: "يقولون أنه مطلب غير الواقعي" مؤكدين أن المجتمع الدولي سيقف ضدها ، وأن الولايات المتحدة ستعارضه - وهذا هراء." يحدث الخلاف انقسامًا. التوجه الانفصالي يلقى معارضة من قِبل منظمات الإيغورالعريقة: "حقيقة أنهم لم يكونوا مستعدين للعمل معنا هو ما دفعنا إلى توضيح هذا الانقسام بين المجموعات كيف أن هناك حاجة ملحة (Shenoy). "الخروج كمنظمة مختلفة لتدخل الولايات المتحدة في قضية حقوق الإنسان هذه. في حال تدخلت الولايات المتحدة سيخفف من مخاوف الجماعات التقليدية الايغورية بأن المساعي غير واقعية، من خلال اتخاذ الولايات المتحدة موقفا وفرض عقوبات اقتصادية ضد الصين. هذا سيدعم الحقيقة العالمية المتمثلة في أن الحرية الدينية حق شامل للجميع.

الإجراءات المقترحة

الحرية الدينية حق عالمي يستحقه كل إنسان على وجه الأرض وفقًا للإعلان العالمي لحقوق الإنسان الصادر عن الأمم المتحدة. ينص هذا الإعلان على أن "لكل شخص الحق في حرية الفكر والوجدان والدين. يشمل هذا الحق حرية تغيير دينه أو معتقده ، وحريته ، سواء بمفرده أو مجتمع مع الغير وفي القطاعين العام والخاص ، لإظهار دينه أو معتقده في التدريس والممارسة والعبادة والالتزام "(الأمم المتحدة). وبالتالي ، فإن محاولات الحكومة الصينية ، من خلال المعسكرات ، لتحويل الإيغور تنتهك العديد من القوانين الإنسانية التي وضعتها الأمم المتحدة ، مثل المادة الخامسة (لا يجوز إخضاع أحد للتعذيب أو المعاملة أو العقوبة القاسية أو اللاإنسانية أو المهينة) وكذلك المادة التاسعة عشرة (لكل شخص الحق في حرية الرأي والتعبير ؛ويشمل هذا الحق حرية اعتناق الآراء دون تدخل والسعي إلى المعلومات والأفكار وتلقيها ونقلها عبر أي وسائط بغض النظر عن الحدود). إن النظر إلى الجرائم ضد الإيغور على أنها انتهاك مباشر للحرية الدينية ، وهو حق دولي ، يسمح لحكومة الولايات المتحدة بالتدخل وتسليط عقوبات على تصرفات الحكومة الصينية.

يتعين على الولايات المتحدة أن تتخذ موقفًا واضحًا من هذه الانتهاكات، مصرحة أنها يجب أن تتوقف. ينبغي على الولايات المتحدة أن تطبق التعريفة الجمركية بحيث تشعر الصين بأن الضغط الأكبر لإيقاف هذه المعسكرات هو التعريفة الجمركية على المعدات والآلات ومنتجات الصلب التي تستوردها الولايات المتحدة من الصين (أكثر دول العالم ثراء). إجمالي كل هذه الواردات يساوي 289.9 مليار دولار (رقم قياسي عالمي) ، والتي من شأنها أن ترسل بسهولة رسالة قوية للحكومة الصينية حول ما تشعر به الولايات المتحدة حول "معسكرات إعادة التعليم" في الصين للإيغور. تثبت الحرب التجارية

التدريبية." هناك العديد من القصص عن الأشخاص الذين تأثرت حياتهم. مثل هذه الحالات ، لم تتلق ما يلزم من التنديد أو الغضب الشعبي التي تستحقها.

نبذة تاريخية للانتهاكات الحالية

بدأت عملية محاصرة الإيغور الأخيرة في عام 2017. "أصبح الآيغوريون في الخارج يشعرون بالقلق لأن الأصدقاء والأقارب في الداخل أصبحوا خارج الاتصال ، في البداية قامت السلطات الصينية بتجريد الايغوريين من اتصالات الهاتف ووسائل التواصل الاجتماعي ثم اختفت قصصهم تمامًا. وبنفس الطريق، اختفى الطلاب الأيغوريين الذين أجبروا على العودة إلى الصين بعد الدراسة في بلدان أجنبية مع حالات الاختفاء هذه ، نشأت أسئلة بين أفراد الأسر. ومع وجود تهديد. (Millward)" عند وصولهم النفقات العامة للحكومة الصينية على الإقليم ، من الصعب معرفة ما حدث بالضبط. على سبيل المثال ، أيدين أنور، لم يتمكن من معرفة ما لمواطنيه الصينيين من موقعه في الولايات المتحدة. ومع ذلك بفضل تجربة والده كناشط حقوق الأقلية الأويغورية ، فهو يعرف ماهية الإجراءات الرهيبة التي تحدث في هذه المعسكرات. أخبره والده أن "الناس في هذه المعسكرات يجبرون على التخلي عن إيمانهم وتبني الإلحاد والتعهد بالولاء للدولة الصينية كإله". وهي تعرف أيضًا أنه من خلال "الحقنة القاتلة والتعقيم القسري والتعذيب والجثث التي يتم حرقها تقوم السلطات الصينية بتدمير الأدلة. هذه كلها (Shenoy)" علامات على الإبادة الجماعية التي تلوح في الأفق.

عاش تيرام في منطقة شينجيانغ. أرسلت شقيقته ، زهرة ، إلى أحد "معسكرات إعادة التدريب" في عام 2016 بعد رحلة عائلية إلى تركيا. بعد أن دفع تيرام حوالي ثلاثة آلاف دولار للحكومة الصينية ليتمكن من التواصل مع أخته ، تمكنت من زيارتها في المخيم. أصيب تيرام بالصدمة لما رآه عندما وصل. تم احتجاز زهرة وآلاف وآلاف من المعتقلين وراء كتلة من الجدران الشاهقة الشائكة التي يبلغ طولها 16 قدمًا. صرحت تيرام بأن "زهرة لم تكن هي نفسها التي تعود على رؤيتها، وقال إنها بدت شاحبة. تشكلت بقع داكنة حول عينيها التي حفرتها بالدموع. . . أخبرت زهرة شقيقها أنها بحاجة إلى إكمال بعض "الدروس" وإجراء اختبار بعد ذلك. إذا نجحت في الاختبار ، فسوف يتم إطلاق سراحها. "(ريجنسيا). لسوء الحظ ، لم يكتشف تيرام أبدًا ما إذا كانت قد اجتازت "الاختبار" أو حتى متى يتم إجراء "الاختبار". بدلاً من ذلك، اضطر تيرام إلى الفرار من شينجيانغ إلى تركيا لمحاولة الهروب من الحكومة الصينية التي يمكن أن تلاحقه هو أيضا لأنه زار أخته. ما يزال يعيش تحت خوف دائم بسبب الخطر الذي قد يلحق به لتحديه الحكومة الصينية. ومع ذلك ، وبسبب مدى إلحاح التهديد للأويغوريين، استمر تيرام في امتلاك الشجاعة للتحدث علانية: "لكن على العالم أن يعرف ما الذي تفعله الحكومة الصينية للإيغور". حتى (الكلاب لها حقوق أكثر من الإيغور في الصين "(ريجنسيا).

عرفت ساراجول ساوتباي ، عاملة في المخيمات ، أن ما حدث كان بوضوح جريمة ضد الأويغور: "أخبرت المحكمة كيف تم نقلها في نوفمبر الماضي من مدرستها إلى وظيفة جديدة لتدريس المحتجزين الكازاخستانيين في "مركز تدريب " والذي صرحت أنهم يسمونه "معسكر سياسي" . . . في الواقع ، كان معتقلاً في الجبال . كان هناك 2500 سجين في المنشأة التي عملت فيها لمدة أربعة أشهر وكانت على علم بمعسكرات أخرى مماثلة. قد يكون هناك الآن ما يصل إلى 1200 معسكر من هذا النوع في

في المجتمع الأمريكي ، هناك تفضيل عام واضح لبعض الديانات على غيرها. لقد تحولت هذه الأمور عبر التاريخ ، ولكن كما هي حال الأمة الآن ، يظهر الامريكيون للمسيحية واليهودية عادة مستوى من الاحترام والحرية أكبر لا تحظى بها الديانات الأخرى مثل الإسلام والسيخية والبوذية والهندوسية والكثير غيرها. هناك خوف ملحوظ من "الآخر" يتغلغل في الثقافة الأمريكية. لقد كان هذا دائمًا موجودًا إلى حد ما ، لكنني أعتقد أن هجمات 11 سبتمبر 2001 لها علاقة كبيرة بهذا الأمر. نفذت الهجمات على مركز التجارة العالمي من قبل المتطرفين الإسلاميين. الأفراد الذين قاموا بالعمل الإرهابي على الولايات المتحدة لا يمثلون بأي شكل من الأشكال جماعة دينية بأكملها ،لكن وسائل الإعلام وبعض التشريعات والإجراءات العسكرية التي أعقبت 11/9 غرست الخوف في الكثير من الناس كان ولا يزال من الصعب عكسه. لأن الكثير من الناس في أمريكا في ذلك الوقت كانوا يفتقرون إلى فهم أساسي للإسلام ، فقد تم جرهم بسهولة إلى الهيجان. قلة التعليم والرؤية المحيطة بغير المسيحيين هي السبب.

أدت الأديان في الولايات المتحدة إلى وضع العديد من الجماعات الدينية غير المسيحية في سلة تُعرف بأنها "أخرى" والتي يعتبرها الكثيرون خطرة. مثال على هذه المشكلة التي اكتشفتها بشكل خاص حديثًا هي قوانين الهجرة. تبذل إدارة ترامب كل محاولة لمنع الناس من الدول ذات الكثافة الإسلامية من دخول أمريكا. لكن إذا حاول شخص من بلد مثل إنجلترا ، يفترض أنه مسيحي في الغالب ، الهجرة إلى الولايات المتحدة ، فستكون العملية أسهل بكثير.

إن الطرق التي أحارب بها أنا والآخرون هذه القضية هي بشكل أساسي من خلال التعليم. إذا أصبح الأمريكيون أفضل تعليماً فيما يتعلق بالأديان غير المسيحية ، فإن شيئًا كان ذات مرة "مختلفًا" و "غير معروف" سيصبح طبيعيًّا. من المهم ، بغض النظر عن الدين الذي يمارسه شخص ما ، أن يُضمن لهم نفس الحقوق والحماية التي وعد بها كل أمريكي. حتى خارج التشريعات الرسمية والسياسة الحكومية ، ينبغي منح الاحترام على قدم المساواة للجميع. بمجرد أن يتم إزالة الالتباس من بعض الأديان التي لا يتعرض لها الأميركيون بشكل يومي ، أعتقد أنه يمكن الوصول إلى الحرية الدينية حقًا.

ميريديث ديويا
الحرية الدينية: حق عالمي يحرم منه الإيغور في الصين

الإيغور هم مجتمع مسلم في الصين يُجبرون على الذهاب إلى معسكرات الاعتقال تحت ذريعة "مراكز تدريب للحد من التطرف". ونتيجة لذلك ، أصبح الإيغور أقلية في المنطقة الوحيدة التي سُمح لهم فيهاسابقاً بأن يكونوا أنفسهم: الإيغور. . . يبلغ عددهم نحو 11 مليون في منطقة شينجيانغ غرب الصين. يعتبرون أنفسهم قريبين ثقافياً وعرقياً من دول آسيا الوسطى ، ولغتهم مماثلة للغة التركية. ولكن في العقود الأخيرة ، كانت هناك هجرة جماعية من قبائل الهان الصينيين (الأغلبية العرقية في الصين) إلى شينجيانغ ، ويشعر الأويغور بأن ثقافتهم وسبل عيشهم معرضة للخطر كنتيجة لذلك"(هيوز). الأويغور ليسوا مخطئين في الشعور بأن سبل عيشهم معرضة للخطر ، لأن هذا ما هو عليه الحال. يُنقل الأويغوريون قسراً من أمن منازلهم إلى السجون القاسية والوحشية. لقد سرقت الحكومة الصينية حقهم في ممارسة دينهم. كانت هناك تسريبات متعددة حول الأهوال التي حدثت داخل جدران هذه "المراكز

أحمل مثل هذا الكلام الكفري داخل الكنيسة. أصبحت روحي أضعف وأضعف حتى لم يتبق لي شيء لأقدمه. كل ليلة بعد الفصل الدراسي ، كنت أذهب إلى المنزل وأبكي لدى التي ، على الرغم من ارتباطها بالكاثوليكية ،كانت تعلمني دومًا أهمية الوقوف أمام أولئك المختلفين وقبول الآخرين بغض النظر عن من هم. لم أتمكن من تبرير إيماني بنظام ديني ويإله لا يحب الناس لمجرد أنهم يعيشون حياتهم بطريقة معينة لا يوافقها الرجال في السلطة سألت نفسي يوميًا ، لماذا يجب على رجال النخبة في الكنيسة إملاء جوانب من حياة الآخرين لا تؤثر عليهم بشكل مباشر بأي طريقة؟

كنت ضد الكنيسة الكاثوليكية بأكملها: كنت أعلم أني لا أستطيع الفوز في هذه المعركة. قررت ، وأنا جالس في صف الدين ، أسبوع واحد ، أنني بحاجة إلى التركيز على مساعدة نفسي والآخرين على اعتناق هويتهم كأفراد لديهم آراء ومشاعر صحيحة بدلاً من أن النقاش حول الكنيسة. بالنسبة لي ، كوني متنفسًا للأشخاص للتعبير عن احتياجاتهم وأولوياتهم المختلفة بعيدا عما تسمح به الكاثوليكية أو لا تسمح به كان تغييرًا جذريًا. لم يقدم لي أحد من أي وقت مضى هذا النوع من الدعم وأردت أن أكون الشخص في مجتمعي لإنشاء هذا الفضاء.

عزز الدين قدرتي على أن أكون قائدا مدنية بطريقة ملتوية. لم تقم الكاثوليكية أبداً بتمكيني بمعنى أنني شعرت بالحب والشمول والإصغاء إلي. حاولت أن أكون قائدة في الفقاعة الصغيرة الخاصة بي من الأبرشية، لكنني لم أتمكن مطلقًا من الوصول إلى أي شخص. بدلاً من ذلك ، مكنتني الكاثوليكية من تحديد معتقداتي وآرائي بنفسي. لأنني لم أتفق مع المواقف الرسمية للكنيسة ، تمكنت من تكوين وجهة نظري للعالم بشكل شامل ومستقل. لقد جعلني الشعور بالوحدة الكاملة ضد كيان ضخم مثل الكنيسة الكاثوليكية أكثر تصميماً مما كان يمكنني فعله كقائدة مجتمعية. من خلال علاقتي بالدين ، أدركت أن كونك قائدا في المجتمع المدني لا يقتصر على تغيير أو "التخلص" من الأنظمة القوية. ولكن كان أيضا حول التمكن من بدء الحوارات ، وتقديم الدعم ، والاستماع بعضنا إلى البعض ، وإنشاء مساحات آمنة أنا أدرك أني واحدة من المحظوظات. لقد تربيت داخل بيت مسيحي داخل بلد مسيحي واسع. على الرغم من أن قراري بمغادرة الإيمان الكاثوليكي جعلني أشعر بالعزلة ، فقد كان من السهل نسبيًا أن أجد أشخاصًا مسيحيين وأصبحوا الآن غير متدينين. إن وضعي الجديد ، رغم أنه لا يُقدَّر في مسقط رأسي ، هو موقف يحترمه عامة الناس في المجتمع الأمريكي في معظمه. امتلائي للمسيحية الكاثوليكية كنقطة انطلاق، تلقائيًا وبشكل غير عادل ، يمنحني امتيازًا.

الولايات المتحدة ، من الناحية النظرية ، تقدر وتقيم الحرية الدينية. في التعديل الأول لدستور الولايات المتحدة ، تُكفل حرية الدين لكل مواطن يعيش داخل الأمة. يشترط على الكونغرس عدم تفضيل أي دين على أي آخر في القانون وأن الممارسات الدينية الفردية غير مقيدة. على المستوى القانوني ، نحن محميون من المعاملة غير العادلة على أساس الدين. بينما أنا ممتنة لهذه الحماية وأؤمن أنه ينبغي منح جميع الأشخاص هذه الحماية أيضًا ، لا أعتقد أن الشروط المكتوبة في دستورنا تؤدي وظيفة كافية لضمان حماية الحريات الدينية لجميع المواطنين.

سام أوينز

لقد نشأت في بلدة صغيرة في ولاية ويسكونسن ، مباشرة على بحيرة ميشيغان و على مسافة نصف ساعة إلى الشمال من أكبر مدن الولاية ، ميلووكي. عندما كنت طفلة ، شعرت بالأمان والدعم في فقاعة ضواحي الصغيرة. في أي مكان ذهبت إليه ، كان هناك دائمًا وجه مبتسم مألوف. كان المجتمع متماسكًا ، ويبدو أن الجميع يعرفون بعضهم بعضًا ، وكذلك خصوصيات وعموميات بعضهم البعض. لقد كنا نهنئ بعضنا البعض على النجاحات التي حققناها ، ونواسي بعضنا بعضًا على الخسائر ، نعرض المساعدة في أوقات الحاجة. تتضمن بعض ذاكرتي الأولى مساعدة والدتي على الطهي وتقديم وجبات الطعام إلى أسرة إحدى أصدقاء الطفولة عندما تم تشخيص إصابة والدته بسرطان الثدي. أتذكر أنني كنت أذهب إلى منزل جاري المسن في عطلة نهاية الأسبوع لمساعدتها في حديقتها إذ لم تعد قادرة على الانحناء لسحب الأعشاب الضارة.

بالنسبة إلى كطفلة صغيرة ، كانت بورت واشنطن بولاية ويسكونسن بمثابة يوتوبيا مثالية. الحياة لا يمكن أن تكون أفضل مما كانت عليه. لكن عندما بدأت في التقدم في السن ، بدأت أدرك أن مسقط رأسي لم يكن خاليا من العيوب كما إعتدت أن أراه.

كانت مدينتي في الغالب بيضاء ومحافظة سياسياً ، والأهم من ذلك هويتها الكاثوليكية. كنت أحضر بانتظام إلى الكنيسة مع عائلتي كل صباح أحد وليالي الاثنين ، ومنذ أن بدأت في روضة الأطفال وحتى المدرسة الثانوية ، كنت أداوم على دورات التعليم الكاثوليكي الأسبوعية. خلال السنوات الأولى ، لم أر شيئاً يثير القلق بشأن التعليم الذي كنت أتلقاه. تحدثنا عن يسوع وسفينة نوح ومن كان الله. علمنا أن الله يحب الجميع على قدم المساواة و يغفر لكل من ضل طريقه. كانت هذه الصورة السعيدة اللامعة مفهومي للكاثوليكية حتى التحقت بالصف السابع أو الثامن. عندما بدأت في التقدم في السن ، بدأ معلمو الدين الذين درسوني التربية الدينية يتعمقون في المذهب والتاريخ الرسمي للكنيسة الكاثوليكية. مع كل عام أكبر من العمر ، كنت ألاحظ ان المدرسين يبدون لي أكثر تعصباً. أعضاء كنيستي الذين علموني عن حب الله وغفرانه عندما كنت طفلاً بدأوا يغيرون الرسالة الآن. كان لمحبة الله وقبوله فجأة شروط.كنت أعيش نصف ساعة فقط من أكبر مدن ولاية ويسكونسن وأكثرها ليبرالية ، وكنت دائماً أتعرض لأفكار بديلة. عملت والدتي أيضًا بجد للغاية لضمان ان أعيش حياتي بطيبة قلب وقبول. مع كل تلك التأثيرات التي تعارض تربيتي الكاثوليكية ، جلست في الصف كل أسبوع ، وازداد الغضب والارتباك والنزاع الداخلي لدي. لقد كنت أؤمن دائمًا أن الحق في اختيار من تحب هو شيء ينبغي توفيره للجميع. لكن الآن،البالغون الذين كنت أثق بهم كانوا يصرون على التحدث على الذنوب والبغض. كما أنني اعتقدت اعتقادا راسخا ، لا سيما أنني امرأة ، أن الحق في الإجهاض هو حق يجب أن يكمن فقط في أيدي المرأة الحامل. لكن الآن ، أخبرني رجال أقوياء ذوو مناصب رفيعة في الكنيسة أنه قرار غير مقبول.

حاولت التحدث أود أن أرفع يدي خلال مناقشاتنا لتقديم رأي أو أن أسأل لماذا لا يوافق الله على مثل هذه الأمور إذا كان من المفترض أنه يحب كل مؤمنيه ويغفر لهم. لقد ناضلت بكل وجودي لجعل صوتي مسموعًا وللتواصل مع البالغين ذوي النفوذ في الكنيسة ، لكن ذلك لم يكن مفيدًا. مع كل محاولة لتوضيح مخاوفي يقال لي بصراحة أن رأيي كان خطأ. قيل لي إنه لم يكن مناسبا لي كطفلة وامرأة ، أن

يمكنهم الدعم
يمكنهم التغيير
يمكنهم الانخراط
يمكنهم فعل أشياء
التي تبقي وحدتنا

لقد تكلمت
لقد شاركت
لقد دافعت
لقد فعلت أشياء
التي تدعم وحدتنا

لقد تحدثوا
لقد شاركوا
لقد دافعوا
لقد فعلوا أشياء
التي تدعم الوحدة

لقد تعلمت
لقد فتحت عقلي
لقد تواضعت
لقد فعلت أشياء
لتعلم معنى المجتمع

نحن نتعلم
نحن نكبر
نحن نفكر
نحن نفعل الأشياء
لنتعلم الوحدة

شالبي هوست

مجتمع

"جميع المهاجرين" قالوا
"أموالي" قالوا
"غير أمريكي" قالوا
لماذا نستمع
إلى الأشياء التي قالوها

هذا خطأ هكذا اعتقدت
ليس حقائق
هذا تحيز اعتقدت
قررت أن أقول
الأشياء التي اعتقدت

"ليس كل شيء" أنا قلت
"أموالنا" قلت
"المواطنون" قلت
هل يمكنك أن تسمع من فضلك
إلى الأشياء التي قلت

يعملون بجد هم
بدأوا لتو هم
مقصون هم
لماذا لا تستطيع أن ترى
كل الأشياء التي هم

الظلم الذي يواجهون
القتل الذي يواجهون
المنع الذي يواجهون
أنت لا تعرف حتى
الأشياء التي يواجهون

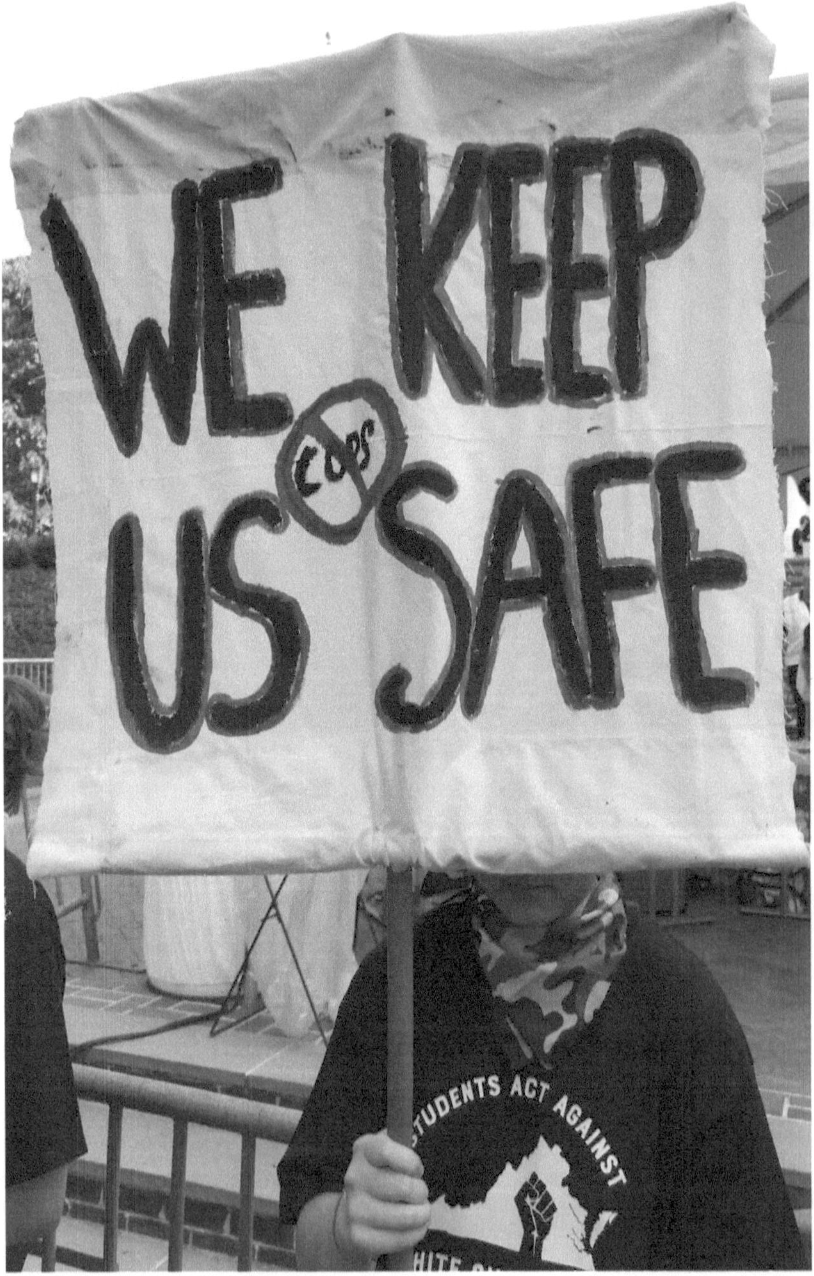
WE KEEP
COPS
US SAFE
STUDENTS ACT AGAINST

"لا يمكنك محاربة النار بالنار" صحيح. لن تشتعل النار إلا إذا كان العنف هو الحل لكل موقف. كانت حادثة ترايفون مارتن ، الشاب الذي قُتل بالرصاص أثناء السير في الشارع ، هي الحادثة التي جعلت الأمور تغلي. قررت والدته ، سيبرينا فولتون ، محاولة تشجيع التغيير بدلاً من الاستجابة للغضب. بدأت تتحدث بعد وفاة ابنها على ضرورة التخلي عن الكراهية والغضب وبناء مجتمع متسامح عندما تحدث أشياء من هذا القبيل. بالطبع ، سيكون هناك غضب وستكون هناك أفكار سلبية ، ولكن كلما كان من الممكن احتواء تلك الأفكار والعواطف ، كلما بدأنا في التحرك نحو مستقبل مختلف. صرحت سيبرينا فولتون خلال إحدى خطبها ، "نحن جميعًا في هذا البلد معًا ، وعلينا أن نتعلم كيفية التواصل معًا. بغض النظر عن العرق. بغض النظر عن التوجه. بغض النظر عن لون البشرة". مثل كل علاقة ، يجب أن يكون هناك إرسال واستقبال ، يجب أن يكون لدينا كلا الجانبين من المدافعين عن طيف التغيير ، وليس واحد فقط. يجب أن نبذل جهدا واعيا لتجاوز ثنائية الأبيض والأسود والتحرك نحو وجهة نظر تتكلم عنا كأخ وأخت. يجب علينا أن ندرك أنك مثلي تمامًا وأنا مثلك تمامًا.

ايرين برانتلي-ريدجواي

تعني العدالة تكافؤ الفرص لجميع الناس ، بغض النظر عن قدراتهم أو لونهم أو #JusticeMeans جنسهم. أنا امرأة ، امرأة سوداء ، يجب أن تتاح لي نفس الفرص مثل أي امرأة بيضاء أو رجل أبيض. لا ينبغي على النساء الكفاح من أجل الحصول على مقعد على الطاولة ، ولا ينبغي أن يضطر السود إلى القتال من أجل حق التصويت. لا ينبغي على الناس النضال والاحتجاج من أجل العدالة بينما الحقيقة أن العدالة هي عصى رحى ومدار ما ينبغي ان تدور حوله أميركا. لكن الحقيقة ليست كذلك.

يمنح الناس العقوبة التي يستحقونها عندما ينتهكون القانون ، مثل ضابط شرطة يقتل #JusticeMeans حياة بريئة. مثل هذه الحالات لا تحصل على العدالة اللازمة. بدون عدالة ، لن يكون هناك سلام. الحكومة لا تريد انتفاضة - فهي لا تريد مسيرات أو اعتصامات. لا يريدون أن يسير الناس ويصيحوا في الشوارع بقبضاتهم في الهواء ممتدة. إنهم لا يريدون للناس أن ينتقموا من أولئك الذين ارتكبوه خطأ. إذا كانوا يريدون السلام ، فلماذا لا يحققون العدالة؟ # العدالة تعني اتخاذ موقف ضد أولئك المخطئون.

كريستيان كافندر

العدالة تعني المساواة بين أفراد المجتمع جميعهم بغض النظر عن الظروف. النظام القضائي في مجتمعنا معطوب ويحتاج إلى التغيير. اعتبر أنه في مجتمعنا يمكن للأثرياء والأقوياء أن يفلتوا من معظم الأشياء ، في حين أن الفقراء والأشخاص الذين يعانون من الفقر سيتحملون المسؤولية. ثم هناك تمييز وتحامل في السجون. يتم سجن المواطنين السود بأكثر من ثلاثة أضعاف من سجن المواطنين البيض. هذه مشكلة سببها أن مجتمعنا الذي وضع هذا النظام موضع التنفيذ ، وهو نظام تسبب في زيادة عدد السجناء بسرعة. حتى عندما يُسمح لأي سجين بالخروج ، فإن معظمهم لا يملكون أي أموال ولا مكان يذهبون إليه ، والثياب التي ارتدوها فقط في اليوم الذي ذهبوا فيه إلى السجن. إنهم يُسمح لهم بالخروج إلى العالم دون مساعدة ولا وظيفة.

بمطاردته؟ أجاب الضابط: "كنت قد سأصرخ 'توقف' وأركض وراءه". وعند هذه النقطة طلبت من الضباط أن يغادروا بيتي ، أدركت أن لون بشرة أحدنا يصرخ بصوت أعلى من الألوان التي داخله.

قصة حقيقية:

تمتلك فانيسا جيرمان ، وهي فنانة من بيتسبرغ ، قطعة من الأعمال الفنية التي تصور الكمان على رأس صبي من بين أشياء أخرى في حوزتها. في هذه القطعة ، استلهمت من شاب كان صديقا لها و الذي كان يتمشى من منزله إلى متجر الحي على بعد بضعة مبانٍ فقط عندما تغيرت حياته كليا. كان صديقها من الكوير ، الأمريكيين من أصل أفريقي ، كان موهوبا جدا على آلة الكمان . أمضى والداه غالبية أرباحهما لإرساله إلى مدرسة خاصة يمكن أن تزدهر فيها مواهبه. في طريق عودته من المتجر ، ادعى ضباط شرطة ، لم يكونوا في حالة الخدمة ، أنهم أخطؤوا به كمشتبه كانوا يحاولون العثور عليه. بدأوا الركض وراءه ، وكشاب في سن المراهقة رؤية السود الناس تطاردك يجعلك تركض. عندما تم القبض عليه ، قاموا بضربه إلى درجة أنه تعرض للشلل التام. تعرض للضرب المبرح لدرجة أنه حتى عندما تعافى ، لم يعد بإمكانه العزف على آلة الكمان. تضع فانيسا جيرمان الكمان على رأسه في هذه القطعة الفنية كبيان ليقول ، إذا رأى ضباط الشرطة عدد المزايا من السمات والشخصية التي كانت بداخله ، مجموعة من المواهب الجميلة ، هل كانوا سيضربون هذا الشخص؟ إنها مغامرة بقول "لا" ، والتي أوافق عليها. هذا البلد له تاريخ في الحكم على شخص ما على لون بشرته بدلاً مما يحتويه. خاصة في حالة الرجال والنساء السود ، يمكننا ببساطة أن نسأل متى سينتهي الأمر؟

تقدم هذه القصص الخيالية والحقيقية أحداثًا تطلب من المستمع أن ينظر في قيمة الحياة البشرية وأهميتها. في عام 2018 ، قضى ضباط الشرطة على حياة شخص ما كل يوم 342 يومًا من أصل 365. "لم يكن هناك سوى 23 يومًا في 2018 لم نشهد فيها قتل الشرطة لشخص" (مرصد عنف الشرطة). لا يوجد سبب يجعل أي شخص يدفعه للاعتقاد بأن 342 شخصًا يستحقون القتل. ما الذي يعطي رجال الشرطة الحق في قتل شخص ما؟ لون بشرتهم؟ الموقع الذي يعيشون فيه؟ كم من الوشم لديهم؟ إذا أسنانهم لديها الذهب عليها؟ إذا ترهل بنطلونهم ؟ ما الذي يعطيهم الحق؟

تنص مقالة بعنوان "تعقب وحشية الشرطة" على أن السود يفقدون حياتهم ثلاثة أضعاف أكثر على أيدي رجال الشرطة. في عام 2015 ، قُتل 30٪ من الأفريقيين الأمريكيين الذين قتلوا على أيدي ضباط الشرطة ، مقابل 21٪ من القوقازيين . على الرغم من هذه الحقائق قليلة ، سيظل الناس يحاولون إنكار وجود عنصرية وقوالب نمطية قائمة في جميع أنحاء هذه الأمة. أظهرت دراسة أن 13 من أكبر 100 إدارة شرطة أمريكية تقتل الرجال السود بمعدلات أعلى من معدل القتل في الولايات المتحدة نفسها. على الرغم من هذه الحقائق غالبة ، فإن 99٪ من الحالات التي تنطوي على هذه الحالات لا يعاقب أصحابها إطلاقا. إذا كان رجل أسود قد قتل هؤلاء الناس ، لكانوا محبوسين أو حتى يمكن أن يحدث لهم أسوأ من ذلك . لكن ، في هذا البلد، نختار تكريم الشرير الذي يصور نفسه كضحية.

في خضم عالم يختار النظر في المواقف ، مثل الظلم ضد الأقليات بغضب وكراهية ، يجب أن نجد طريقة لرؤية التغيير والعمل على تحقيقه . كلما زاد غضبنا كلما حصلت أشياء أسوأ. القول القديم ،

مما يجب علينا القيام به. لسوء الحظ ، هذا هو العالم الذي نعيش فيه. يجب أن نستمر في السعي لتحسينه ، ولكن لا ننسى أبدًا أنه مليء بالأشخاص غير المثاليين. نحن بحاجة إلى التمسك بهؤلاء الذين قد يحتاجون إلى مساعدتنا.

بيريس جونز
قصة قصيرة (بناءً على أحداث حقيقية في كثير من فصولها):

بدأ ذلك اليوم كيوم إعتيادي ، إبني الأكبر جاستن ذهب إلى المدرسة الثانوية ، ونهضت ماري وأنتونيو الأصغر سنا ليذهبا إلى المدرسة بعد ذلك بقليل. ذهبت أنا وزوجي للعمل بعد وقت قصير من رحيل صغارنا ، كان كل شيء كما كان يجب أن يكون، هادئًا. الآن، تكاد تكون الساعة الثالثة ظهرا، جاستن يصل إلى البيت من المدرسة. سألته ماذا يريد أن يأكل على مائدة العشاء ، أجاب قائلاً أنه يريد طبقه المفضل: معكرونة بالجمبري. أنا أحب أن أطبخ لابني ، وافقت وأرسلته إلى متجر البقالة على بُعد مبنيين سكنيين للحصول على بعض الجبن والمعكرونة الإضافية. بمجرد أن أرسلته في حوالي الساعة 3:30 مساءً ، بدأت بتحضير العشاء. عادت ماري وأنتونيو بعد ذلك بقليل وبدءا في أداء واجباتهما بعد محادثة قصيرة معي حول يومهما المدرسي . حوالي الساعة 5 مساءً ، يصل زوجي إلى المنزل جائعًا ومتعب كما هو الحال دائمًا. بينما أواصل الطهي، بدأت أفكر في اللاوعي بنفسي أنه قد مضى بعض الوقت على مغادرة جاستن ، لكني طمأنت نفسي عندما تذكرت أنه يلهو مع أصدقائه أحيانا في الطريق، لذلك هونت على نفسي . عندما انتهيت من طهو الجمبري والصلصة ، انضممت إلي زوجي والأولاد في غرفة المعيشة في انتظار وصول جاستن من المتجر. بينما نحن ننتظر،قمنا بتشغيل التلفزيون واذا بنشرة الأخبار المسائية تعرض عنوانا حول اطلاق نار على بعد عدة مبان منا.

تقريبا بنفس توقيت الخبر كان هنالك طرق على الباب. هرعت لأفتح الباب و إذا بالباب ضابطان بعلو وجهيهما الفزع، أكبرهما سنا قال: "سيدتي ، لدينا بعض الأخبار لنخبرك بها ، قد ترغبين في الجلوس". أدركت من النظرات على وجهيهما أن إبني الصغير كان ضحية الرصاصة التي أذيعت على التلفاز. سقطت على الأرض أصرخ من شدة الألم و الحزن و الارتباك. رفضت أن أصدق أنه قتل، كنت أصرخ في داخلي : لا يمكن أن يكون ذلك صحيحا، كنت قد رأيته للتو، والآن غادرني إلى الأبد؟ هذا مستحيل، أنا أرفض أن أصدق ذلك . لم يكن جاستن مجرما. لم يرتكب أي ظلم ، لكنه كان ضحية لواحدة من المظالم. حملني زوجي وأجلسني على الأريكة ، وأمسك بي كما أوضح له الضباط. وجدت نفسي أحدق في شفاههم وهم يتحركون . بينما هم يتحدثون، وجدت نفسي أنجرف للتفكير بابني من دون أن أسمعهم.

ثم التقطت عبارة "أطلق عليه النار بطريق الخطأ". غضبت على الفور وسألته لماذا؟ لماذا تأخذ حياة ابني في حادث بالخطأ؟ لام يكن بإمكان أي إجابة قدموها لي أن تخفض من حدة غضبي. أخذوا يرددون أنهم اشتبهوا به بأحد الشباب الذين كانوا يتعقبونهم بتهمة المخدرات، وأنهم عندما حاولوا التوقف لمواجهته، ركض، لذلك كانوا يعتقدون أنه مذنب وأطلقوا عليه النار. ولكن كنت أعرف أن ذلك ليس هو السبب. لذلك، سألته سؤالا واحدا، " لو كان الهارب رجلا أبيضا وركض، أكنتم ستطلقون النار عليه؟ أم أنكم كنتم ستصرخون 'توقف' وتقومون

و من المهم كذلك أن يكون المرء صريحا و لا يخشى أي شيء عند قوله الحقيقة. صحيح أن ردة فعل الناس قد تكون مخيفة في بعض الأحيان و لكن

عَنْ أَبِي سَعِيدٍ رَضِيَ اللَّهُ عَنْهُ قَالَ: قَالَ رَسُولُ اللَّهِ صَلَّى اللَّهُ عَلَيْهِ وَسَلَّمَ: "لَا يَحْقِرْ أَحَدُكُمْ نَفْسَهُ، قَالُوا: يَا رَسُولَ اللَّهِ كَيْفَ يَحْقِرُ أَحَدُنَا نَفْسَهُ؟ قَالَ: يَرَى أَمْرَ اللَّهِ عَلَيْهِ فِيهِ مَقَالٌ، ثُمَّ لَا يَقُولُ فِيهِ، فَيَقُولُ اللَّهُ عَزَّ وَجَلَّ لَهُ يَوْمَ الْقِيَامَةِ: مَا مَنَعَكَ أَنْ تَقُولَ فِي كَذَا وَكَذَا؟ فَيَقُولُ: خَشْيَةُ النَّاسِ، فَيَقُولُ: فَإِيَّايَ كُنْتَ أَحَقَّ أَنْ تَخْشَى" رواه ابن ماجه بسند صحيح.

بالمختصر، الإسلام جعلني شخصا أفضل من خلال تعليمي حس المسؤولية، التواضع، التقبل، الاحترام و الصراحة و هذه كلها خصائص القائد المدني.

فيكتوريا هانتر

أتذكر ذات مرة خلال سنتي الثانوية الاخيرة ، كنت في فريق شكسبير مع مدرسة جان ماسيو للصم والمكفوفين. كانت هذه سنتي الثانية في الفريق وكنا نذهب إلى جامعة جنوب يوتا في مدينة سيدار بولاية يوتاه للمشاركة في مسابقة. أنا لست صماء ، لكن كل الممثلين كانوا من الصم. الأشخاص ذوي حاسة السمع (مثلي) يقومون بإصدار اصوات لمايغنيه الممثلون. في المسابقة ، يكون الممثلون الصم على خشبة المسرح بينما كان ثلاثتنا الذين نصدر الاصوات على جانب المسرح غير مرئيين، لكنهم يسمعوننا. قضيت وقتًا رائعًا كل عام وأحببت زملائي في الفريق. كلنا عملنا بجد كل عام لنكون من المتنافسين في هذه المسابقة.

كنا نقوم بالأداء أمام ثلاثة حكام. اثنان منهم كانا رائعين و ودودين للغاية. حتى أن أحدهم بكى أثناء أدائنا لأنه تمتع بدمج ثقافتين. ومع ذلك ، لم يستمتع حكم واحد بفكرة ممثلي الصم. لا أظن أن هذا الحكم أدركت أننا نحن الثلاثة يمكننا أن نسمعها وهي تتحدث أثناء أدائنا حول عدم اعجابها بأي من حركات اليد التي قام بها الممثلون (وهي الطريقة التي يغنون بها). ذكرت أن الأشخاص الصم لا يمكن أن يكونوا ممثلين لأنه لا أحد يمكن أن يفهمهم أبدًا. أعلم أنها لم تكن تتحدث عني ، لكنها كانت تتحدث عن أصدقائي الذين أصبحت قريبة منهم. لم يكن من السهل الجلوس وترك الأمر يحدث.

في نهاية العروض ، تحدثت أنا وآخر ممن كانوا يصدرون الصوت معي إلى الحكم حول ما قيل عن أصدقائنا. صرحت الحكم بأنه لا يمكننا أن نكون ضمن هاته المنافسة مع ممثلين صم. تحدثنا إلى معلمنا ، الذي تحدث إلى قيادة المنافسة. تلقينا اعتذارًا ولكنهم أوضحوا أيضًا أنه لا يمكنهم فعل أي شيء حيال ذلك. في النهاية ، حصلنا في النهاية على أوراق النتائج الخاصة بنا. كان القاضيان اللطيفان قد منحونا درجة عالية بشكل لا يصدق ، أحدهما أعطانا درجة كاملة. ومع ذلك ، فإن الحكم الثالث قد وضعنا في مرتبة منخفضة للغاية وكانت معظم تعليقاتها غير مهذبة تجاه ممثلينا الصم. لحسن الحظ مع الملاحظات العالية التي تلقيناها من الحكمين الآخرين ، تحصلنا على المرتبة الثانية.

على الرغم من ذلك ، لن أنسى سماع حديثها عن أصدقائي بتلك الطريقة ، ونعلم جميعًا أن الطريقة التي قيمتنا بها كانت تستند إلى حد كبير على حقيقة أنها لا تحب أن يكون الأشخاص الصم ممثلين، وهذا غير عادل تمامًا. إضافة إلى التحدث إلى الأشخاص المسؤولين عن المنافسة ، لم يكن هناك الكثير

"الحلم الأمريكي" هي أساس الجريمة لأن بعض الناس إما يصابون بخيبة الأمل عندما يدركون مدى جور النظام بالنسبة لهم ، أو أن البعض الآخر يطمحون بشدة لتحقيق هذا الحلم فيحاولون الوصول إله بأي طريقة. أعرف بعض الأشخاص الذين أخذوا بهذا الخطاب ، هم دائما ممن يتلقون النشرات و يسيئون استخدام النظام ، في حين أنهم هم أنفسهم عملوا بجد ولم يحصلوا على أي شيء في المقابل. في الواقع ، هم ليسوا أفضل من الأشخاص الذين يعتقدون أنهم سبب لمعاناتهم. كان بإمكانهم الاستفادة من بعض هذه البرامج مثل الرعاية الصحية الميسورة التكلفة و المساعدات المالية التعليمية ، وما إلى ذلك ، لكن شدة انهماكهم بالغضب جعلتهم يضيعون تلك الفرص. لذلك ، أفهم تمامًا كيف يمكن لهذا النسق أن يكون محبطا للغاية وكيف يمكن لأي شخص أن يشعر بأنه عديم الجدوى فيصبح متشائمًا وغير واثق، دون أي أمل في التغيير.

عيسى صديقي
هذا صحيح ، لكن سياستنا الجزائرية مختلفة تمامًا. يلعب السياسيون في سياق متناقض.

ميريديث غالاغر
أوافق على أنه لا يوجد مجتمع مثالي. أعتقد أن هذه طريقة جيدة لوصف أن النقص الحالي ليس سببًا للاستسلام ، إنه بالأحرى سبب للاستمرار. إذا نظرنا إلى شيء يشبه الإعلان العالمي لحقوق الإنسان الصادر عن الأمم المتحدة ، فقد يبدو بعيد المنال ، لكن طالما تستمر المجتمعات و البلدان في السعي لتحسين نفسها للحصول على حقوق لشعوبها ، فهناك شيء نحتفي به.

شيماء هاشمي
نعم هذه هي النقطة التي يجب إبرازها.

مزيد من المشاركة

شيراز رتيمي
يعود الفضل كله إلى ديني الإسلام في تكوين ما أنا عليه اليوم. الفتاة المستقلة, المتفهمة و الحكيمة. و هذه كلها صفات القائد المدني. لقد نما الإسلام الشعور بالمسؤولية في نفسي فلا يجدر بي أن ألوم أي شخص على خطأ ارتكبته . يقول الله تعالى:" و لا تزر وازرة وزر اخرى" سورة النجم – الاية 18 علمني أيضا أن جميع البشر متساوون كأسنان المشط و لا فرق بين عربي و أعجمي إلا بالتقوى.

لهذا السبب لا أحكم على الناس وفقا لمعايير شخصية ولا أنحاز في معاملاتي مع أي شخص كذلك . أؤمن بأن لدى جميع الناس نفس الحقوق و لا فرق بينهم . كذلك من المبادئ الأساسية في الإسلام تقبل الآخر و احترام الآراء المغايرة، لذلك لا أفرض رأيي على أي أحد وأحاول أن أكون دائما متفتحة الذهن لتقبل وجهات النظر المختلفة و النقد البناء، لأني اظن أن هذا ما يكون مجتمعا متحضرا .قال أبو بكر الجزائري , عالم مسلم جزائري" إذا قمت بالشيء الصحيح فساعدوني و إذا ارتكبت خطأ فأرشدوني. الصدق هو ثقة مقدسة و الكذب هو خيانة.

حقوق الإنسان هي حقوق أساسية تنبع من الضروريات في الحياة. البشر لديهم القدرة على صياغة الآراء ، لذلك يجب أن يكونوا قادرين على التعبير عنها دون تحيز. على أقل تقدير ، يجب إعطاء الحقوق الصحية الأساسية ، مثل العيادات أو غرف الاستعجالات ، بحيث يمكن لأفراد المجتمع الحفاظ على صحتهم. يجب أيضًا الحصول على الغذاء والماء والمأوى ، لأنه بدون هذه الأشياء ، سيكون من الصعب للغاية البقاء على قيد الحياة. يجب أن تكون القدرة على الحصول على التعليم متاحة أيضًا للناس، على الأقل إلى مستوى معين ، لأن البشر لديهم فضول طبيعي ومن الضروري تغذية أدمغتنا بالمعرفة. فقط بالحفاظ على حقوق الإنسان ، يكون المجتمع في ذروته.

عيسى صديقي

لقد قضيت وقتًا رائعًا في قراءة هذا الحوار، لكن يبدو أنني لست بنفس التوجه مع البقية.

بادئ ذي بدء ، كل ما أقوله صالح فقط للتطبيق على المجتمعات العربية ، لأني لم أحصل على تجربة خارج السياق العربي.
"اجعل كلبك جائعًا ، يتبعك".
" جوع كلبك يتبعك "

هذا التصريح أدلى به أحد أكبر السياسيين وأكثرهم نفوذاً في الجزائر. من خلاله ، يمكننا أن نطرح بأمانة وبشجاعة عددًا من الأسئلة: هل نتمتع حقًا بإرادة حرة للتعبير عن مصالحنا الجماعية؟ هنا ، بالطبع ، أعني بوضوح ما إذا كانت المظاهرات الجارية في الجزائر (2019) تدار حقًا بإرادة الناس الخالصة أم أنها لعبة يتم لعبها مرارًا وتكرارًا من قبل لاعبين آخرين يرغبون في إضافة ديكورهم إلى المشهد الحالي. باعتباري من كبار المعجبين بنظرية المؤامرة ، أعتقد اعتقادا راسخا أنه لا يمكن لفرد واحد داخل نسيج اجتماعي عربي أن يفرض نفسه على إرادة من هم في قمة التسلسل الهرمي للسلطة. علاوة على ذلك ، لا يمكن له / لها المطالبة بحقوق مختلفة بخلاف الحقوق الأساسية. وأقصد "الأساسيات القاعدية" ، هنا ، أعني الحق في ملاذ آمن ، هواء / مياه نظيفة ، حق التعليم وحرية التعبير ، وبالتالي ، لا أستطيع أن أخفي قلقي العميق بأننا سنضطر يوما ما إلى وضع عداد على أكتافنا لحساب كمية الهواء الذي نتنفسه لكي ندفع ثمنه لاحقا.

بشكل عام ، إن المجتمع المدني هو أكبر كذبة يقوم بها السياسيون لإبقاء الجمهور ينافس بعضه البعض وينسيهم حقهم المشروع في اختيار من يقودهم كخادم أكثر منه كرئيس. نحن مسيطر علينا بواسطة رقابة هائلة تحيط بنا في كل لحظة نهض فيها للمطالبة ببعض الاحتياجات فضلا عن الحقوق أتمنى أن تكون كلماتي المتواضعة واضحة.

ميريديث غالاغر

عيسى ، لا يمكنني ادعاء معرفة ما الذي تشعر به من تشاؤم حول النظام أو التجارب التي أدت إلى تطور رؤيتك، لكي أستطيع رؤية ذلك. السياسيون الأمريكيون هم أيضا على دراية جيدة بالتكتيكات التي تختلق للفقراء والطبقة المتوسطة صراعا لإبعادهم عن الأنظار. حتى أن البعض يقولون أن فكرة

عيسى صديقي

الوعظ دون اتخاذ خطوات جادة وعملية هو مجرد متاهة أخرى مصممة للناس لإهدار جهودهم على" القناة الخطأ". كل ما قلته صحيح ، لكن لا يتم تجسيده في العالم الحقيقي.

عيسى صديقي

هل يمكننا كمواطنين تحقيق هذا المجتمع المثالي؟ لا أعرف لماذا أنا الوحيد الذي يستشعر العالم بالأسود والأبيض. كلمات رائعة! تفاؤل كبير. مبروك.

نجوى الحريزي

هو مفهوم بعيد كل البعد عن الواقع المعاش، و لكن The Ideal Community مفهوم المجتمع المثالي بناء مجتمع مدني فعال و متطور ليس بالمستحيل،و يعد حلم كل فرد في هذا العالم. تبنى المجتمعات المتطوره على أسس متينة و على مبادئ و قيم إنسانيه تشمل المساواه،السلام ،العدل و الحرية. كما ترتكز على سياسات سليمة و قوانين صارمه و قرارات متزنه و هذا من جانب نظري. أما الجانب التطبيقي و هو الاهم من نظري فيتمثل في تطبيق ما يسمى بالمواطنه و التي تتمثل في تمتع المواطنين بحقوقهم الاساسيه و آدائهم الواجبات و المسؤوليات التي من شأنها المساهمه في ازدهار المجتمع المدني. تشمل أهم الحقوق المدنية في : الحق في حياه كريمه،حق التعليم،الرعايه الصحيه،حريه الدين و حريه التعبير. علاوة على ذلك،و من منظور شخصي، الحق في الأمن هو أهم تلك الحقوق، فالعيش في بيئه آمنه بعيدا عن الصراعات العرقيه،الحروب الاهليه،التهديدات و غيرها من مظاهر العنف يساهم في بناء جيل سليم بدنيا،عقليا و نفسيا و بالتالي جيل واعي،كفؤ فاعل في المجتمع. المجتمع الآمن و الذي لا يقوم على اي عنصريه عرقيه او دينيه او ما شابه هو مهد للحضاره و التقدم. مجمل القول، ارى ان الحقوق و الواجبات هي وجهين لعمله واحده،فالتمتع بالحقوق المدنيه في ظل مجتمع مبني على قوانين بنائه سيقود حتما الى مواطنين مسؤولين يأدون واجباتهم على اكمل وجه. و بالتالي ركيزه المجتمع المدني القوي و المزدهر تكمن في العلاقه الوطيده و المتكامله ما بين الحقوق و الواجبات. و في الاخير تبقى التربيه و التعليم منذ نعومه الاظافر هي جوهر النجاح و الاستقرار مادو نابا المجتمع المدني عبارة عن مجموعة من الأفكار والرؤى التي يعبر عنها المجتمع ويتم توحيدها بطريقة أو بأخرى من خلال بعض القواسم المشتركة بين أفراد المجتمع. يتم التعبير عن هذه الأفكار بشكل مثالي دون خوف من كيفية استقبال الآخرين لها. بدلاً من ذلك ، يجب أن يعمل الناس معًا لدمج آراء بعضهم البعض بطريقة يمكن أن تخدم البيئة التي هم فيها بشكل أفضل. يمكن أن تكون العوامل الموحدة هي الجنسية أو المعتقدات أو حتى القرب المكاني. يجب أن يكون المجتمع المدني الصالح حاضر لعوامل موحدة ، بحيث يمكن أن تنبثق أفكار أكثر تنوعًا من المجتمع. كلما كانت الخلفية أكثر تنوعًا ، كان التصور العام للقضية المطروحة أفضل . على سبيل المثال ، إذا كانت الميزة المشتركة الوحيدة بين أفراد المجتمع هي حقيقة أنهم جميعا يحبون الآيس كريم ، فعندما يقررون ما هي النكهات التي يجب بيعها في متجر الآيس كريم ،كلما كان من الصعب على المجتمع اتخاذ القرار. ولكن ، إذا كان لدى المجتمع بعض الأعضاء الذين يحبون الآيس كريم والشوكولاتة ، والذين يحبون الفانيليا ، فهناك مقاربة أكثر تقاربا وبساطة لمعضلة متجر المثلجات.

حوار

شيماء هاشمي

قبل الحديث عن المجتمع المدني ، يجب أن يتمتع أي مجتمع بالحق في مساحة مدنية تسمح للفرد بالتحدث نيابة عن شعبه.

سامانثا أوينز

أعتقد أن أساس المجتمع المدني ينبغي أن يكون شاملاً. يجب أن يكون هناك مساحات للجميع داخل المجتمع المدني حتى يكون فضاءا فعالا. أعتقد أنه من المهم أن يكون لدى الناس حوار مفتوح يعبر حدود الجنس والعرق والأصل.

هناك العديد من حقوق الإنسان التي أعتقد أنه يجب أن يكون الجميع قادرين على المطالبة بها. من الواضح أنه يجب لكل شخص الحق في المياه النظيفة والمأوى وجميع الاحتياجات الأساسية الأخرى للحياة. بعض حقوق الإنسان الأخرى التي أؤمن بشدة أن الجميع يجب أن يكونوا قادرين على المطالبة بها تشمل الحق في التعليم ، والحق في المشاركة بفعالية في الحكم، والحق في حرية التعبير ، والحق في حرية الممارسات الدينية والعرقية ، والحق في الاستقلال الذاتي للشخص بجسمه. أعتقد أن الجميع يجب أن يكونوا قادرين على المطالبة بهذه الحقوق لأن الاضطهاد والقسر لا يفضيان إلى التقدم. إن أفضل الأفكار وأفضل القادة و أحسن العلاقات تنمو من الحرية ، على الأقل في رأيي.

نجاة بوشريط

حسب ما أرى، يجب أن يكون المجتمع المدني مجتمع المبادئ والقيم والفضيلة والأخلاق التي تستدعي الخير بعيدا عن قيم الرذائل والعداء والكراهية. يجب أن تكون في وئام مع مبادئ وقيم جميع الأديان السماوية. يولد جميع الناس أحرارًا متساوين ويجب معاملتهم بالطريقة نفسها. يمكن للجميع المطالبة بحقوقهم بغض النظر عن اللغة والدين والعرق، وكذلك الحق في المساواة أمام القانون ، والحق في حرية التعبير، والحق في الخصوصية ، والحق في اللجوء.

علاوة هشام خليل

أنا أتفق مع كل ما تم ذكره تقريبا ، أعتقد أن معظم ما قلته موجود بالفعل. أعتقد أنك اتخذت الخطوة الأولى في هذه المحادثة ، وستكون الخطوة الثانية هي دحض حجج أولئك الذين يحملون وجهة نظر أخرى ، حيث أفترض أن لا أحد منا يختلف مع أي مما قلته. كان القمع والقوة دائمًا السبب وراء سقوط الديكتاتوريات بعد فترة ليست بطويلة من قيامها. السبب الرئيسي هو أن مثل هذه المجتمعات لم تستوعب أبدًا كيف تقدم العالم ، واستوعبت حقيقة أن العالم يحترم حقوق الإنسان التي يجب أن تكون شاملاً.

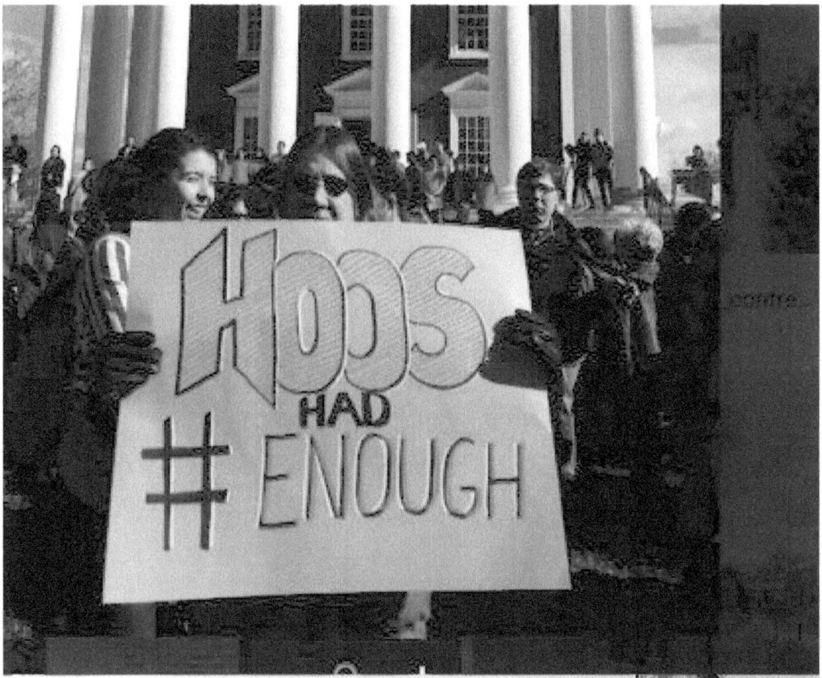
HOOS
HAD
ENOUGH

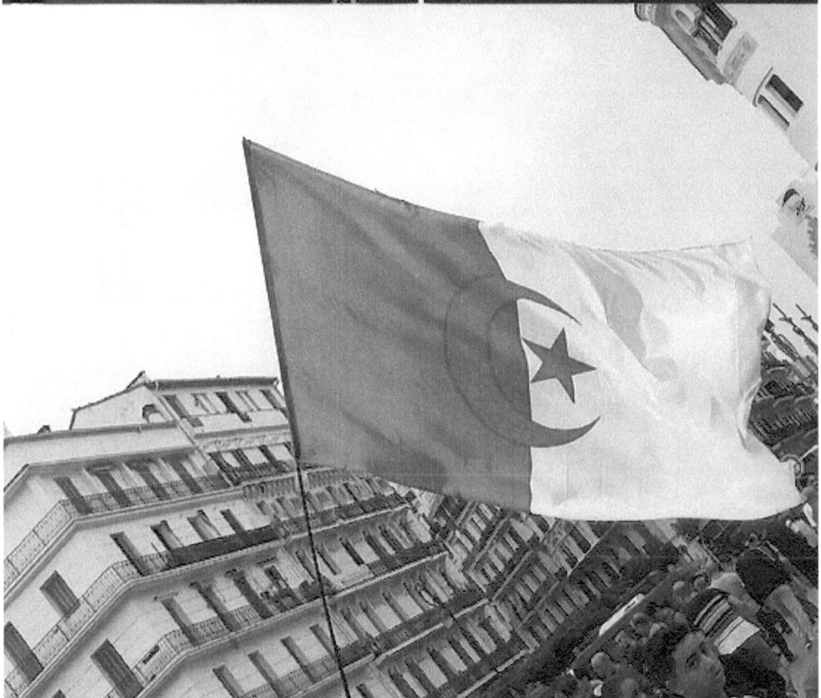

حب إنسان وطني — محي الدين عوفي

الاستقلال لا معنى له.
كل شيء بعده كان شائن. مجيد،
هو بلدنا ، ولكن يكتنفه الظلام.
فقدنا البصيرة ، لكننا لم نتجاهل.

وطني فخور بلا نحاس لديه ؛
الحب والشرف هو كل ما يملك.
فقط الحجارة ، بينما يجلس الفساد على العرش.
على قيد الحياة ، ولكن اليأس حطم صحته.

هتفت نغمة مترنمة في رأسه.
أصوات بلا صوت ، لكن أبلغ من الكلام.
أطلقت العنان لشجاعته ومحت فزعه
للظلم ، قال انه لن يبق مطيعا.

مشى الرجل الفخور مثل السهام.
مع ملايين من مواطنيه ، سار.
كان من المفترض أن تبدأ ثورة جديدة
لتطهير العلم والمجد ، ابتسموا.

طاف الوطنيون بلا خوف حول أعدائهم.
قريباً ، ينسحب الفساد ويغادر
لأنهم لم يعرفوا إلا الشيء اليسير
تقرير المصير يسكن في قلوب الوطنيين

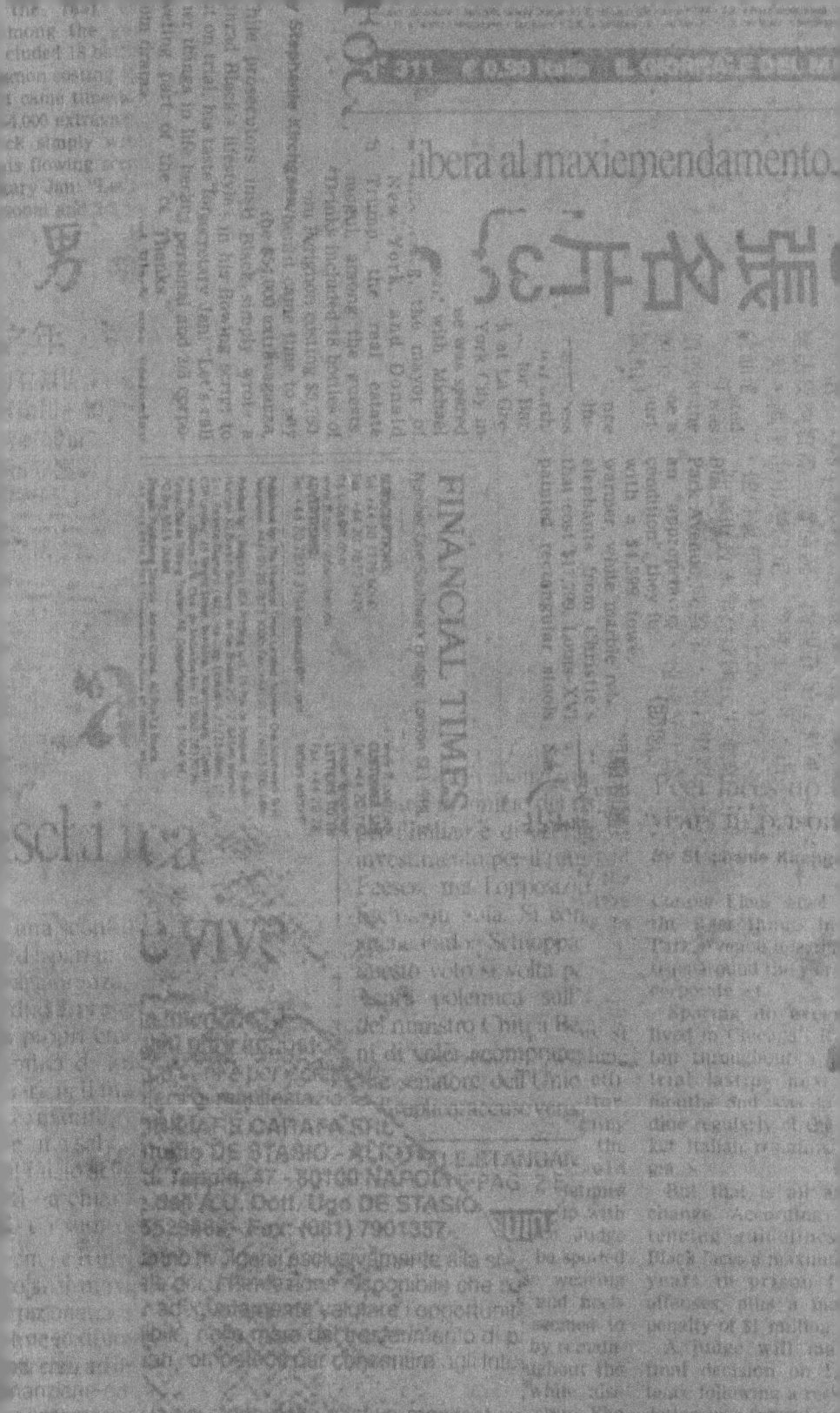

الفصل الثاني:
المجتمع المدني
والمظالم

أفكار ختامية

بشرى رحموني

أريد فقط أن أضيف أنه بالنسبة لي كمدرسة مستقبلية ، سأعمل على منح طلابي الفرصة للتفكير بالطريقة التي يريدونها والتعبير عن أنفسهم بحرية لأن مهمتي ستكون توجيههم وعدم فرض أفكاري الخاصة أو تلك الدروس المبرمجة في أذهانهم لأني أعتقد أن هناك بعض الموضوعات الأخرى المهمة هي الأخرى شأنها شأن الرياضيات أو العلوم لطلبتنا ليتعلموها ، بما في ذلك شيء ذكره أستاذي ، الأستاذة حشلاف ذات مرة ، والذي قال أنه ينبغي معاملة الطلاب كمواطنين حاليين وليسوا مواطنين في المستقبل. هنا ، على سبيل المثال ، يمكن تنظيم فصول المحادثة بطريقة يكون فيها المعلمون مستمعين إلى أفكار وآراء الجميع لأن معرفة من ذوات الطلبة تؤدي إلى نتائج أفضل فيما يتعلق بإعدادهم ليكونوا قادة ومواطنين صالحين.

شيلي وايمونت

أعتقد أنه خلال تجربتي في التعليم العالي ، تعلمت أن أنتقد و أتساءل عن العالم المحيط بي، و بذلك تعلمت المهارات اللازمة للإنخراط في المجتمع المدني. لقد تعلمت حتى المهارات اللازمة للإحتجاج على السياسات والإجراءات التي لا أتفق معها - على سبيل المثال ، قمت مع زميلتي في الغرفة بتنظيم في العام الأول من الجامعة Utah State Capitol احتجاج صامت على عتبات مبنى.

أعتقد أن بعض هذه المهارات التي اكتسبتها تأتي من خلال التخصصات الأساسية والفرعية التي اخترتها في الجامعة. خلقت هذه الفصول الدراسية مزيجًا فريدًا من المعارف / المهارات بالنسبة لي ، حيث تعلمت المزيد عن تنفيذ السياسات في حكومتنا وكيفية التحدث بفعالية ، بينما علمتني بقية الفصول الدراسية أن أتحدى عالمنا المحيط بنا وان أشكك فيه. أعتقد أن كل هذه الأمور تساهم في القدرة على المساهمة الإيجابية في المجتمع المدني. أعتقد أنه يجب أن تكون لديك القدرة على التشكيك في العالم من حولك ، ولكن أيضًا المعرفة لفهم كيفية تحدي هذا العالم. هذه مهارات لا أعتقد أني كنت لأمتلكها لو لا تجربتي الجامعية.

ومع ذلك ، على الرغم من أن تجربتي قد عززت هذه المهارات بنجاح ، إلا أنني أعتقد أن نموذج التعليم ككل ليس سهل الولوج لجميع فئات المجتمع إلى حد كبير. تكاليف التعليم مرتفعة، ومع ارتفاع تكاليف المعيشة في حين تستمر الأجور في الركود بشكل أساسي، لا يمكن الوصول إلى الجامعة لكثير من سكاننا. أعتقد أن نموذج التعليم الخاص بنا يعزز هذه المهارات بنجاح ، ولكنه يوفر هذه المهارات فقط لعدد قليل يحظى بالامتيازات.

هاشمي شيماء

أنا على دراية بمصطلحات مثل القيادة والقادة. لقد نشأت وأنا أستمع إلى قصص عن القادة. لدي أيضا والدي كمثال حي للقائد المثالي. أستطيع أن أقول إن أساتذتي في المدرسة المتوسطة بذلوا قصارى جهدهم. على سبيل المثال ، يتبادر إلى ذهني أستاذتي بدارنية مباركة التي كانت مثالا حقيقيا للقائدة. إنها تحاول إيقاظ القائد في داخلنا ليس عن طريق إلقاء المحاضرات أو إملاء الأفكار والنصائح. إنها تلك القائدة التي تطلب منا أن نراقبها وأن نعمل معها. في الواقع ، أراد كل أساتذتي تشكيل مواطنين صالحين. لقد ساعدوني دائمًا وشجعوني على التحدث في الأماكن العامة. بالإضافة إلى ذلك ، اعتادوا على جعلي أعمل في مجموعات. أرادوا مني المشاركة مع الغير، والقيادة و الإتباع. أتذكر كل ما اعتادوا قوله وكل ما اعتادوا فعله. كانوا متحدين وعملوا معا. أرادوا لي رؤية النموذج أمامي.لقد أظهروا لي المقصود بكلمة "نحن". في ذلك الوقت ، لم أكن أدرك ذلك لأنني لم أكن أعلم ما الذي كانوا يفعلونه أو يقولونه. اليوم، كلما قرأت شيئًا ما عن القيادة - سواء أكان ذلك مقالًا عن خصائصها أو سلوكياتها أو الأشياء التي يجب قولها أو القيام بها ، أو كتاب حول ذلك - أبتسم فقط لعلمي أنه ذات مرة ، كان لدي مدرسون ممتازون.

لتصبح قائدًا سياسيًا يمكنه تغيير القوانين أو السياسات أو الأنظمة لصالح عدد أكبر من الناس. وأنا حاضر في العديد من الأحداث المدنية ، وأنا حاضر في المسائل السياسية. في انتخابات البرلمان عام 2017 ، كنت منظمًا لحملة انتخابية لأحد المرشحين في مسقط رأسي.

لا يوجد مثال أفضل على المشاركة السياسية للمرأة من الاضطراب الذي يحدث اليوم في الجزائر مع النساء غالبًا في الخطوط الأمامية. إنها تحتج جنبًا إلى جنب مع الرجل لتغيير ظروف البلاد كما يرغبون في ذلك. حضورها ليس مباشرًا فحسب ، بل قد يكون غير مباشر أيضًا ، اعتمادًا على قدرات كل فرد وقدراته. إنها حاضرة حتى مع أبسط الطرق ، إما بإعداد الحلويات والكعك للمتظاهرين ، أو توزيع المياه عليهم من الشرفات ، أو حتى فتح أبواب منزلها للصحافة لتغطية الأحداث. وكما هو الحال مع أي امرأة جزائرية أنا حاضر دائمًا. (الشكل 8)

(الشك 8) امرأة جزائرية في احتجاجات اليوم

المراجع:

(1). مجلة التعليم والسياسة الاجتماعية المجلد. 5 ، رقم 2 ، / (2011 ، ONS) مكتب الإحصاء الوطني يونيو 2018

(2). jesp / 10.30845 :doi 2018 June ,2 .No، مجلة التعليم والسياسة الاجتماعية (السنة) المجلد. 5 .v5n2p10 / page 16

(3). 2013 مايو مركز المعلومات والبحوث حول التعلم المدني والمشاركة (w.w.w.civicyouth.org)

(الشكل 7) مشاركاتٍ في أحداث مختلفة

إلى أن الفتيات يؤدين أداءً أفضل Civicstest في الواقع ، تشير نتائج التقييم المدني للتقدم التربوي في ، إن لم يكن أفضل من الأولاد في اختبارات المعرفة المدنية (4). المرأة الجزائرية اليوم ، شأنها شأن جميع نساء العالم ، تقدم إلى نظيراتها الذكور في العديد من مؤشرات المشاركة المدنية ، بما في ذلك العمل التطوعي والعضوية في الجمعيات المجتمعية والتصويت. ما هو واضح هو أن النساء أكثر عرضة للانخراط في العمل المجتمعي الشعبي من خلال العمل التطوعي ومن خلال المنظمات المجتمعية. تظهر النساء أيضًا رغبة أقوى في مساعدة المحتاجين أكثر من الرجال. على سبيل المثال ، في مسقط رأسي ، تعتمد الكثير من الجمعيات الخيرية التطوعية على وجود الإناث. في رمضان ، وهو الشهر التاسع من السنة المسلمة ، حيث يصوم المسلمون من الفجر حتى غروب الشمس ، تتنافس النساء الجزائريات ، وخاصة الأصغر سناً ، في المشاركة في "مطاعم الرحمة" المعروفة بتقديم الطعام للفقراء والعاملين الذين لا يستطيعون العودة إلى المنزل.

ومع ذلك ، لا تقتصر المشاركة المدنية للمرأة على المطبخ فقط. يمكن أن نلاحظ أيضًا أن الشابات يشاركن في جميع جوانب المجتمع المدني ، من النشاط في مجتمعها من خلال قيادة جمعيات محددة ذات أغراض مختلفة (التعليم ، التدريب الاجتماعي ، الرياضة ، الموسيقى ، وما إلى ذلك) ، إلى التقدم في المشاركة في الأحداث الدولية حيث تجد نفسها تمثل بلدها وثقافتها. على سبيل المثال ، تنشط النساء وهي جمعية تمثل مؤسسة دولية معتمدة من قبل المجلس الثقافي البريطاني في الجزائر ، "Learn In" في وكذلك تمثيل الجزائر في المنتديات الدولية مثل، L. Annissa ، والتي تقودها امرأة ناشطة ، هي السيدة مسابقات النقاش التي جرت في قطر.

تحاول النساء الجزائريات أيضًا أن يكون أقرب إلى السياسة ، رغم أن التواجد في هذا المجال أقل من الرجال. لا تزال هناك أمثلة في حين تتلقى الشابة التي تشارك في المجتمع الدعم والتشجيع والتوجيه

ومع ذلك ، يبدو أن التوقعات الاجتماعية قد تغيرت قليلاً فقط مع مرور الوقت. إذا نظرنا إلى الوراء إلى السنوات العشر الأخيرة ، أصبحت المرأة الجزائرية حرة في اختيار وظيفتها بغض النظر عن تقاليد المجتمع. المرأة الجزائرية اليوم لا تحدى الرجل والمجتمع فحسب ، بل إنها تحدى نفسها أيضًا. ومع ذلك فهي تكافح لتحقيق التوازن بين العمل والحياة المنزلية لأن وضعها الجديد كعاملة أنثى لم يغير مسؤولياتها التقليدية تجاه منزلها وزوجها وأطفالها. والجدير بالملاحظة أن النساء الجزائريات أظهرن دائمًا قدراتهن ورغباتهن في أن يصبحن مهنيات في العمل وفي نفس الوقت كن هناك من أجل منزلها.

(الشكل 6) العرض الذي قدمته في جلسة السيد حشاف في ديسمبر 2018

المرأة الجزائرية كعنصر منخرط بشكل جيد في المجتمع

ماذا بعد أن أكملت المرأة جميع مهام المجتمع ، وحصلت على الدرجة ، وكانت المهنة ناجحة ، وتم تأسيس العلاقات؟ ما هو مستقبل هؤلاء النساء المتعلمات؟ أعتقد أن التركيز سيكون على تحديد اهتماماتها خارج متطلبات عملها ومتطلبات الأسرة. هذه خطوة مهمة في تحديد الفرص المتاحة لها للمشاركة المدنية ، "الطرق التي يشارك بها المواطنون في حياة المجتمع من أجل تحسين ظروف الآخرين"(3)

من خلال التجربة الشخصية ، يمكنني القول أنه بصفتي طالبًا في الكلية ، كانت هناك فرص لي لكي أكون أكثر نشاطًا وأكثر انخراطًا في الحياة المدنية. شاركت في أنشطة وفعاليات مختلفة. تم تعييني نائبة للأمين العام لنادي ثقافي في كليتنا. شاركت في تنظيم بعض ورش العمل التي تتناول القراءة والصحة. نظمت بعض الحملات التطوعية للمرضى. شاركت أيضًا في صنع أول مكتبة لبيع الكتب في الشوارع في مسقط رأسي (الشكل 7). أكثر من ذلك أعمل مع أحد أعضاء تويزا لدينا ، شيراز ، لتقديم دروس صيفية مجانية لتدريس اللغة الإنجليزية لتلاميذ المدارس الابتدائية لتغيير الثقافة الفرنسية مع اللغة الإنجليزية

بحلول عام 2005 ، عندما بدأت الدراسة في عمر 6 سنوات ، كان الوصول إلى التعليم قد تغير بشكل كبير. كما هو الحال مع أي طفل جزائري ، بدأت عملي التعليمي في المدرسة الابتدائية في سن السادسة (في عام 2005). في السنة الخامسة من التعليم الابتدائي ، يتعين على كل تلميذ اجتياز امتحان وطني دراسة امتحان بريمير / امتحان شهادة التعليم الابتدائي). يسمح لكل تلميذ يتلقى ما لا يقل عن 5 (BEP من كل 10 طلاب بالانتقال إلى المدرسة المتوسطة. تلقيت 8 ، وهو نجاح غير مسبوق لفتاة في عائلتي تستمر المدرسة المتوسطة في الجزائر لمدة 4 سنوات. من 2010 إلى 2014 ، كنت أدرس بجد ونتيجة لذلك حصلت على درجات جيدة. في السنة الرابعة من المرحلة الإعدادية ، يجب أن يجتاز كل طالب اختبار اللغة الفرنسية / اختبار اللغة الإنجليزية) امتحان وطني آخر يسمى BEMاختبارًا وطنيًا آخر باسم اختبار امتحان اللغة الإنجليزية / اختبار شهادة التعليم المتوسط). يُسمح لأي طالب يحصل BEM على 10 على الأقل من 20 بالانتقال إلى المدرسة الثانوية. حصلت على 16 من أصل 20. ثم ذهبت إلى المدرسة الثانوية. في السنة الثالثة من المدرسة الثانوية ، يجب على كل طالب اجتياز امتحان وطني آخر لكي تكون قادرًا على الحصول على القبول في الكلية ، يحتاج الطلاب إلى (BAC). يسمى اختبار البكالوريا الحصول على المعدل التراكمي أو ما يزيد عن 10/20. لقد نجحت في امتحان البكالوريا في عام 2017 (وحصلت على 14 من أصل 20 (الشكل 5)

(الشكل 5) آخر أيامي في المدرسة الثانوية مع أصدقائي وأفضل مدرس 2017

اجتياز كل هذه السنوات الاثنتي عشرة في الدراسة والانتقال من مرحلة إلى أخرى أمر ممكن لأي طالب جزائري. الفرق الوحيد هو الحصول على درجات جيدة. سمح لي الحصول على 14 من أصل 20 في الخاص بي بالحصول على المزيد من الخيارات في اختيار ما سأدرسه في الكلية. (BAC) امتحان البكالوريا كلما ارتفعت درجاتك ، زادت الخيارات المتاحة في الكلية. لقد سمح لي النجاح في حضور معهد تعليم المعلمين الذي يعتبره معظم الجزائريين أفضل من أي جامعة عادية. أنا هنا لأصبح مدرسًا للغة الإنجليزية في المدرسة الثانوية. تستمر دراستي لمدة 5 سنوات ، مما يعني أن لديّ أكثر من 3 سنوات لإنهاء دراستي.

ولدت أمي في عام 1963 ، أي بعد عام من الاستقلال الوطني. رغم أن الظروف في الجزائر كانت سيئة في ذلك الوقت ، إلا أن أمي كانت واحدة من الفتيات القلائل في مسقط رأسي الذين التحقوا بالمدرسة. عندما لم تنجح في امتحان البكالوريا ، سُمح لها بحضور مؤسسات أخرى. في الواقع ، واصلت دراستها في (الشكل3).بعد ، عندما دخلت القوى العاملة ، فرضت المعايير الاجتماعية قيودًاei) معهد التكوين المهني على) النساء عند اختيار المهن. نتيجة لذلك ، انتهى الأمر بالعديد من المهنيات إلى العمل في مجالات مثل التمريض والتعليم والتي كانت تعتبر أكثر قبولًا اجتماعيًا ومناسبة للجنس. عندما أكملت أمي دراساتها ، أصبحت معلمة في مركز التكوين المهني (مركز لأولئك الذين لم يتمكنوا من الالتحاق بالجامعة). بعد 32 عامًا كمدرس ، حصلت على تقاعدها في عام 2019.

(الشك 3) أمي في معهد التكوين المهني 198

(الشكل 4) أول أيام أمي في العمل 1986 (اليمين) / تقاعد أمي 2019 (اليسار)

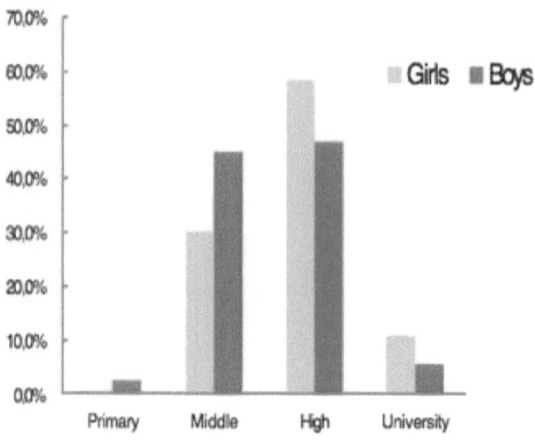

، (الشكل 1) نسبة الأشخاص غير المتزوجين الذين تتراوح أعمارهم بين 15 و 19 سنة في المدارس في عام 2002 حسب مستوى التعليم (2)

ويمكن ملاحظة ذلك في تاريخ المرأة داخل الأسرة ؛ أنا وأمي وجدتي ، ثلاثة أجيال من النساء اللائي جرين النظام التعليمي في الجزائر. على سبيل المثال ، جدتي في 76 سنة. لم تحصل على أي وصول تعليمي كبير. مرت بجزء من نظام التعليم الاستعماري ، لكنها منذ ذلك الوقت وحتى اليوم هي مثال لامرأة منزل (الشكل 2).

(الشكل 2) جدتي

الطلاب فقط مناهج دراسية متساوية، فسنرى أقل من هذه اللحظات غير المتوقعة حيث نشعر كما لو أننا سُرِبنا من الحقيقة. أحداث مهمة مثل فينغر هيل تنزلق من خلال الشقوق. إنها تعمينا عن القدرة على رؤية العالم حقًّا. اعتدت أن أمشي في مقهى ميب وأفكر فقط في الطعام الرائع والثقافة الجذابة، لكن الآن، أرى بامتنان الصورة الأكبر التي تشمل الرحلة التي مر بها هذا المبنى والمجتمع. إذا تم تعليم الطلاب فقط مناهج دراسية متساوية، فسنرى أقل من هذه اللحظات غير المتوقعة حيث نشعر كما لو أننا سُرِبنا من الحقيقة.

خديجة خليد

في الجزائر، كان الالتحاق بالتعليم منذ فترة طويلة امتيازًا يتمتع به الرجال، الذين لديهم تاريخًا معدلات أعلى من الالتحاق بالمدارس، ومعدلات أعلى من الإلمام بالقراءة والكتابة كبالغين، والدبلومات العليا التي حصلوا عليها، ومستويات التعليم الأعلى حسب العمر، وما إلى ذلك. بعد سنوات من الاستقلال، تغير مستوى التعليم. لم يثبت التعليم المجاني والإلزامي للأطفال حتى سن 16 عامًا أنه يكفي لتوفير التعليم الأساسي لجميع الأطفال فقط، ولكن بمجرد التحاقهم بالنظام المدرسي، وجد أن الفتيات أكثر عرضة للاستفادة الكاملة من تعليمهن ومواصلة دراساتهم في المدرسة الثانوية والجامعة. منذ الألفية الجديدة، أصبحت هذه الظاهرة واضحة بشكل متزايد في سجلات وزارة التربية والتعليم والمكتب الوطني للإحصاء. هذا الخلل بين الرجل والمرأة من حيث الإنجازات التعليمية يميل الآن بشكل واضح لصالح المرأة. في المدارس الثانوية والجامعات، يتجاوز معدل التخرج للبنات نسبة الأولاد، والتي لها علاقة قوية مع حركة الجزائر نحو شبكة أكثر انفتاحًا للمشاركة المدنية. لقد أثبتت المرأة الجزائرية نفسها دائمًا كعنصر نشط في المجتمع المدني، والآن تثبت أنها رائدة قوية في المجتمع. على الرغم من أنني لن أزعم أن الجزائر مجتمع مثالي، إلا أنني سأحاول إظهار التقدم الذي أحرزته النساء وإبراز العمل المهم الذي يتعين القيام به.

المرأة الجزائرية كعنصر عالي التعليم في المجتمع

كما هو الحال مع الكيانات الأبوية الأخرى في المنطقة، كان المجتمع الجزائري عالماً يسيطر عليه الرجال، عالمٌ كانت فيه المرأة في وضع أدنى من الولادة وحتى الموت. في أعقاب صراع الاستقلال، بعد 132 سنة من الحكم الفرنسي، وجدت الدولة نفسها موجودة داخل أنقاض النظام الاستعماري. فإن 75٪ من، (2011، ONS) كانت الغالبية العظمى من السكان أميين. وفقًا لتعدادات عام 1966 الأشخاص الذين تبلغ أعمارهم 10 أعوام فما فوق لا يستطيعون القراءة أو الكتابة. كانت هذه النسبة 85٪ للنساء مقارنة بـ 62٪ للرجال (1). عملت الحكومة بنشاط لتغيير هذا الوضع. بحلول عام 2000، نجحت الجزائر في تحقيق بعض هذه الأهداف. كانت سياسة الحكومة التي كانت بلا شك الأكثر أهمية هي الوصول الشامل إلى التعليم، والذي أصبح إلزامي ومجانيًا للأطفال الذين تتراوح أعمارهم بين 6 و 16 عامًا. وقد كان هذا أكثر فائدة لتحسين وضع المرأة. تتلقى البنات الآن نفس التعليم الابتدائي الذي يحصل عليه الأولاد، ثم واصلت النجاح في الجامعات. (الشكل 1). ونتيجة لذلك، تمكنت بعض النساء من الاستفادة من هذا الوضع الجديد للحفاظ على الاستقلال الذي تم العثور عليه حديثًا، وشاركت بنشاط في تطوير الدولة الجديدة.

الإنصاف والعدالة

جايدن ويليامز

مقهى ميل هو مهرب من الجامعة. من الجانب الفيزيائي، لأنه خارج الحرم الجامعي [بعيدا عن جامعة فرجينيا]، ولكن من الجانب المعنوي أيضا. يمكنني الدخول والنظر حولي وإيجاد الوجوه المبتسمة المألوفة. الجو في ميلز يعادل متجر حلاقة لذوي البشرة السوداء. يمكنك الذهاب إلى هناك وأن تشعر تاريخي جدًّا، عندما نكون هناك في Mel's Café بالقبول وأن تشعر بأنك جزء من المجتمع. نظرًّا لأن تشعر كما لو كنت جزءًا من التاريخ. كان لدى شارلوتسفيل الكثير من عمليات التجديد ولكن ميلز ظل دائمًا كما هو. من ضمن عمليات التجديد أو ما يعرف ب ("التجديد الحضري") الأكثر تدميرًا في تاريخ شارلوتسفيل هي فينجار هيل. اعتاد ميل نفسه على العيش هناك ، و المقهى الذي ابتكره ميل يشبه المجتمع الأسود المزدهر القديم.

أروي هذه القصة لأشير إلى النقطة التالية: منذ أن تم قبولي في جامعة فرجينيا ، كان لدي في البداية انطباع بأن تعليمي السابق يوجهني تجاه النجاح في الحياة. كأمريكي من أصل أفريقي ، علمت أني لم أتعرف على تاريخي في هذا البلد بنفس القدر مع الأمريكيين البيض. نتيجة لذلك ، أشعر أن نظام التعليم قد منعني من تكوين رؤية دقيقة حول العالم من حولي. في الآونة الأخيرة ، كانت هناك أوقات تعرفت فيها على التاريخ الأمريكي الإفريقي من خلال أقراني أو من خلال الإنترنت. لقد تساءلت كيف لم يتم ذكر هذه الأحداث من قبل في الفصول؟ مثال على ذلك هو فينيغر هيل ، في شارلوتسفيل فيرجينيا المذكورة أعلاه. كان فينغر هيل مجتمعًا أسود مزدهر داخل المدينة المفصولة عرقيا. كانت تحتوي على مدرسة ، منازل ،والعديد من الشركات المزدهرة. غضب الجزء الأبيض من المدينة من أن المزيد من الناس كانوا يذهبون لاقتناء البضائع من الشركات المملكة من طرف السود بدلاً من الشركات المملكة من طرف البيض. رغبة في الانتقام ، قاموا بتدمير المجتمع متذرعين بمبادرة "التجديد الحضري" التي دمرت حوالي 30 شركة مملكة للسود. وأجبرت ما يقرب من 140 أسرة على الانتقال ؛ وكان معظمهم من الأمريكيين الأفارقة. (انظر سميث ، https://timeline.com/charlottesville-vinegar-hill-demolished-ba27b6e-a69e1

لقد تعلمت عن هذا التاريخ عندما كنت جالسا في الفصل على وشك المغادرة. كانت المعلمة تخبر الفصل أنها تضطر للمغادرة مبكرا للذهاب إلى حدث في مركز التراث الأمريكي من أصل أفريقي في مدرسة قبل أن يتم تهجير السكان قسرًا. كلامها هذا Vinegar Hill جيفرسون ، حيث كان لديهم معرض لصور أدى إلى الكثير من الاستغراب. شعرت على الفور بالحرج. ليس فقط بسبب قلة معرفتي بفينيغر هيل، ولكن لأني عشت طوال حياتي على بعد 40 ميلاً من المدينة. في وقت لاحق من ذلك الأسبوع كنت أتناول فطوري في مقهى ميلز وكنت أفكر في المأساة التي حدثت. كان السؤال المكرر الذي طرحته على نفسي هو "كيف لم أسمع بهذا مطلقًا؟" بعد التفكير في كل الحقائق التاريخية المحلية التي لا تعد ولا تحصى والأقل أهمية من الناحية التاريخية من هذه المأساة ، أدركت أنه "ليس خطأي لكوني جاهل. إنه خطأ مدرستي السابقة، ومناهجها الغير مناسبة. يبدو كما لو أنه عندما يتعلق الأمر بالتاريخ الأمريكي الإفريقي ، فإن أحداث مهمة مثل فينيغر هيل تتسلل من الشقوق وتختفي. إنها محاولة لمنعي ومنع الآخرين من رؤية العالم حقًّا. اعتدت أن أمشي إلى مقهى ميلز وأفكر فقط في الطعام الرائع والثقافة الجذابة ، لكن الآن ، أرى بامتنان الصورة الأكبر التي تشمل الرحلة التي مر بها هذا المبنى والمجتمع. إذا تم تعليم

إليك شيئا واحدا أريد أن أخبرك به: لا تحدي رؤيتك على مجرد الأهداف النهائية. نجاحك لا يرتبط بالضرورة على اسم كليتك ولا درجة الامتياز التي حصلت عليها والتي ستتحصلين بموجبها على الرضا. بدلاً من ذلك ، إنها المعرفة والتصرفات التي تتخذينها بناءً على الرغبة. منذ العام الماضي ، اكتشفت اهتماماتي في مختلف المجالات التي لم أكن أعرفها أبدًا. أرغب في اكتشاف طريقة لتحسين أساليب الإتصال من خلال البحث في علم أمراض النطق واللغة. أريد أن أعود إلى المدرسة لمعرفة المزيد عن علم اللغة الإجتماعي وتأثيره على بنياتنا الإجتماعية. أريد أن أرشد الطلاب الآسيويين والأمريكيين من أصول آسياوية للمساعدة في انتقالهم، وغالبًا في لحظاتهم الضعيفة.أريد القضاء على مخاوف الأسر ذات الدخل المنخفض للوصول إلى مقدمي الرعاية الصحية وبناء مجتمع يمكن أن نلتمس فيه العافية البدنية والنفسية. وأريد إعطاء والداي التعليم الذي يستحقانه والسماح لهم بالحصول على فائدة من ذلك التعليم ، وحصولهم على الاستقلالية: القدرة على قراءة اللافتات والسفر بمفردهم ، والقوة لمكافحة العنصرية ، والشجاعة لإيجاد انتماء لمجتمع.

إنها هذه الرغبة في التصرف ، مدعومة بالمعرفة التي تكسبها من التعليم. وهذا ، بمعنى ما ، هو الامتياز والحرية اللذان تمناه آباؤنا لنا.

من السريالي أن أكتب هذا لك وأنا على وشك الانتهاء من دراستي الجامعية في غضون أربعة أسابيع فقط. أشعر بوخز غامض في قلبي في كل مرة أفكر بك. كنت تعتقدين أنك لن تخرجي من هذه المدينة الصغيرة. لقد كنت مكانك، ولا أتمنى أبدًا لأي شخص آخر أن يشعر بنفس ألم الإنتقال الذي شعرت به. تعد سنوات المراهقة وقتًا عصيبًا بما يكفي ، وعليك الآن أن تتعلم لغة جديدة بمستوى أكاديمي وثقافة لتكوين صداقات، وقوة لرعاية نفسك. لا يوجد سوى طريق واحد للخروج من الألم ، على الرغم من أنه ليس من السهل على ضعيفي القلب ؛ تعلم ، حرك عضلة، و غير فكرة. عندما تشعر بأنك لا تنتمي إلى أي مجتمع ، إعلم أن لديك القدرة على تكوين مجتمع.

بكل ود،

كلير

تايلور بلاكلي

أشعر أنه على الرغم من أن نموذجنا التعليمي الحالي يعزز أحيانًا بعض المهارات اللازمة للمشاركة الإيجابية في المجتمع المدني، فإنه غالبًا ما يهمل الآخرين. هناك العديد من القضايا داخل الأوساط الأكاديمية تجعل من الأهداف التربوية بعيدة المنال. في بعض الأحيان يبدو الأمر كما لو أن التعليم ، على المستويين العام والخاص ، موجه نحو نوع معين من الطلاب ونوع معين من المخرجات ويتم قصره على هذا الافتراض. أيضا، يتم التغافل على الكثير من الخطابات من التعليم العام. لماذا لا أتعلم الآن سوى تاريخ وراء بعض الانقسامات العرقية المريرة الموجودة في المجتمع الأمريكي؟ يجب أن تكون هذه القصص جزءًا أكثر من مجرد تعليم فنون ليبرالية. لإشراك الطلاب بطريقة تعزز مشاركتهم الإيجابية في المجتمع المدني ، يجب تقديم هذه القضايا بطريقة حساسة ومثمرة.يحتاج الناس إلى تعلم كيفية مناقشة المواضيع المثيرة للجدل بطريقة محترمة وعادلة.

الأشياء التي تجلب لنا السعادة. هناك مساحة فارغة كبيرة في ألبوم الصور العائلي لدينا خلال سنوات الدراسة المتوسطة والثانوية. قضينا معظم وقتنا في حفظ المفردات لنعتاد على اللغة الأكاديمية المكتوبة في الكتب المدرسية والامتحانات. لقد كتبنا العديد من المقالات، نحلل فيها معاني النصوص الادبية في حين لم نتمكن من فهم الاعتداءات الصغيرة التي أحاطت بنا في حياتنا اليومية و حوادث العنصرية داخل وخارج المدرسة، غياب دور الوالدين بسبب عملهم وحاجز اللغة سرق الكثير من الأفراح في حياتنا لكننا تسامحنا. لأننا اعتقدنا أن هذا لن يحدث مرة أخرى، نحن في الكلية مرة واحدة فقط. لقد كانت، تذكرة ذهبية للنجاح والسعادة.

تقمصنا هوية أخرى في الكلية، تدعى كلير. لقد واصلت جعل والديك فخورين، حيث حضرت كلية مرموقة في جامعة فرجينيا بمنحة دراسية كاملة. بدا أن كلير تتلاءم أفضل من جيمين في كلية من الدرجة الأولى التي احتلت المرتبة الثالثة بين أفضل المدارس العامة في الولايات المتحدة.

بالنسبة لكلير، فإن معنى التعليم الأمريكي قد تغير كثيرًا. كما ترى، كان التعليم الذي فكرت فيه يعتمد فقط على النتائج: الدرجات، والقبول بالكلية، والدبلوم، مما يوصل إلى مهنة تكفي للاعتناء بك وبوالديك. اعتقدت أن التعليم الذي آمن به آباؤنا كان حسن النية، لكنه كان ساذجا. فكرت في مكانهم، أن الحصول على شهادة من شأنه أن يضمن حياة أفضل من حياتهم ؛ مريحة، مرضية، وأكثر إسعادا. لكن بالكاد عرفنا نظام التعليم الأمريكي، حول سبب اضطرارك إلى الحصول على درجة أعلى من غير الآسيويين لإتاحة الفرصة لك للدخول إلى الكلية ذاتها. فجوة الثراء توجد حتى بين الجيل الأول والثاني والثالث من الأميركيين الآسيويين الذين يتحدثون الإنجليزية، وهي اللغة الأكاديمية التي يستخدمونها حتى داخل أسرهم. تأثير الخلفية الاجتماعية والاقتصادية على صعوبات العثور على مجتمع تنتمي إليه حتى بعد القبول في مدرستك التي طالما حلمت بالولوج إليها.

كانت الكلية أرضًا موعودة حيث اعتقدت أنني سأستعيد كل الفرح الذي سُرق مني أثناء انتقالي إلى أمريكا. اعتقدت أنني سوف أكون أندمج تمامًا، لأن جامعة فرجينيا بها عدد من السكان الأميركيين الآسيويين أكثر من مسقط رأسي. اعتقدت أنني سأكون أكثر تلقائيّة وثقة أثناء مزاولة الجامعة. جئت إلى جامعة فرجينيا، وأنا واثقة من أنني سأدرس العلوم لأتخصص في مجال الرعاية الصحية لأن ذلك كان أكثر الأعمال النبيلة والمحترمة التي عرفتها. اعتقدت أن الحصول على درجة واستقرار مالي وتكوين للثروة يعني أن الناس سوف يتوقفون عن إساءة معاملة والداي بسبب لون بشرتهما و كثرة تلكئهما عند التكلم باللغة الإنجليزية.

بدلًا من ذلك، اكتسبت رؤية جعلتني أدرك التباين في إمكانية الوصول إلى التعليم والرعاية الصحية و غيرها بين الأفراد ذوي الخلفيات العرقية والاجتماعية والاقتصادية المختلفة. لقد اكتشفت مشاكلا في نظام التعليم والرعاية الصحية، وليس في نفسي لعدم كوني ذكية أو ثرية بما فيه الكفاية. لقد اكتشفت رغبتي في استخدام امتيازي كخريجة جامعية للتواصل مع الناس وبناء مجتمع بدلًا من أن أختزل نفسي لأتناسب معايير الانتماء لواحد.

المتعة. كافحنا لإيجاد منزل في بلدة زراعية تقع على بعد 20 دقيقة من الحدود المكسيكية. قد تكون المدينة مليئة بالأقليات ، لكننا لم نكن جزءًا منها ، لعدم قدرتنا على التحدث باللغة الإسبانية أو الإنجليزية بشكل كامل.

كثيراً ما تساءلت عن مدى سعادتهم ، إذا كان- ترك أجدادنا وأصدقائنا للعيش بين الغرباء الذين لا يستطيعون فهم ثقافتنا ولغتنا تمامًا - يستحق كل هذا العناء. للمرة المليون ، كانت والدتنا تقول نعم بابتسامة تعلو وجهها. قبل ثماني سنوات من الآن ، الجواب لم يتغير بعد.

لست متأكدّة تمامًا إذا كان بإمكاني تقديم نفس الإجابة لك. كان من الصعب للغاية رؤية آبائنا يتنازلون عن حياتهم في كوريا و عائلتهم و أصدقائهم و مهنهم. لقد شاهدتهم يعملون من الصباح إلى الليل، 7 أيام في الأسبوع في المتاجر الصغيرة لأن شهاداتهم الجامعية في كوريا لم تعادل الولايات المتحدة. رأيت كيف كان والدنا يعاني مرارة ذنب ترك والدته وحيدة في كوريا. شعرت بالمرارة كلما عوملت والدتنا بلهجة متعالية - من أشخاص خارج منزلنا - في محلات البقالة والبنوك و متعاملي العقارات ومدرسي وأحيانًا في متجرنا بسبب تلكئها المستمر و هي تحاول أن تتكلم باللغة الإنجليزية.

بالنسبة لوالدينا، كان التعليم الأمريكي يعني سلمًا خارج البئر ، تعليما مثل ذلك الذي استخدماه للهروب من فقر مدنهم الريفية الصغيرة في أندونج بكوريا. لقد أدركا كيف كان الحال عندما انقلب عالمهما رأسًّا على عقب انتقالهما إلى مدينة كبيرة مثل سيول. الجلوس على مكتب في فصل دراسي واحد بعد الآخر ، والانتقال من المدرسة إلى دروس الدعم والدروس الخاصة، ودراسة 13 موضوعًا مختلفًا من الصباح حتى الذهاب إلى السرير. كانت هذه مصائر حتمية كان يجب أن أواجهها أنا وأخي لو نشأنا في سيول. عندما سافرا عبر البلدان للعمل، إكتشفا أن هناك عالما أوسع. بدلا من ذلك ، أخذوا قفزة وقدموا حبهم ، حنانهم ، و رؤاهم لنا.

بالنسبة لك ، كان التعليم الأمريكي يعني تبرير تضحيات والديك. لقد كانت وسيلة لك للدفاع عن سعادتك في بلدك الذي تبنيته ، لكونك الشخص الوحيد الذي وجد الأصدقاء والمجتمع والبيت. كان التباين واضحاً. كانت حياتك تتغير باستمرار ، في حين يبدو أن حياة والديك قد توقفت. سبب هجرة عائلتك تسبب لك الكثير من الإثارة. في المدرسة بدأت تتعلمين أشياء عن كوريا باللغة الانجليزية، مكتوبة ويدرسها أجانب. بدت قصص كوريا خاطئة و متحيزة ومُصممة لتناسب الكتاب المدرسي الأمريكي. في الوقت نفسه ، كنت تلعبين، تتعلمين و تكبرين بلغة جيرانك. كنت جزءًا من كل شيء ، ولكن لم تكن جزءًا كاملا من شيء ما. كلما ابتعدت خارج عائلتي نحو المدرسة ، منازل الأصدقاء ، البلدات خارج إل سنترو ،كنت أجنبية ، فتاة آسيوية خجولة. كلما وطأت قدماي المنزل، كنت أمريكيَّة بدأت في مزج الكلمات الإنجليزية مع الجمل الكورية.

كنا الأقلية النموذجية. لقد نجحنا في المدرسة ، وتخرجنا بتفوق. أردنا أن نجعل والدينا فخورين ، لإثبات أن ساعات عملهم الدؤوبة في المتجر كانت تستحق كل هذا العناء. في خضم كل هذا، كنا منهمكين فلم نحتفل بالسنة القمرية الجديدة و لا بأعياد شوزوك ، ولم نقم بإجازات عائلية ولم نتحدث عن

التي نحتاجها. ربما سيكون هناك تعاون بين الطلاب وأعضاء هيئة التدريس والمسؤولين على جميع المستويات،أعتقد أن سماتنا الفريدة لها قيمة للجامعة: لدينا الانضباط للحصول على ما نحتاج إليه. نحن مستمرون في النضال. نحن نخلق الحلول التي يعتقد البعض الآخر أنها غير محتملة. كفاحنا يمنحنا تعاطفا ولطفا مع معاناة الآخرين. نحن بحاجة إلى الشعور بقيمتنا للتعبير عنها.

جذورنا ضمان لبقائنا على قيد الحياة. مع الدعم ، جذورنا ستسمح لنا بالنمو.

بإتمامي ل 4 سنوات هنا في جامعة فرجينيا، أتأمل تجربتي. لقد حصلت على تعليم جيد و أعتزم استخدامه. أنا أسف لعدم وجود مجتمع كبير لأولئك الذين يشتركون في خلفيات مماثلة لتجربتي. أفكر في الكثيرين الذين لا يصلون إلى خط النهاية. أعلم أن كفاحي ليس كفاحا خاصا بي وحسب، وأنا أتساءل كيف تمكنت بطريقة ما من التغلب على الصراعات التي تحملتها.

قصصنا قوية، لذلك دعونا نشاركها لتمكيننا نحن والآخرين من إحداث التغيير. من خلالنا ، جامعة فرجينيا هي جامعة رائعة وجيدة. دعنا ندعو جامعة فرجينيا لتجلس معنا على طاولة واحدة لنتحاور، و سنرى ما إذا كانت تستجيب

كلير سونغ

عزيزتي نفسي عندما كنت أصغر سنا،

جيمين ، كيف تشعرين اليوم؟ لقد مر وقت منذ أن تحدثت إليك آخر مرة ، أخيرًا أنا هنا ، مكان لم يكن ليخطر على بالك، أنا اتحدث معك قبل يوم من تخرجي من جامعة فرجينيا - مكان يبعد عنك أكثر من 2000 ميل

لقد كنت أفكر كثيرًا فيك مؤخرًا - في مئات الأسئلة التي لم تتمكني مطلقًا من طرحها على والدينا حول الانتقال إلى بلد آخر ، كم كان غريبًا الانتقال من مدينة كبيرة في كوريا أين يتحدث الجميع بلغة عائلتنا وأصدقائنا ، إلى أرض جافة صغيرة في ولاية أريزونا والتي غالبا ما تصل درجة الحرارة فيها إلى ثلاثة أرقام (فهرنهايت) خلال فصل الصيف. لقد شاهدتُ والدنا يرتدي قميصًا وسروالاً غير رسمي بدلاً من بدلة رسمية على طاولة الإفطار. رأيت بأم عينك كيف أن والدتنا لم تعد تعزف البيانو أو تدندن أسطرها المفضلة من فالس شوبان. كان المنزل صامتا طوال اليوم. فقط في الليل عند عودتها إلى المنزل من العمل سرعان ما امتلأ المنزل برائحة الأرز المطهو على البخار وصوت البرامج التلفزيونية الكورية. كانت حياتنا تتغير.

خلال طفولتنا ، لم أفكر مطلقًا في حياة والدينا في إل سنترو ، وكيف كان يبدو عالمهم صغيراً، الذي لم يمتد إلى ما وراء منزلهما ومتجرهما. يومهم كان مثل اليوم الموالي والذي بعده. لقد قمت بترجمة المحادثات من نفس الزبائن الذين يأتون للحصول على اللوازم المنزلية ، والوجبات الخفيفة في الصباح، والمشروبات الغازية والحلوى بعد الظهر. كان هناك القليل جدا في هذه المدينة الريفية من يمنحهم

في بعض الأحيان ، طلب المساعدة لا يكفي. عليك أن تقاتل من أجل ما تحتاجه. أتذكر أنني أخبرت في قد استلم رزمة الأوراق السنوية المطلوب مني (SFS) شهر مارس / آذار أن مكتب المساعدات المالية ملؤها. حل أغسطس، وبدأت الفصول الدراسية و لكن حتى تلك اللحظة لم يتم صرف أي منحة دراسية لي. قلت لنفسي "لا تقلق. المنحة الدراسية تتأخر معظم الفصول الدراسية. فقط كن صبورا". بعد ذلك استلمت رسالة بالبريد الإلكتروني تقول:

"لديك 3 أيام لدفع الرسوم الدراسية الخاصة بك قبل أن يتم الغاء التسجيل".

كل الفصول الدراسية التي كنت مسجلا بها كانت ممتلئة. بمجرد إلغاء التسجيل، لن أعود مرة أخرى الى هاتة الفصول. قال مكتب المنح إنني لم أكمل كافة المستندات. بعد إظهار التأكيد من الفصل الدراسي السابق ، قالوا إن طلبي سيتطلب معالجة من أسبوع إلى أسبوعين ، حيث يتعين على حالتي الانتظار في الطابور. لم يكن لدي هذا الكم من الوقت.

لحسن الحظ ، تذكرت حديثًا أدلى به عميد الطلاب في الفصل الدراسي السابق. ذكر العميد غروفز أنه يبدأ يومه في السابعة صباحًا بالرد على رسائل البريد الإلكتروني. أرسلت له عبر البريد الإلكتروني في تلك الليلة و أرفقت رسالة ببيان تأكيد التسجيل في شهر مارس. لم أفعل شيئًا خاطئًا ، وبالرغم من أنني كنت معزولًا في جامعة فرجينيا لم أكن لأرمي الفرصة الوحيدة التي منحت لي في الحياة. في صباح اليوم التالي ، أرسل طلبي إلى المدير المالي وتمت معالجت مشكلتي المالية بطريقة سحرية. السحر يتطلب معارف واتصالات مميزة. الكثير منا بالكاد يفهمون طريقة الحصول على المساعدات المالية ، ناهيك عن كيفية الوصول إلى عميد. لقد كان درسًا يجب أن أتعلمه.

واصلت رحلتي في جامعة فرجينيا معتقدا أنني كنت الوحيد الذي واجه هذه القضايا. ثم في شهر مارس ، اكتشفت مؤتمراً في واشنطن العاصمة لطلاب الجامعات من الجيل الأول الذي يزاول الجامعة، وذوي التحالف من أجل ذوي الدخل المنخفض وطلبة) AL1GN كان يطلق عليه (FGLI). الدخل المنخفض الجيل الأول ممن يزاولون الجامعة). بدافع الفضول، سجلت وحضرت. لقد غير المؤتمر حياتي. هناك تعلمت أنني لم أكن الوحيد الذي يواجه مثل تلك المشكلات. لقد وجدت مجتمعًا يمكن أن يتفهم معاناتي.

أصبحت متفائلا لدرجة أنني أحضرت المؤتمر إلى جامعة فرجينيا. كنت أعلم أنني أردت إحداث تغيير قبل التخرج وكان هذا المؤتمر هو ذلك التغيير. كان المؤتمر تجسيدا لبحثي عن مجتمع ، عن مكان أنتمي إليه. أردت أن ينتبه المسؤولون إلينا ويعلموا أننا هنا. نحن بحاجة لمساعدتهم. من السابق لأوانه معرفة ما إذا كان المؤتمر قد أنشأ هذا التغيير ، وبما أنني على وشك التخرج من هذا المجتمع وتركه، فقد لا أعرف ذلك أبدًا.

مع أوان مغادرتي ، لا يمكنني إلا أن أتمنى قدوم اليوم الذي يكون لدينا فيه مجتمع لتبادل خبراتنا والموارد التي لدينا. في يوم من الأيام ، ربما سيكون لدينا المزيد من المدافعين للمطالبة بالموارد

أخرى. لم يكن هناك مجتمع يتحد.

لحسن الحظ ، وجدت العزاء في العاملين في قاعة الطعام. كان لدينا في كثير من الأحيان جذور مماثلة. لم يكن ذلك دائمًا كافيًا لأنني لم أرهم طوال الوقت ، لكي كنت دائمًا ما أجد شخصا ما للتحدث إليه أثناء تناولي للطعام. قد لا يفهمني زملائي وأساتذتي ، لكن هؤلاء العمال يفهمونني دائما.

لم تكن الحياة في الجامعة مع منحة دراسية كاملة تذكرة للخروج من الفقر كما كنت أتوقع. في الواقع، كنت عالق بين عالمين. التوفيق بين الدراسة والمنزل كان صعبا للغاية. عائلتي استمرت في المعاناة وظللت أنا أساعد. اعتدت على التعامل مع حياتي في المنزل لوحدي. كانوا يدعوني. وأنا أستجيب:

يكلمونني بالهاتف: الشرطة داهمت المنزل في الليل ، وتمنع أمي من المغادرة للذهاب إلى العمل. لقد تم طردها من العمل. يعتقلون أخي.

أرد: أنا أتكفل بالإيجار حتى تجد عملاً وأرسل المال لشراء أدوات النظافة والطعام لأخي أثناء وجوده في السجن. ثم أنهي المكالمة وأعود إلى ورقتي.

يرن الهاتف: أخوك البالغ من العمر 13 عامًا أصيب بمرض وقيل انه لن يستيقظ. يتغيب زوج أمي عن العمل لنقله إلى المستشفى و يتم تسريحه بسبب ذلك.

أجيب على الهاتف: سأدفع فاتورة الكهرباء والبقالة بينما يجد عملاً. ثم أمشي إلى المحاضرة الأولى في اليوم.

يهاتفونني مجددا: يسمع مالك المنزل عن مداهمة الشرطة ، وينهي عقد الإيجار ، ويحترق منزل جدتي.

ومن ثم أتوجه إلى وظيفتي بدوام جزئي GoFundMe أجيب : لقد قمت بجمع 2000 دولار من موقع.

دفعتني معاناتهم إلى العمل بجد وتحقيق المزيد. بالنسبة لي ، كانت الدراسة أكثر من مجرد تحصيل علامات جيدة. كان علي أن أتعلم ليس فقط دعمهم ، لكن أن أدافع عن نفسي أيضا في جامعة فرجينيا، وكذلك المدافعة عن أولئك الذين يعانون من مواقف مماثلة. على سبيل المثال ، في وقت متأخر من إحدى الليالي، كنت أعمل على واجب منزلي كان علي تسليمه في الساعة الثامنة صباحًا في اليوم التالي. اتصل بي والدي من السجن ، وطلب المساعدة. بحلول نهاية المكالمة ، كانت الساعة 11:30 مساءً. كانت الأعمال متراكمة على منذ عدة ليال آنفا. ترددت قليلا قبل أن أرسل رسالة بالبريد الإلكتروني إلى أستاذي، حيث كشفت قليلاً عن حياتي ، ولأول مرة في الكلية ، طلبت تمديدًا. ولحسن الحظ أنه منحي التمديد. لقد اكتشفت أن طلب المساعدة أمر صعب ، ولكنه قد يكون مجزيًا أيضًا.

"لأن لدي الكثير من مدمني الكحوليات في عائلتي ولا أريد أن أعرف ما إذا كنت أحدهم".

ثم تنتهي المحادثة دومًا بنفس الطريقة:

"حسنا. تعرف ماذا! يجب أن تقابل صديق لي. دعني أقدمك!"

بالنسبة لهم، كانت قصتي رواية. بالنسبة لي، كانت قصتي طبيعية.

غالبا ما أتناسى هذه الحقيقة.

كنت أرغب في الانتماء، وأن يكون لدي أصدقاء وعلاقات، ولكن ليس على حساب جذوري. إن ماضي جزء من هويتي. لقد نشأت في مجتمع ريفي صغير في شاسفيل بولاية فرجينيا، حيث يعيش حوالي 1000 شخص فقط، حتى الغرباء كانوا مألوفين. نحن نفخر بتضامننا المتبادل، سواء كان بتوقُفنا لمساعدة شخص ما بسيارة معطلة، أو لجمع الأموال لمفجوع بموت مفاجئ لأحد أفراد أسرته، كنا دائمًا هناك لبعضنا البعض. فقُرُبنا جعلنا أكثر ابتكارا في كيفية حل مشاكلنا. لقد تعاملنا مع ما كان لدينا وشجع والدينا إبداعنا في كثير من الأحيان. أرى مجتمعي في شخصي مجسدا.

أرى أيضًا أجزاء من عائلتي في نفسي. لدي إصرار أمي المتقد. بغض النظر عما حدث لنا، كانت دائما تجد حلا. إذا كنا بحاجة إلى معاطف لفصل الشتاء، سألت جيش الخلاص. إذا احتجنا إلى الطعام، فستقدم طلبًا للحصول على طوابع الغذاء والعثور على مخزن للأطعمة. إذا كنا بحاجة إلى الدفع عندما يكون الجو باردًا، فسوف تطلب من الكنيسة دفع الكهرباء. رغم كل عيوبها، علمتني أمي أن أكون مبتكرا وان اطلب المساعدة. أمي علمتني القوة.

لدي كاريزما والدي. والدي من النوع الذي يتحدث إلى أي شخص. انه يجعل حتى الغرباء يشعرون وكأنهم أصدقاء لم يروهم منذ زمن. على الرغم من كل عيوبه، والدي غالبا ما كان سخيا. كان يعمل كسائق مقطورة جرار. عندما ذهبت معه في رحلات، كثيرًا ما واجهنا المتسولين. حتى لو لم يكن لوالدي الكثير من المال، فقد كان دائمًا يشتري لهم وجبة. من خلال والدي، كان كل كياني يتدرب على اللطف والكاريزما والإبداع.

هذه الجذور ساعدتني على البقاء. في البيئة المثالية، تسمح لي جذوري بالنمو والازدهار.

بعد فترة وجيزة من وصولي إلى جامعة فرجينيا، وبعد كل هذه المحادثات الافتتاحية، بدأت في البحث عن مجتمع يشاركني نفس الجذور. لقد وجدت مجموعة طلابية اسمها يونايتد للتنوع الاجتماعي والاقتصادي (UFUSED) والتي كانت تزمع عقد اجتماعها القادم. أتذكر أنني كنت أركض في يوم عاصف، تبللت من رأسي إلى أخمص قدمي، وصلت و وجدت حجرة دراسية بها حوالي خمسة طلاب للحضور، اثنان منهم هما القائدان. لم يناقشوا الكثير وانتهى الاجتماع بعد فترة وجيزة. لم تكن هناك اجتماعات

جوشوا فارس

في الأول من كانون الأول (ديسمبر) 2014 ، غيّرت رسالة إلكترونية حياتي. قرأت فقط الكلمات الثلاث الأولى (UVA). "عزيزي جوش ، تهانينا!" لقد تلقيت للتو منحة دراسية كاملة لجامعة فرجينيا لي ، كانت هذه المنحة هي تذكرتي الذهبية إلى واحدة من أفضل الجامعات في البلاد. كنت أحلم بهذا اليوم لأكثر من سبع سنوات. كانت فرصة لحياة مستقرة. حفزني هذا الحلم بما يكفي للالتحاق بمدرستين بالإضافة إلى العمل في مطعم ماكدونالدز المحلي وتناول العشاء طوال سنوات الدراسة الثانوية. كنت أستيقظ كل يوم

في الخامسة صباحًا لأخلد للنوم بعد كل منتصف ليلٍ متعبا ، كنت أكافح للحفاظ على هذه الوتيرة.

بعد ثمانية أشهر من استلامي لرسالة المنحة ، غادرت المنزل بحماس وتوجهت إلى جامعة فرجينيا.

لسوء الحظ ، شعرت بغربة شديدة لحظة وصولي إلى الحرم الجامعي. شعرت بأن الأعمدة الرخامية على الطراز اليوناني مختلفة تمامًا عن المنازل المؤقتة المتراصة والمجمعات السكنية المبنية من الطوب والتي اعتدت على العيش فيها.أما عن تكوين صداقات، فالأمر كان صعبا أيضا. أتذكر أنني في أحد حفلات سُئلت تلك الأسئلة النمطية التي يطرحها الطلاب ، "ما اسمك؟ ما هو تخصصك؟ من أين أنت؟ "كان هناك دائمًا سؤال واحد يؤدي في النهاية إلى السقوط في الارتباك:

"ماذا يفعل والداك؟"

حسنًا ، أمي لا تعمل الآن. والِدي بالتبني هو حارس في السجن وأبي مسجون " عادة ما آخذ رشفة ماء وأنا أقول ذلك.

"هاه؟"

وعادة ما يؤدي هذا إلى سلسلة من الأسئلة التي أشعر بالراحة في الإجابة عليها ، لكنها غير مريحة للمستمع:

"حقا؟ ، هل يمكنني أن أسأل لماذا سجن أبوك؟"

"المخدرات ، معظمها من نوع الكوكايين."

"هذا فضيع. ماذا تشرب أنت؟"
"الماء". آخذ رشفة ماء".

"لماذا؟" مع جبين مجعد.

معظم أساتذتي ملتزمين بالمناهج الدراسية حرفيا وركزوا فقط على تقديم الدروس التي بين أيديهم. كانوا مهتمين في الغالب بإنهاء المقررات وتحقيق الأهداف المسطرة لهم، وهي أهداف لم تتغير منذ عقود.

أعتقد أن النظام التعليمي نفسه محاصر في منطقة الراحة الخاصة به لأن معلمي المدارس والإداريين لا يفكرون خارج الصندوق. هذه الحقيقة يمكن أن تعزى لأسباب عديدة. أولا بالنظر إلى الفجوة العمرية، لا يمكنهم الارتباط بالطلاب و معرفة ما يريدون. مسؤولوا قطاع التربية ينشئون مدارس لا تراعي آراء الطلاب في تصميمها. إنه نظام هرمي للغاية. يبدو محصنا ضد الابتكار والخروج على المألوف. لسوء الحظ، ما زلنا نستخدم نفس النظام التعليمي الذي أكل الدهر عليه وشرب، ونفس المواد الدراسية والاستراتيجيات نفسها لتدريس كل جيل، على الرغم من فجوة التفكير الواضحة وعلى الرغم من الاختلافات الشاسعة بين الواقعين. وبالتالي، يصبح من المستحيل تقريبًا على المعلمين إضافة بعض المواد الجديدة من أجل مواكبة ما يحدث في العالم. هذا على الرغم من وجود العديد من الدراسات الجديدة التي يمكن الاعتماد عليها من أجل مساعدة الطلاب والمعلمين على العمل بشكل أفضل في الفصل، هذه التقنيات التعليمية من شأنها أن تناقش القضايا العالمية وتتطرق إليها، والتي ستنتج تطورًا في مستوى الطلاب وطريقة تفكيرهم. بالطبع، هناك مدارس خاصة تتماشى مع العالم وتطور أساليب جديدة، لكن ليس كل شخص في الجزائر قادر على تحمل تكاليفها. التمدرس بالمدارس الخاصة ليس شائعًا جدًا، خاصة في المدن الصغيرة مثل مدينتي.

بمجرد وصولي إلى الجامعة، أتيحت لي الفرصة لتوسيع أفاق. على الرغم من أن النظام التعليمي والمناهج على المستوى الجامعي ليسا مبدعين حقًا أيضًا، إلا أنهما يتضمنان منظورًا أحسن قليلاً عندما يتعلق الأمر بالمعرفة. يستخدم بعض أساتذتي في الجامعة طرقًا مختلفة ومبتكرة عند التدريس، وهي أساليب لها دور كبير في تشكيل قدراتي القيادية بشكل أكبر. يشجع الكثير منهم القراءة والمناقشات والتفكير النقدي، وهو مفهوم رئيسي في بناء قائد طموح مبدع، من أجل تعليمه / ها التفكير المستقل، ورؤية الأشياء من وجهات نظر مختلفة. سمح لي التواجد في الجامعة أيضًا بالمشاركة في المؤتمرات الوطنية والدولية، والتعرف على أفكار الآخرين وقصصهم ورؤاهم ونقدهم الإيجابي، كما أتيحت لي الفرصة للمشاركة في العديد من الأنشطة، مثل الأندية الجامعية، والنشاطات اللاصفية، وحتى فرص التبادل. كل هذه لا تزال تساعدني ولكل منها دور رئيسي في إعدادي لأصبح قائدة في المجتمع المدني.

أعتقد اعتقادا راسخا أن الفصول الدراسية النشطة، مع المعلمين المتحمسين، سواء في المدارس المتوسطة أو الثانوية أو الجامعة، ضرورية لإنتاج جيل من القادة المستعدين لإجراء التغيير. كمُدرِسة مستقبلية، و بالرغم من أنه يجب أن أعمل وفق المناهج المقررة حيث لا يسعني إلا أن أعمل وفقه، أعتقد أنه يجب على جميع المعلمين التوصل إلى أفكار واستراتيجيات مبتكرة لنشر المعرفة والوعي في الفصل الدراسي. إذا كان المعلم "مخدرًا"، فسيكون الطلاب كذلك وسيخلقون فقط كأعضاء سلبيين في المجتمع. سوف يكبر هؤلاء الطلاب ليصبحوا بالغين متشائمين مهمشين، والذين يفضلون الجلوس وترك الحياة تمر بدلاً من التحرك نحو شيء عظيم. من شأن الطلاب المتعلمين بشكل صحيح أن يمارسوا ضغطًا كبيرًا على من هم في السلطة من خلال انتقادهم وإيجاد حل للمشاكل التي square تواجه بلدانهم.

ثم يضايقونني لأخبرهم من أحب الآن،
أبدأ بسؤال أي شخص يرغب في الاستماع،
فقط لكي أجد شخصًا غيرهم للجلوس معه عند الغداء.

أنا أدعي أني بخير عندما يقول كل شخص لا.

هل تتذكر الطريقة التي يمكن أن يتحول بها اللون القرمزي إلى وصمة عار على بشرتي الشفافة؟

في الصف السابع:
أفضل صديقة لي تحصل على خليل
عند ترتيبنا في المجموعة على أساس مدى جاذبيتنا.
أحصل على صفر.

في الصف الثامن
ألف ذراعي حول كتفي داني
كما فعلت عدة مرات من قبل.

العضة التي خلفتها لا تتلاشى
حتى بعد أشهر
عندما كنت منعزلة مع نفسي
في الحمام في الطابق السفلي
، و أخواتي تركلن الباب
وأنا أضغط بسكين
في فخذي للمرة الخامسة.

الحرب التي أخوضها كل يوم ، أصعب في الليل
لذلك أهاتف كايل وأبكي.

لكن أنا هنا.
وأنا على قيد الحياة.

جمانة هديل بوغازي

تعد سنوات المدرسة المتوسطة والثانوية جزءًا أساسيًا في عملية بناء شخصياتنا. في غضون ذلك الوقت نبدأ في معرفة من نحن ، ما نريد ، ونستخدم كل شيء لبناء شخصيتنا ، لنصبح قادة الغد. كل ذلك يأتي من خلال المعلمين والمناهج الدراسية. ومع ذلك ، أود أن أقول أن مدرستيَّ الإعدادية و الثانوية لم تقدما حقًا أي مساهمة كبيرة في بناء كريادية في المجتمع المدني أو بالأحرى لم تسهما فيها إطلاقا. كان

المساواة مهمة للغاية خاصة وأن المراهقين لا يزالون في طور النضوج ومن المهم تشكيل وجهات نظرهم بشكل عام. هذه مشكلة مستمرة داخل المجتمع تحتاج إلى معالجة وتطوير.

غابريال هيرسي
المدرسة الإبتدائية

آخر مرة حدث هذا ، لم ينته الامر بهذا الشكل.

ولكن مرة أخرى ، لم تكن حياتي سهلة.

تبدأ مشاكلي في الصف الثاني:
يسألني كيلي إن كنت أريد ركوب الدراجات في طريق مسدود.

ذاكرتي تتخطى إلى الأمام.

مزيج مربك من الألوان غير الواضحة والحركات السريعة
في حين يتم رشقي بالصخور من اتجاهات غير مرئية ،
ضحك الأطفال الذين يلقون الحجارة من كل مكان ،
كيلي تصرخ بألفاظ نابية لم أسمع بها في حياتي ،
وميا تجرني إلى الممر ،
قميص أبيض يضغط على الجرح أسفل ذراعي.

لن أنسى أبدًا الطريقة التي يبدو بها الدم أثناء الانزلاق ببطء فوق الجلد.

في الصف الثالث
كل ما أعرفه هو عندما قرصني ولوى القرصة ليؤلمني أكثر ،
بكل قوته ،
آلمني ذلك
أسوأ من ذلك حين سقطت من سفينة القراصنة ذات شكل شجرة الكمثرى.

كانت كيلي هناك ، لكنها ترفض أن تخبرني.

في الصف السادس
أصدقائي يفصلونني عن أجمل ولد قابلته على الإطلاق.

إسمي مليسا. بالنظر إلى أني نصف بيضاء ونصف فلبينية ، اعتدت أن أكون أعمق شخص في الغرفة لوناً من حيث البشرة. لم يزعجني ذلك أبدًا ، ربما لأني لم أكن ضحية للعنصرية أبدًا. ومع ذلك ، فإن الأشخاص الآخرين من ذوي اللون من مدرستي الثانوية لم يحالفهم نفس الحظ. المدرسة الثانوية التي التحقت بها كان بها 28% من طلاب الأقليات. بسبب هذا ، كان من الشائع جدًا أن يشعر الأشخاص ذوو اللون في مدرستي بأنهم دخلاء. من حين لآخر يتعرض هؤلاء للازدراء العنصري وفي أحيان أخرى يشهر بعض الطلاب العلم الكونفدرالي بالكامل ، ولا يتم فعل أي شيء على الإطلاق حول هذا الأمر. أعتقد أن التمييز لم يكن موجَّهًا إليَّ أبدًا ، ولم ألاحظ مدى سوء الأمور حتى السنة الإعدادية في المدرسة الثانوية ، والمعروفة بالسنة التي انتخب فيها دونالد ترامب رئيسًا.

في البداية كانت الأمور متحضرة للغاية. لم يكن سراً أن غالبية مدرستي كانوا جمهوريين أيدوا ترامب ، لذلك إذا كان لديك آراء سياسية مختلفة ، فقد تم فحصك تلقائيًا ، وهذا ربما كان السبب في أني لم أكن أتحدث بصوت عالٍ عن بلدي في المدرسة الثانوية. كانت هناك مجموعة من الأشخاص في مدرستي على الرغم من أنهم يتشاركون الآراء مع الأغلبية ، إلا أنهم كانوا "The Hicks" يشار إليها غالبًا باسم هم الذين أخذوا الأمور أبعد مما كانت عليه. لقد أدلوا باستمرار بتعليقات تمييزية وقحة ، خاصة تجاه الطلاب ذوي الأصول الأسبانية. إحدى صديقاتي المقربات كانت من بورتوريكو وانتهى الأمر بها أن كانت من بين طلاب الأقليات العديدين الذين تلقوا تهديدات عديدة قبل الانتخابات. حتى أنا تلقيت بعض التهديدات. على الرغم من كون هذه التهديدات غير محتملة الحدوث بشكل أساسي ، إلا أنها كانت تهديدات. اختلفت التهديدات في الجدية والقساوة، بعضها شفهي والبعض الآخر عبر وسائل التواصل الاجتماعي. كان اليوم الذي أعقب فوز ترامب بالانتخابات أحد الأيام القلائل في حياتي التي كنت خائفة فيها من الذهاب إلى المدرسة. لحسن الحظ ، لم أكن من الذين استهدفتهم مجموعة "هيكس" في مدرستي. ظهر العلم الكونفدرالي ليس فقط في موقف السيارات ملحقا بشاحنة بيك آب عملاقة ، بل ظهر أيضًا على عدة مبان في المدرسة. قبل لي عدة مرات أني سأتعرض للترحيل ، لكن هذا كان أقسى ما مررت به ، وهذا ليس سيئًا مقارنة بما تعرض له الآخرون في مدرستي. اقتربت مني أفضل صديقة عندما كنت أهم بفتح خزانتي والدموع في عينيها. كنت في حالة صدمة كاملة عندما أظهرت لنا خزانتها التي تعرضت للتخريب وكتب عليها عبارات مهينة و تهديدات ، وبالطبع ، تم إرفاقها بإشارة تقول "لنجعل أمريكا عظيمة مرة أخرى". لم تكن صديقتي هي الوحيدة بل إن الكثير استُقبِلُوا ذلك الصباح بخزائن مخربة وعبارات عنصرية. رغم أننا أبلغنا على الفور بالحادث ، ومع ذلك ، لم يتم فعل أي شيء، لأن الكثير من الأشخاص كانوا متورطين ولم ترغب مدرستي في أي دعاية سلبية أكثر مما كانت عليه المدرسة بالفعل. كانت هذه هي المرة الأولى التي أدركت فيها حجم العنصرية في مدرستي. كانت مجموعة من الأطفال في مدرستي عنصرية بشكل علني ولم تفعل مدرستنا شيئًا حيال ذلك. هذا أغضبني أكثر من أي شيء منذ فترة. لم أكن أعرف ماذا أفعل أو كيف أساعد ، لكني عرفت بعد ذلك أن هناك حاجة لتغيير شيء ما.

إن معرفة أن هذه الأحداث قد حدثت يجعلنا ندرك أن التغيير ضروري للقضاء على التمييز العنصري الذي يحدث في المدارس. بينما نعلم أنه لا يمكن إصلاحه تمامًا ، فإن خطة العمل ستكون خلق المزيد من التعليم حول ماهية التمييز بالضبط وكيف يؤثر على غالبية سكاننا. تعتبر معاملة الجميع على قدم

ميليسا ميركادو و ديفيا باريتي

من الصعب أن نفهم كيف يمكن لشخص ما أن يكره شخصًا آخر بسبب بسيط كلون بشرته ؛ ومع ذلك ، لا يزال هذا الامر يحدث في زمننا. يضع الناس افتراضات حول الآخرين من دون حتى محاولة التعرف عليهم. كنا محظوظتين لأننا لم نخض تجارب مع العنصرية بشكل شخصي، لكن هذا لا يعني أننا لم نشهدها على الإطلاق. في الواقع ، نشأنا في مجتمعات بيضاء في الغالب لكننا شاهدنا بأم أعيننا العنصرية بشكل متكرر. على الرغم من أن بلدنا قطع شوطًا طويلًا في مكافحة العنصرية، إلا أنها لا تزال قضية رئيسية منتشرة ليس فقط في الولايات المتحدة ، ولكن في جميع أنحاء العالم. هذا شيء لا يدركه الكثير من الناس، ولديهم الكثير من المفاهيم الخاطئة حول العنصرية. التعريف الرسمي للعنصرية هو التحيز أو التمييز أو العداء الموجه ضد شخص من جنس مختلف على أساس الاعتقاد بأن جنس الفرد هو الأفضل. سواء كنت قد لاحظت ذلك أم لا ، فإن أعمال العنصرية لا تزال حوادث شائعة ، لا سيما في الأوساط الأكاديمية. من العار أن يشعر بعض الطلاب بعدم الأمان في المدرسة أو الجامعة بسبب
العنصرية.

منذ أيام المدرسة الثانوية، شهدنا نصيبنا الأوفر من الظلم العنصرية وهنا قصصنا:

اسمي ديفيا وأنا هندية ولدت وترعرعت في نابرفيل،إلينوي، في مجتمع ليس متنوعًا كثيرا ، حيث 68% من سكانه من البيض. منذ أن كنت طفلة ، اضطررت إلى التكيف مع المعايير الاجتماعية المتعلقة بالثقافة. أتذكر بوضوح عندما كنت في الصف الثاني، أحضرت طعامًا تقليديا من المنزل، وعندما هممت بتناوله، أخبرتني إحدى الفتيات أنه يبدو مثيرا للاشمئزاز ورائحته غريبة. ثم أخبرتني أن لون بشرتي لون خاطئٌ وأنني لا أنتمي إلى هناك. بعد ذلك ، لم أتجرأ على إحضار الطعام الهندي للمدرسة مرة أخرى. على الرغم من أن هذا كان أمرا صغيراً ، إلا أنه ما زال يؤثر علي بطرق لن أنساها أبدًا. كان والدي يحضّر لي علبة الأرز لأخذها معي، أما أنا فكنت أختلق الأعذار لعدم أخذه. اعتدت أن أقول أنه كان يتناثر ويسبب لي الفوضى أو أنه يصبح باردًا جدًا بحلول وقت تناول الغداء. استمرت هذه الأعذار تتراكم وأعتقد في ذلك الوقت أني كنت أصدق ما كنت أخبر والديّ به. ومع ذلك ، بالنظر إلى ذلك الآن ، أستطيع أن أرى أنني كنت أحاول الحفاظ على صورتي كهندية "بيضاء". مع تقدمي في السن ، كنت أحاول بصعوبة أكبر وإخفاء ثقافتي والتصرف بمزيد من تصرفات ذوي "اللون الأبيض" من أجل الاندماج. وإذا اضطررت للذهاب إلى المعبد ، فسأقول إن عليّ الذهاب إلى الكنيسة أو تكوين كذبة مختلفة. عندما وصلت إلى المدرسة الثانوية ، كنت معتادة على إخفاء هويتي الهندية. الحدث الوحيد الذي شهدته والدي كان أكثر أثراً في كان في سني الإعدادية. جاء أحد التلاميذ يلف العلم الكونفدرالي حول جسده وكان اكتشفت أن الطالب فيما بعد. (MAGA) "يرتدي قبعة مكتوب عليها "لنجعل أمريكا عظيمة مرة أخرى تم إيقافه ؛ ومع ذلك ، فإن حقيقة اعتقاده أنه من الجيد الترويج لتلك المُثل العنصرية جعلني غير مرتاحة للغاية. طوال المرحلة الثانوية ، شاهدت أحداث مختلفة كالعدوان الخفي والعنصرية الموموة؛ ومع ذلك ، لم أكن متأكدة تمامًا من كيفية الرد عليها. كل ما كنت أعلمه هو أنه يلزم القيام بشيء ما حيال هذه المظالم.

الدراسي. إن تعليم طلاب الرياضيات الصعبة بكل بساطة يزيد من التوقعات ويعلم المعارف الجديدة. هذا هو النضال بالنسبة لي. ثانياً ، أتت هذه التجربة بثقة كانت تكمن في داخلي في السابق. أستاذي بالجامعة ناقش معنا نظرية المعرفة والسلطة بطريقة غيرت تماما فهمي لكلا المفهومين. بدأت أقدر معرفتي الخاصة والمعرفة الخاصة بالمجموعات المهمشة الأخرى ، وهو شيء لم أفعله من قبل. هذا غرس في داخلي شعوراً بالقوة. أتفهم الآن أن هناك أشكالًا مختلفة من المعرفة ، يمكن أن تبدو القوة بأشكال عديدة ، وتكمن القوة في كل شخص. ثقتي المكتسبة حديثًا وفهمي النظري أصبح القوة الموجهة لنضالي.

على المستوى الجزئي ، لقد نجحت في نضالي. لسوء الحظ ، لا تؤدي أفعالي إلى القضاء على المظالم المجتمعية المتعلقة بالمنظومة ككل ، والتي ترسخ نفسها داخل أنظمة حسنة النية مثل برامج الولوج إلى الجامعة ، ولا على المستوى العالمي حيث يمكن أن يكون الظلم أكبر. مع ذلك ، سأكون مجحفة إذا لم أعترف بأن الولايات المتحدة تتفوق كثيرًا على العديد من البلدان الأخرى في الكفاح من أجل المساواة في التعليم. يوجد حاليًا بلدان لا يُسمح للنساء فيها بالحصول على التعليم. يسود الظلم التعليمي في جميع أنحاء العالم بعمق عند الأشخاص الذين يعانون من تدني الموارد الإقتصادية و الأشخاص الملونون والنساء. تماما مثلما يهدد انعدام العدالة في صفي الدراسي بنشر انعدام العدالة خارج الفصل ، فإن الظلم التعليمي للمجموعات المهمشة يهدد عدالة المجتمع ككل، وفي العديد من الحالات يهدد وجودهم. المجتمع يعكس التعليم والعالم مكان غير متكافئ. كما أوضح هوريس مان ، فإن الكفاح من أجل العدالة التعليمية هو الكفاح من أجل المساواة بين البشر، الامر نفسه أشار إليه الدكتور كينغ بقوله: إذا كان الظلم موجودًا في مكان ما ، فإن العدالة مهددة في مكان آخر.

أليكس جرانر

ركز جزء كبير من إصلاح التعليم خلال القرن التاسع عشر على محاولة القضاء على التمييز ومنح الحقوق للأقليات داخل النظم المدرسية. ركزت التشريعات الرئيسية مثل الباب الأول (1965) ، والباب السادس (1964) ، وقانون التعليم العالي (1965) جميعها على تحسين المدارس الفقيرة ، وخاصة المدارس التي تضم أعدادا كبيرة من أبناء الأقليات. الكثير من هذا يرتبط بحركة الحقوق المدنية الأمريكية الأفريقية في الولايات المتحدة خلال الخمسينيات والستينيات ، والتي عملت على تعزيز المساواة. ومع ذلك ، فإن تكوين الأقليات العرقية داخل الولايات المتحدة قد تغير خلال العقد الماضي. بالإضافة إلى زيادة عدد المهاجرين اللاتينيين ، فقد شهدت الولايات المتحدة في السنوات الأخيرة تدفقًا هائلاً من المهاجرين من الشرق الأوسط وشمال إفريقيا أيضا. لم يتم تأهيل نظام التعليم الحالي لاستيعاب هؤلاء الطلاب الجدد - ولا يبدو أنه نجح في إعادة بناء نفسه للاعتراف بالمهارات التي يجلبها الأمريكيون الأفارقة إلى الفصول الدراسية. على هذا النحو ، غالبًا ما يُنظر إلى ثقافة ولغة ودين طلاب الشرق الأوسط وشمال إفريقيا على أنها حواجز أمام نجاحهم. من أجل تلبية احتياجات جميع الطلاب ، يجب إعادة هيكلة النظام بأكمله. تكون فيه الفصول مصممة للطلاب حيث اللغة الإنجليزية القياسية ليست هي اللغة الوحيدة ذات القيمة ، حيث يوجد احترام للممارسات الدينية ، والقبول المنهجي لجميع الثقافات ضروري لجعل مدارس الولايات المتحدة شاملة ومصممة خصيصًا لنجاح جميع الطلاب بدون استثناء.

هو الحال
دائمًا ، فقد ظلوا عالقين في نظام يفشل باستمرار في خلق تحد لطلاب مثلهم.
الرياضيات هي بوابة الولوج للجامعة. يمكن أن يكون بمثابة حاجز يعيق دخولهم للجامعات ، أو يمكن أن يكون نافذة للحصول على شهادة جامعية. بمجرد الالتحاق بالكلية ، يكون الطلاب الذين لم يكملوا برنامج الجبر 2 في المدرسة الثانوية أقل احتمالًا في الالتحاق ببرنامج الرياضيات الذي يمكنهم من الحصول على الأرصدة الأكاديمية، وهذا بدوره غالبا ما يحدد ما إذا كان الطالب سيستمر في الجامعة أو يتسرب منها. يتجسد هذا المشكل بشكل أكثر لدى الطلاب ذوي الدخل المنخفض والطلاب الملونين.
تعد الرياضيات في المدرسة الثانوية عاملاً محددًا في نجاح الجامعة ، كما أن الطلاب الذين يتركون الدراسة بالجامعة بسبب ذلك هم من هذه الفئات المجتمعية. لذا ، أين هي العدالة في دروس التقوية للطلاب لمادة الرياضيات من أصحاب ذوي الدخل المنخفض والطلاب الملونين؟ لا يوجد. إنه في الواقع يزيد من فرص الفشل في الكلية ، وبالتالي المساهمة في عدم المساواة ، مما يهدد العدالة التي يسعى البرنامج للحصول عليها. عندما جلست شاري وألانا في فصل تقوية مادة الرياضيات ، كانت حظوظ شاري في أن تصبح مهندسة في خطر. الطلاب البيض والأثرياء الذين أرادوا أن يصبحوا أطباء سيكون لديهم قدم أسبق على ألانا، أما أنا فقد تعهدت بالكفاح لتصحيح أخطاء هذا الظلم ، ضد برنامج لم يكن بالتأكيد يخدم الطلاب الذين يعانون من التهميش والذي صمم أصلا لخدمة هذه الشريحة.

كثير من الناس لديهم توقعات متدنية للطلاب ذوي اللون وذوي الدخل المنخفض. والسبب في ذلك: العنصرية. لا يزال "تعصب التوقعات المتدنية" يؤثر على الطلاب لفترة طويلة بعد التخرج من المدرسة الثانوية. برامج حق الولوج إلى الجامعة لا تفعل سوى ما يشير إليه هذا الاسم : منح حق الولوج. معظمهم لا يفعلون شيئاً لمساعدة الطلاب بمجرد التحاقهم بالجامعة. هذا يشير إلى أن برامج الولوج إلى الجامعات متجذرة في الظلم والتهميش ، مما يؤدي إلى استمرار عدم المساواة وتوسيع فجوة الفرص. كان هذا الإدراك صعب للغاية بالنسبة لي. كان علي أن أسأل نفسي "ماذا يمكنني أن أفعل؟" لقد قمت بتدريس الرياضيات في المدرسة الثانوية لفترة كافية ورأيت هذا الظلم من قبل مع العديد من الطلاب. المدارس تفشل في خدمة الطلاب ذوي اللون والطلاب الفقراء في كل وقت. لا يتم تلبية احتياجات الطلاب على مستوى واحد وهذا يؤدي إلى الفشل في المستوى اللاحق. يحدث ذلك مرارًا وتكرارًا ولكنه ليس أقل من ذي قبل. وهكذا ، فهمت أن التقاعس من جانبي سيكون مكلفًا للغاية بالنسبة لطلابي ومن ثم اخترت إعادة كتابة منهج الرياضيات الخاص ببرنامج الولوج إلى الجامعة.

كانت الحصة التي أدرسها تعقد مرة في الأسبوع ولكن ما تعلمته لا يقدر بثمن. أولاً ، لقد تعلمت التعريف الحقيقي للنضال، وهو ليس معقدًا كما كنت أعتقد سابقًا. جلب أستاذي في الجامعة العديد من المتحدثين إلى الفصل وتحدثوا عن التعبئة المجتمعية. كانت كل قصة من قصص المتحدثين مختلفة ، لكن كان لديهم جميعًا نقطة مشتركة في نسيج رواياتهم: يمكن أن نكون جميعًا نشطاء مناضلون. النشاط يعني أن المرء يستخدم سلطته الخاصة لإحداث التغيير ، مهما كان صغيرًا. يمكن أن توجد في أصغر الأشياء التي نقوم بها كل يوم. باستخدام برنامج الولوج إلى الجامعة ، استخدمت معرفتي بتدريس الرياضيات للتخلص من التعصب الخاص بالتوقعات المتدنية لشرائح مجتمعية معينة داخل الفصل

أنني مسؤول عن العثور عليها بنفسي.

مزيد من المشاركة:

مونيكا ميلز

ذات مرة كان لديّ طالبين والذين سأدعوهما ب"شاري" و"ألانا" لأخفي اسميهما. كانتا توأمين متطابقتين و ذكيتان للغاية. نعم ، كل طلابي أذكياء للغاية ، ولكن "شاري" و"ألانا" مميزتان. كانتا أكثر الذين قابلتهم عبقرية في حياتي. شاري كانت ترغب في أن تكون مهندسة، أما ألانا فكانت تحلم بأن تصبح طبيبة. لطالما توقعت أن تقوم شاري بتصميم مستشفى يوفر إمكانية العلاج الشامل بطرق مبتكرة في حين أن ألانا ستكتشف الأجسام المضادة الذاتية التي لديها القدرة على علاج الألم الأكثر حدة. بعد ذلك ، سوف تفوزان بجائزة نوبل للسلام المشتركة لابتكاراتهما التي تعمل جنبا إلى جنب لمساعدة أولئك الذين يعانون من الألم الجسدي.

بقولي هذا من الممكن حتى أني قللت من قدراتهم.

في اليوم الأول من الفصل الدراسي ، كانت شاري و ألانا أول الطلاب هناك ، تجلسان جنبًا إلى جنب ، في الصف الأمامي الأوسط. ابتسامتهما تملأ محياهما، وبشرتهم المخملية المتلألئة وتجاعيد الشعر النابض الكبير جعلتهما مميزتين حتى أثناء وجودهما في غرفة ممتلئة عن آخرها بالطلاب. ولكن كان حماسهما للتعلم يعادل حماسة بقية الأطفال لفترة الاستراحة، هذا ما جعلهما أكثر تميزا. لقد جاءتا إلى الفصل لتعلم أكبر قدر ممكن ، آملتين في استخدام التحصيل والتميز للدخول إلى أفضل كلية ، وبدء حياتيهما المهنية بنجاح.

في يوم سبت، قمت بإجراء اختبار لحل المعادلات التربيعية. كعادتي قمت بتمشيط الفصل الدراسي أثناء تقييم طلابي. قام كل من شاري و ألانا بعمل ممتاز تمامًا. كانت علاماتهما متساوية دائمًا وكُتبت كل خطوة بترميز رياضي مثالي. مثل أي عالم رياضيات تقومان بعملهما بدقة تشبه الكمال ، وقد قام التوأم بعمل بارع في مجال الرياضيات العددية البالغ التعقيد. كلاهما أنهيتا بسرعة و وضعتا أقلام الرصاص على الطاولة. أثناء انتظار زملائهما في الفصل لإكمال اختباراتهم ، نظرت بعمق في وجهيهما في لحظة سأتذكرها ما حييت. رأيت فيها عاطفة لا يمكن للمرء أن يفهمها إلا من خلال التجربة. لم تعودا " شاري وألانا" اللتان عرفتهما في اليوم الأول من الفصل. تحول حماستهما إلى الملل. لقد بدتا وكأنهما تتساءلان عن وجاهة دراستهما لهذه المادة، والعمل الذي يتعين عليهما القيام به من أجلها. تعبيرات وجهيهما كانت تبعث بإشارة واضحة لخيبة الأمل بطريقة فريدة. كان من الواضح لي أنهما تحتاجان إلى أكثر بكثير مما كنت أعطي.

في وقت لاحق ، جلست و أوراق أجوبة الاختبار مكدسة أمامي. تلقى الجميع تقريبًا علامات كاملة. لم أكن أعتقد مطلقًا أنني سأشعر بالضيق بعد اتمام مثل هذا العمل الهائل. شعرت بنوع من الإحباط ، مشابهٍ لما رأيته على وجهي شاري وألانا. جالت بفكري كلمات واحاسيس أخرى من دون كلمات ، تخبرني أن طلابي يريدون أشياء أكثر مما في المنهاج الدراسي للرياضيات المطلوب للولوج إلى الجامعة. ومثلما

كيف يمكن للمدارس تعليم مهارات التفكير والتحليل النقدي بشكل أكثر فعالية؟ حسنًا ، في نظري ، يتعلق الأمر بالتفكير بشكل مستقل وقبول وجهات النظر الأخرى. هناك بعض الاستراتيجيات التي يمكن للمدرس استخدامها في الفصل الدراسي لإثارة هذه المشكلات والمناظرات ، بدء الجلسة الصفية بسؤال يحتوي على إجابات متعددة تجعل الطلاب يتساءلون عن موضوع ما هذه طريقة رائعة لفتح مناقشات مفيدة. أؤمن أيضًا أن تشجيع التعلم القائم على المشاريع وحل المشكلات يمكن أن يضمن النجاح في العالم الحقيقي خارج المدرسة وليس فقط داخلها.

بشرى رحموني

أعتقد أننا نتشارك نفس الفكرة هنا. يعطي العديد من المعلمين في بلدنا لطلابهم فكرة خاطئة مفادها أنه إذا حفظ الطالب حفظا عن ظهر قلب، تحصل على علامات جيدة، وهذا بدوره يعني أنهم أذكياء و مجدون!

أعتقد أنه يجب أن يكون هناك طريقة مختلفة لتقديم الدروس واختبار قدرات الطلاب لإعدادهم لمستقبلهم. تلك الموضوعات التي تناولناها في المدارس الابتدائية والمتوسطة والثانوية مفيدة - لا أحد ينكر ذلك، لكن إشراك الطلاب في شؤون المجتمع والاستماع إلى آرائهم سيحدث فرقًا. تحصل الشخصية على شكلها الكامل بدءًا من الطفولة. إذا كان هذا يعني شيئًا، فإنه يعني أنه ينبغي على المربين اكتشاف الطاقات الداخلية لكل طفل وغرس المبادئ والقيم الصحيحة بما في ذلك "القيادة". يمكن أن يحدث هذا فقط من خلال التعليم. أود أن أذكر ما قاله نيلسون مانديلا ذات مرة ، " التعليم هو أقوى سلاح يمكنك استخدامه لتغيير العالم. "من خلال تثقيف الآخرين يمكننا أن نجعلهم قادة.

ميرديث غالاغر

لدي نفس الشعور. لا أشعر أن أنظمة التعليم الحالية تفعل أي شيء لمعالجة هذه القضايا الاجتماعية أو إعدادنا لنكون مواطنين وبشر صالحين. كان أكثر ما أعدني للقيادة المدنية هو مواقفي الناقدة لما كنت أراه في مدرستي من طلاب ومدرسين آخرين.

لقد نشأت في مدرسة متنوعة الأعراق، لكني بعد ذلك انتقلت في المرحلة المتوسطة إلى مدرسة ريفية. في مدرستي القديمة، كان أفضل أصدقائي من جميع أنحاء العالم ، من إفريقيا ، ومن الشرق الأوسط. مع أحداث الحادي عشر من سبتمبر 2001 ، كنت قد انتقلت إلى المدرسة الريفية. هناك واجهت الكثير من العنصرية والجهل لدرجة أني شعرت أني مضطرة للتحدث علانية ضدها. قاومت كل الجهل من خلال تثقيف نفسي. لقد بحثت عن نصوص دينية ووجهات نظر عالمية للحصول على حقائق لتعزيز حججي. لقد تحدثت وعارضت ليس فقط الطلاب ولكن المعلمين أيضًا. لم أستطع فهم الكراهية التي كنت أراها. كنا مجرد أطفال ، لكنني شعرت بالاشمئزاز. حتى يومنا هذا ، أشعر أني محظوظة لأنني تعرضت مبكرا لهاته التجارب وفرصة النمو، ومن حولي عائلات أصدقائي المسلمين الباكستانيين والنيجيريين وأولئك الذين ينحدرون من أوروبا الشرقية. أشعر وكأني اكتسبت لقاحا مضادا للكراهية التي أصبحت معدية بشكل رهيب. لذا ، في حين أن المدرسة لم تعطيني تلك المهارات أو تلك القيادة ، إلا أنها جعلتني أدرك

حوار

شيراز رتيمي

القائد في تعريفه الأساسي هو الشخص الذي يقدم التوجيه والإرشاد لتابعيه، ولديه ثقة في كل ما يفعله، بصراحة تامة، أعتقد أن نظامنا التعليمي يركز بشكل أساسي على الحفظ بدلاً من تطوير التفكير النقدي والتحليلي وهذا ما يدفع على الإحباط. في بلدي ، الدرجات الجيدة هي العلامة الوحيدة على الذكاء والتميز الدراسي ، ولكن الحقيقة هي أن الامتحان لم يكن أبدا محددا للمستوى الفكري للأشخاص. إذا اعتقد الطالب أنه لا يمتلك ما يلزمه ليصل الى معايير "الذكاء" ، فسيفقد مفتاحًا أساسيًا ليكون قائدًا، وهو الثقة. شخصيا ، لم يكن إعدادي التعليمي ليمكنني من مواجهة العالم بكل تحدياته ، كان عليّ أن أتعلم ذلك بنفسي من خلال التجارب الشخصية.

سام أوينز

ما قلته حول التعليم الذي يركز على التحفيظ يجعلني أفكر في تجربتي الشخصية أنا أيضا. أنا بالتأكيد أتفق مع ما قلته حول أن الثقة هي مفتاح القيادة. لا أعتقد أن الحصول على درجات مثالية في المدرسة يستلزم بالضرورة أن تصبح قائدًا جيدًا. في الولايات المتحدة، أعتقد أيضًا أنه عندما لا يتفوق الطلاب على أسلوب الاختبار القائم على الحفظ ، فمن السهل أن يشعروا بالإحباط وبأنهم ليسوا أذكياء، أو أنه ليس لديهم ما يقدمونه. أنا فقط أتساءل كيف يمكن للمدارس تعليم مهارات التحليل النقدي بشكل أكثر فعالية. أعتقد أن العديد من المعلمين يرغبون في قضاء وقت أكثر في غرس تلك المهارات ، لكن ربما يشعرون أنهم لا يستطيعون ذلك لأن الذين يشغلون مناصب عليا يفرضون متطلبات صارمة عليهم.

شيراز رتيمي

أنا سعيدة لأننا على وفاق حول هذا الموضوع، لأني بصراحة ، أعتقد أن بعض المعلمين لا يدركون حتى مدى عدم جدوى إعطاء "قاعدة تعليمية مؤقتة" للطلاب واستهداف أدنى مستويات الحفظ والتفكير البسيط. ولنأخذ مثلا أسئلة الخيارات المتعددة. الجواب موجود بالفعل في الخيارات المحددة. يحتاج الطالب فقط لتشغيل ذهنه وسيجد الإجابة بسهولة ، لكنه سوف ينسى كل شيء درسه لأنه لن يكون بحاجة إلى هذه الكمية من المعلومات بعد الاختبار.

فضلا على كون اختبار الطلاب اعتمادًا على مهارات الحفظ الخاصة بهم أمرا سهلا، من السهل أيضًا تعليمهم عن طريق الحفظ.. ليس مهما ما إذا كان المدرسون يفقهون الموضوع المراد تدريسه أم لا ، يمكنهم التحدث إلى الطلاب من خلال السياق، وإظهار روابط مفاهيمية لهم ، أو ربما قراءة بعض الكلمات من الكتاب المدرسي والإشارة إلى أقسام منه. يمكنهم بعد ذلك جعل الطلاب يعيدون سلسلة قصيرة من القواعد لحل المشكلات البسيطة جدًا.

كيف يمكن للمعلم تطوير الشعور بالقيادة لدى الطالب عندما لا يستطيع حتى جعل الطالب يقدر "قيمة المعرفة التي يتم تدريسها؟ جعل الطلبة يتعلمون المادة الدراسية فقط باعتبارها شيئًا "إلزاميا" ينبغي اجتيازه و هو عين الفشل في اعتقادي.

أسباسيا تسامباس - كلمات متّقدة

قالوا لي أنني بحاجة إلى العلاج.
لأني أدرت لساني بنطق الأر
وشددت على الراء في كلمة تذكرر.
بدل نطقها كالبقية

حينما كتبت ، كنت مثالية، كذا قالوا ،
ولكن عندما تحدثت اعتبروني "مفتقرة للتثقيف".
أمي ، بدرجة الماجستير
لكن بلهجة أثخن من زيت الزيتون
على بساتين أجدادنا قبلها ،
اعتذرت لي بالقول:
"أعدك أنك ستبدين ذكية
كما أنت حقيقة يا أغابي مو".

في سن الثامنة ، ذهبت إلى معالج أمراض الكلام
أمراض الكلام.. باثولوجي، كلمة من أصل يوناني هي الأخرى ،
باثوس لاتقاد العاطفة
لوغوس للكلمات ،

حيث كلماتي الشغوفة المتقدة ،
الرابط الأكثر مجدا بين
هويتي ومصدر فخري كأمريكية من أصل يوناني ،
تعرضت للضرب حتى
أتقنت تحدث الانجليزية القياسية.

بينما لساني قد يكون تعلم الحد من الألحان المتقدة
في لكنتنا اليونانية ،
لكن جسدي مازال يتذكرر.
وعندما أكون في قمة غضبي ،
فتأتي اللكنة، مثل موجة أيونية.

فأشدد على حرف الأر
في كلمة تذكر ،
لأني سأتذكر دائما.

الفصل الأول:
التعليم و القيادة

، داخل كل وحدة من الوحدات ، حاولنا اختيار العمل الذي يمثل مجموعة متنوعة من الخبرات والأفكار والاستنتاجات. في مشروع معتمد على الحوار، لم نحاول تقديم إجابة موحدة ، ولكن مشهدًا منوعا لتشجيع حوار أكبر.

على وجه الخصوص ، تمت مناقشة القضايا التالية:

التعليم والقيادة

إن معنى وقيمة التعليم متأصلان بعمق داخل جميع المجتمعات. على هذا النحو ، يلعب التعليم دورًا مهمًا في فهم الأفراد لدورهم في ثقافاتهم الخاصة و ثقافات الأمم ككل. يعزز التعليم أيضًا آلية تخل الفرد لدوره المدني في المجتمع ، وكيف يكون دوره في إحداث تغيير إيجابي.تستكشف هذه الوحدة تجربة الطلاب للتعليم العام كتعليم مدني. على هذا النحو ، تتحدث المقاطع عن النجاحات وأوجه القصور والتغييرات الضرورية التي عاشها المؤلفون في التعليم ، فضلاً عن طرق سن هذه التغييرات. الأعمال كانت متفردة ولكن مترابطة فيما يبدو ، كما تصور الأعمال الحالة الراهنة للتعليم عبر سياق دولي. بالنظر إلى دور التعليم في تشكيل الأفكار والمعتقدات حول معنى المجتمع المدني والتغيير الاجتماعي ، يمكن لهذه الوحدة أن توفر السياق للأقسام الأخرى من الكتاب.

المجتمع المدني والظلم

هناك لحظة لحظة عندما يتم فهم ما يبدو تجربة شخصية من التمييز ، والقمع ، على أنه هيكل اجتماعي أكبر. في هذه اللحظة الفارقة يتكشف الظلم المجتمعي، ويتوضح ما ينبغي فعله لازالة هذه المظالم. في هذه الوحدة ، يشارك الكتاب تجاربهم الخاصة في التمييز وكذلك أعمال الدعم لأولئك الذين يتعرضون للاضطهاد. يناقش المؤلفون حدود هذه الظلم في الكلية والمجتمع والحدود الوطنية. يبدأون في ربط الصلات بما يدعم مثل هذه الممارسات. من خلال هذه الوحدة ، يمكن اعتبار ما يبدو شخصيًا في الغالب ، على أنه سياسي في طبيعته. وبمجرد فهمها على أنه سياسي ، يبدأ إمكانات التغيير في التجلي.

وسائل التواصل الاجتماعي والنشاط

يعتبر تأثير الفراشة ظاهرة مثيرة للاهتمام ، حيث يمكن أن تؤدي حركة صغيرة على ما يبدو إلى سلسلة من الأحداث ، مما يؤدي إلى نتيجة أكبر بكثير من المقصود. سواء كان الأمر يتعلق بتغريدة" على Twitter أو الانضمام إلى مسيرة لدعم التغيير السياسي ، فإن هذه الكتابة تستكشف التغييرات الشخصية ، والعامة التي نتجت عن أفعال صغيرة على ما يبدو. في هذه العملية، يأخذ هؤلاء الكتاب القارئ في تجربة دعم طالبي اللجوء المودعين من قبل الشرطة الفدرالية في أميركا بدون دعم ولا مأوى؛ إلى الاحتجاج على الناشطين النازيين في شوارع شارلوتسفيل وحرم جامعة فرجينيا ؛ والمشاركة في الجهود الوطنية لخلق مجتمع مدني وسياسي أوسع في الجزائر. بين هذا وذاك، يمتد الإيمان بمستقبل أفضل من خلال المقاطع على الصفحة. على هذا النحو ، لا ينبغي قراءة هذه القصص على أنها منفصلة ، بل باعتبارها قصة متداخلة حول كيفية معالجة الظلم على مستوى العالم. كيف ذلك؟ ربما ، رؤية هذا الجيل تتشكل في جميع أنحاء العالم الآن.

الكتابة حول اللحظة التاريخية

برز عملنا الجماعي من خلال الحوار ، مع إدراك كل شخص لتعقيدات الماضي ، وصعوبة خلق مستقبل أكثر إنصافًا ، والحاجة إلى التعاون عبر الحدود . تم اختيار النصوص المنتقاة لتضمينها في هذا الكتاب اعتمادا على قدرتها على التقاط هذا التعقيد ، وإبراز اليقظة إلى مستقبل تسمع فيه كل الأصوات وتحترم .

الكتاب ، إذن ، لم يوسم بخاتمة بشكل متعمد ، إذ كنا نعني أنه يجب على كل نص أن يستدعي أي نوع من أنواع الكتابة ، وأن يعيش داخل هذا النوع ، وأن يقدم حلولاً واضحة للمشاكل التي يتم معالجتها . الكتابات المختارة لكتابنا تتجاوز الأنواع والتوقعات . مثلا قد تأخذ مقالة مدرجة تقاليد الكتابة الأكاديمية ، ولكنها تتحول إلى حكاية شخصية ، أو لغة شعرية . تتم مناقشة اللحظات السياسية ، ثم مقارنتها بمشاريع فنية في الفصل الدراسي تم إنتاجها . بذلك تصبح نظريات التغيير الاجتماعي منسوجة في قصص الجدات ، وقصص أولئك الأسر الذين اضطروا إلى اجتياز الحروب والصراع الأهلي . يتحدث الكتاب بأصوات ناشئة بطريقة تطور وتحول الفضاء المدني . يسن هذا النوع من الكتابة لغة تحول صراع لمزج اللحظات الشخصية مع مجموعة من الالتزامات العامة . وبهذه الطريقة ، فإنه يحمل قوة تجاوز خطاب الفصل الدراسي النمطي .

كتابتنا كانت أيضا طوباوية عمدا . سيحدد الوقت ما إذا كانت المشاركة المدنية التي تم تسليط الضوء عليها في هذا الكتاب يمكن أن تحقق أهدافها - شارلوتسفيل خالية من العنصرية ؛ جزائر مفعلة مجالا مدنيا شاملا . لا يمكننا أن نعد بأن الأهداف الفردية التي أعرب عنها الكتاب سوف تتحقق - تحقيق شهادة جامعية ، وخلق فصل مدني ، وتعزيز التسامح في مجتمعهم ، وتحويل الحوارات الوطنية - سوف تحدث . ولكن شعرنا بالحاجة إلى تسليط الضوء على الشجاعة والقوة التي تكمن في هذه الجهود . شعرنا بالحاجة إلى مكافحة الرؤى التي جعلت هذا الجيل "ليس بأقل" سابقيه من الأجيال ، ليس قاصرا على مهمة خلق مستقبل أفضل . نعتزم إظهار جيل يتولى بالفعل هذا العمل .

المستقبل ، كما يقولون ، قد بدأ بالفعل .

نأمل أن تنضم إلينا في إنشائه .

فهم هيكل كتابنا

لقد صممنا هذا الكتاب ليعكس الديناميكية التي عززت إنشائه . لهذا السبب ، أنشأنا ثلاث وحدات فريدة من نوعها: التعليم والقيادة . المجتمع المدني والظلم ؛ وسائل التواصل الاجتماعي والنشاط . يبدأ كل قسم بـ "خاطرة افتتاحية" ، وهي عبارة عن مقتطفات من الحوارات الأولية مع بعضها البعض . هذه الحوارات تأطر القضايا المركزية التي تجري مناقشتها . بعد ذلك نعرض عنوان "مزيد من المشاركة" نقدم فيه كتابات من إنتاج أعضاء مشروعنا بالإضافة إلى أولئك الذين قدموا العمل من مختلف البلدان . ثم من خلال الأفكار الختامية ، نعود إلى أفكار زملائنا المشاركين لالتقاط بعض الدروس على الأقل من الموضوع المتناول . على الرغم من أن ترتيب الوحدات يعكس أصول ونمو عملنا معًا ، إلا أنه لا يلزم قراءتها بالترتيب . نعتقد أن كل فصل من الكتاب يمكن اعتباره جزءا مستقلا يعالج القضايا المطروحة فيه . أخيرًا

بلورة الدروس المستفادة

الجهود الجماعية للشعب الجزائري قاطعت كما أوضحت قيم كتابنا المقترح. كما قدموا لنا الصورة المجازية المركزية التي من خلالها قمنا باختيار الاعمال للإدراج: كل ما له علاقة بالصحوة. كتب العديد من المؤلفين الذين ساهموا في هذه المجموعة عن لحظات تحولية عندما شهدوا أو كانوا هدفًا للقمع أو الظلم. في العديد من المجالات ، الدين ، السياسة ، التعليم ، الجنس ، ساعدت خبراتهم الشخصية على تشكيل تصور لكيفية فهم هؤلاء الكتاب للمجتمع. نرى مثل هذه القصص مفيدة للغاية. في الواقع ، لقد توصلنا بشكل جماعي إلى الاعتقاد بأن تجربة واحدة ، يعيشها فرد واحد ، يمكن أن تغير الطريقة التي نفكر بها حول مجموعة أو بنية أو قضية بأكملها. يمكن أن تكون هذه التجارب مرعبة ومربكة ومسببة للعزلة بالتأكيد. في البداية ، يقول هؤلاء الكتاب ، إن مثل هذه التجارب يمكن أن تجعل المرء يشعر بأنه صغير ، لا أهمية له ، وهو وحده الذي يجادل بأن شخصًا واحدًا غير قادر على تصحيح مثل هذه المظالم. في الواقع ، يشهد هؤلاء الكاتب على أن فهم مثل هذه اللحظات كجزء من أنماط أكبر في المجتمع أمر مخيف ولكنه باعث على القوة في آن واحد. تضعك هذه الرؤى كعضو فاعل في مجتمع ما ، ولكنها تُظهر أيضًا مدى الصراع المستقبلي الذي ينتظرنا. في النهاية ، يثبت هؤلاء الكتاب أن هذه المشاعر الشخصية يمكن أن تربطنا سويًا في جهد مشترك من أجل التغيير.

وبما أن هؤلاء الكتاب الطلاب قد خبروا مثل هذه الصحوة ، فقد بدأوا أيضًا في تطوير نظرية لكيفية حدوث التغيير. في البداية ، قد يكون التغيير شخصيًا في المقام الأول ، قد يكون صغيرا جدا ، وغاليًا ما لا يتم اكتشافه إلا في الإيماءات الصغيرة. قد ينتقل مثل هذا التغيير إلى الخارج ، إلى منشورات الوسائط الاجتماعية ، محاولا إيجاد مجتمع رقمي يدعمه. ويوضح هؤلاء الكتاب أن الانخراط في المشاركة المدنية يعني استخدام مثل هذه الموارد والمنصات الرقمية لتمكين وتثقيف أنفسنا والآخرين. يجادلون بأن توفير أماكن آمنة للحوار أمر لا يقل أهمية عن أي شكل آخر من أشكال النشاط. (وهنا قد نستخدم الفصول الدراسية لدينا كمثال واحد.

بينما يتحرك الطلاب إلى الخارج ، بعيدًا عن وسائل التواصل الاجتماعي وإلى الشوارع ، يتغير العمل قليلاً. يصبح الجهد منصبا على العثور على مفردات يمكنها عبور المجتمعات ، وتعزيز التعاون المستمر ، وتحمل ردود من معارضي الأهداف المقترحة لمجتمع مدني واسع. يجادل الكتاب بأن هذا العمل يتطلب الشجاعة أيضًا. يستغرق قوة تحمل فقد الاشياء ذات القيمة بالنسبة لك. لتناصب المحرضين العنصريين في بلدتك. لتتحدث بصوت عالٍ إلى السلطات التي قد لا ترغب في الاستماع. هذه هي الأفكار والقيم والخبرات لكتابنا الذي بين يديك.

خلال فترة وجودنا معًا ، تعلمنا أن الطريق إلى إنشاء مجتمع مدني مثالي يتم فيه تحقيق الديمقراطية وحماية حقوق الإنسان هو مسعى متفرد لكل مجتمع. لا ينبغي لنا أن نتخيل أن استراتيجياتنا وهياكلنا يمكن أن تنقل بسهولة إلى بلدان مختلفة. ومع ذلك ، يجب علينا أن نتخيل ، ويجب أن نصدق أنه يمكن أن يكون هناك هدف مشترك - لبناء مجتمع مدني جامع ومنفتح ومشترك ، حيث يمكن للجميع المشاركة في التأسيس الجماعي لمجتمعهم. وعلى الرغم من الإحباط الذي قد ينشأ عنه كتابنا ، والاضطهاد الذي لا يزال الكثير منا يواجهه ، فإننا متفائلون بشأن المستقبل.

بالطبع ، لم تمر كل هذه الأمور بسلاسة. بعد تواصلنا الأولي مع المشاركين عبر الأسئلة التأملية، لم نتلق أي استجابة تقريبًا. خلال الفصل الدراسي ، كنا نحاول باستمرار العثور على منصة رقمية لضمان أنه بإمكاننا التحدث مع بعضنا عبر الحدود الدولية وفروق المناطق الزمنية. على مدار شهر واحد ، بدأنا في تلقي الردود. في النهاية ، كان لدينا ما يقرب من 300 طالب يكتبون إلينا من مواقع مختلفة في جميع أنحاء الجزائر وكذلك من جامعات مختلفة في الولايات المتحدة - مثل جامعة يوتا ، وجامعة ولاية ميشيغان ، وجامعة تيمبل ، وغيرها ، في الواقع ، سرعان ما أصبحنا غارقين في بحر من الكتابة. على هذا النحو ، كما هو مذكور أعلاه ، سرعان ما أصبح الفصل الدراسي في الولايات المتحدة مجموعة مناقشة أسبوعية حول الكتابة المقدمة - تقييم مدى ملاءمتها للكتاب ، مع الأخذ في الاعتبار ما قد يحتاج إلى مراجعة، وإرساله للمؤلفين.

كان الأمل الأولي هو أن يعمل الطلاب الجزائريون معنا أيضًا في تقييم الطلبات في كل مرحلة من مراحل العملية ، لكن عجلة التاريخ تدخلت في شكل احتجاجات جزائرية من أجل الإصلاح السياسي.

تفعيل المجتمع المدني

بدأت حواراتنا من خلال النظر في كيفية إعداد التعليم للفرد ليصبح منخرطا في مجتمعه. في منتصف هذه الحوارات ، بدأ الجزائريون انتفاضة سلمية لتوسيع الديمقراطية والحقوق السياسية. وكانت النتائج الأولية للمسيرات والاحتجاجات هي استقالة الرئيس والدعوة إلى انتخابات وطنية جديدة. يبدو كما لو أن أهداف كتابنا قد تجسدت في شوارع الجزائر.

انغمس الجزائريون في حماس يومي وحيوية جماعية كبيرة لتمكين الجزائر من تحقيق مصيرها التاريخي كأمة. فشاركوا في حوارات عميقة حول المستقبل ، وشاركوا في مسيرات قانونية ، وسنوا قيما من خلال رعاية الأفراد المشاركين في هذه الجهود. وكتبوا أيضا.

لم يكتبوا الكثير ، ربما ، في الحوارات الأسبوعية المخططة مع الطلاب في الولايات المتحدة. وربما ، لم يكتبوا مقالات أكاديمية تستند إلى مقالات أكاديمية- والتي واصل طلاب الولايات المتحدة القيام بها. بدلاً من ذلك ، فقد كتبوا قواعدًا جديدة لما تعنيه الجزائر للجزائريين بأجسادهم في الشوارع ، ناشرين أفكارهم على لوحات المفاتيح.

بطريقة غريبة ، أدت الأحداث في الجزائر إلى تعطيل المشروع. المحادثات الأسبوعية أصبحت شهرية. ودردشة المجموعة بالكاد استمرت. لم يتم الوفاء بالمواعيد النهائية للكتاب في كثير من الأحيان. ولكن هنا ظهر قيمة الثقة في المشروع ومجتمع الحوارات المفتوحة. كان الطلاب الجزائريون يعرفون أن زملاء الولايات المتحدة قد دعموا أهدافهم ، واستمروا في العمل المطلوب ، وسوف يرحبون بهم مرة أخرى في المشروع عندما نأمل أن تتحقق الأهداف المدنية ، عندما يمكنهم العودة إلى الإحساس التقليدي للطالب وهذا ، في الواقع ما حدث.

بسبب الخطاب السياسي الأخير في العديد من البلدان ، فقد تم طرح مزاعم جذرية ومناقشتها وتشجيعها في بعض الأحيان. هذه الادعاءات الجذرية يمكن أن تؤدي إلى الظلم من قبل الجماعات أو الأفراد مما يسبب الضرر للآخرين. يتعين على قادتنا اتخاذ قرارات بشأن الظلم في مجتمع اليوم ، وكذلك الأمر بالنسبة لنا كمواطنين نشطين.

صف حادثة شاهدت فيها ظلمًا وكيف عرفت أنه ظلم وكيف استجبت له

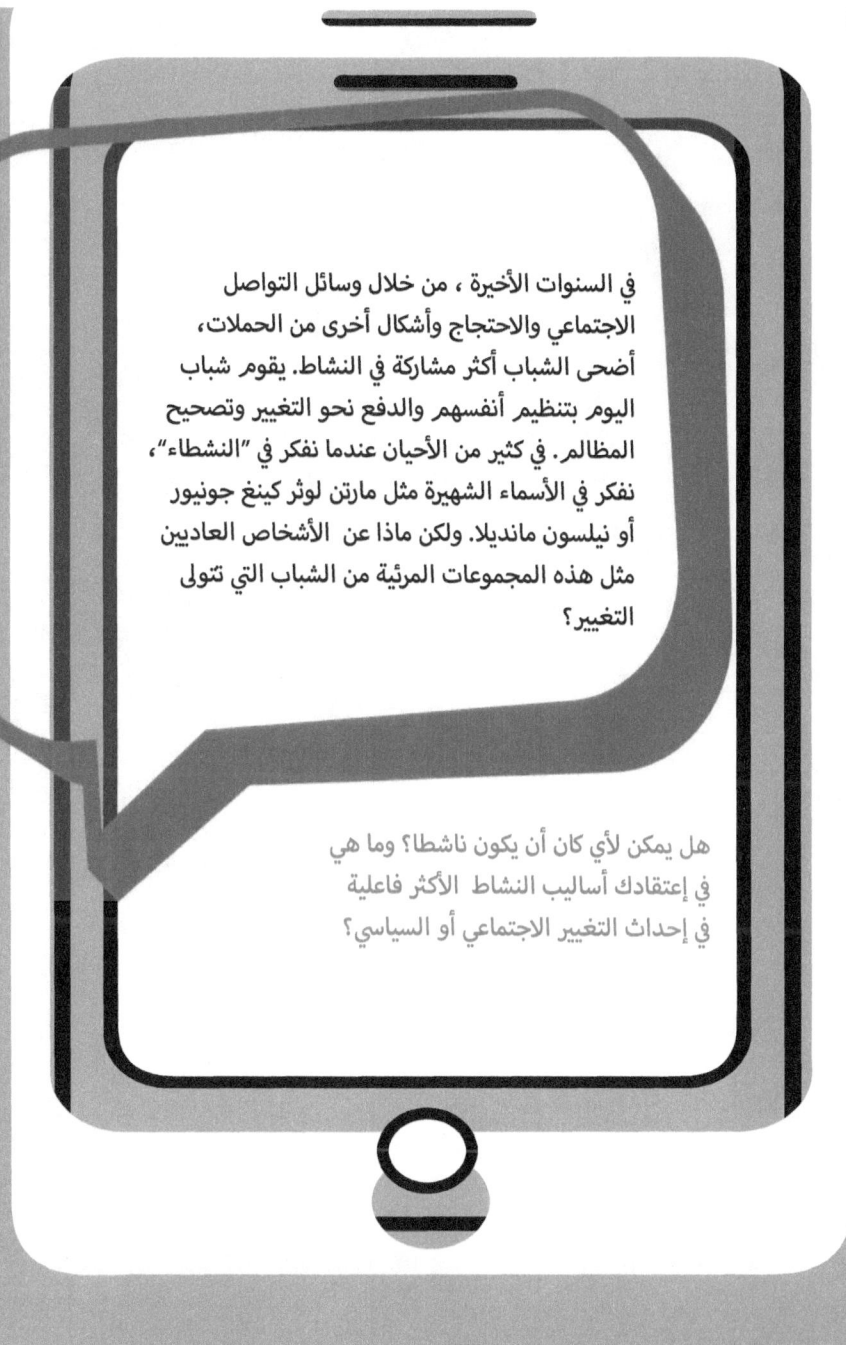

في السنوات الأخيرة ، من خلال وسائل التواصل الاجتماعي والاحتجاج وأشكال أخرى من الحملات، أضحى الشباب أكثر مشاركة في النشاط. يقوم شباب اليوم بتنظيم أنفسهم والدفع نحو التغيير وتصحيح المظالم. في كثير من الأحيان عندما نفكر في "النشطاء"، نفكر في الأسماء الشهيرة مثل مارتن لوثر كينغ جونيور أو نيلسون مانديلا. ولكن ماذا عن الأشخاص العاديين مثل هذه المجموعات المرئية من الشباب التي تتولى التغيير؟

هل يمكن لأي كان أن يكون ناشطا؟ وما هي في إعتقادك أساليب النشاط الأكثر فاعلية في إحداث التغيير الاجتماعي أو السياسي؟

التعليم هو أكثر من مجرد عملية لتعلم القراءة أو الحساب. يتعلق التعليم أيضًا باكتساب الحكمة والبصيرة بالعالم من حولنا والمهارات اللازمة للتعامل مع ذلك العالم.

هل يساهم نموذج التعليم الحالي بنجاح في غرس المهارات اللازمة للمشاركة الإيجابية في المجتمع المدني؟

بناء منشورنا الخاص

مع هذه الأفكار الجديدة ، بدأنا في وضع مقالات لإنشاء الكتاب.

كانت خطوتنا الأولية هي إنشاء سلسلة من الأسئلة التأملية للتداول عبر مجموعتينا، وإذا أمكن ، عبر الجامعات في الولايات المتحدة والجزائر. كان هدفنا هو طرح سلسلة من الأسئلة القصيرة ، ثم السماح للطلاب بالرد في أي نوع - مقال أكاديمي ، أو مقالة شخصية ، أو قصيدة ، أو عمل فني - على وجه أفضل يلبي احتياجاتهم. قمنا بعد ذلك بتطوير قائمة بالأفراد والفصول وأعضاء هيئة التدريس والهيئات الطلابية للاتصال للمشاركة. من الحوارات التي أجريناها، ظهرت مواضيع متعددة بدءا من تأثير التعليم في خلق قادة مدنيين ، إلى كيفية تحديد ومعالجة الظلم وعدم المساواة ، وكذا ماهية الفاعلية المجتمعية ومن يمكن أن يكون ناشطًا وكيف يمكن تعريف النشاط. كان هدفنا دعوة المجيبين للنظر في القضايا التالية:

دور التعليم في إعدادهم ليكونوا نشطين في الحياة المدنية لمجتمعهم وبلدهم.

الفجوة بين الخطاب العام حول التعليم / المشاركة المدنية وتجربتهم الفعلية كطلاب.

الفجوة بين الخطاب العام على المساواة السياسية بين الجنسين / الإرث الثقافي، وتجربتهم الفعلية ك كأعضاء في المجتمع.

الأفكار المستقاة من المشاركة في مشاريع الانخراط المدني المصممة لتوسيع ممارسات المجتمع المدني .

معنى القيادة داخل المجتمعات المدنية الملتزمة بالمساواة والانصاف في الحقوق.

مع وضعنا تصورا لما أردنا أن يتناوله الكتاب ، قسمنا أنفسنا إلى مجموعات مهام بناءً على نقاط القوة لدينا. مجموعة المحتوى التي عملت على الأسئلة التأملية للكتابة لإنشاء محتوى للكتاب. قامت مجموعة التواصل بصياغة رسائل البريد إلكتروني ليتم إرسالها إلى المؤلفين المحتملين.أوضحت مجموعة التصميم مطالبات الكتابة وبدأت العمل على العناصر المرئية للكتاب.

ببطء ، بدأت الأمور تأخذ مكانها، وما بدا ذات يوم كأنه حلم بعيد المنال، أصبح حقيقة تتراءى بشكل متزايد. بمجرد أن بدأت تصلنا الردود على الأسئلة التأملية، بدأت عملية التقييم في الفصل بتحديد الموضوعات الناشئة ، واختيار الأعمال لإدراجها ، وإرسال الأعمال مرة أخرى لمزيد من المراجعة. لقد أخذنا دور المحررين في صياغة الكتاب الذي تولد من رؤيتنا الإبداعية.

منظروا هذا المشروع أن مثل هذه السياسة أدت إلى زيادة جرائم الكراهية في المجتمعات المحلية وزيادة في التعصب العالمي تجاه اللاجئين السياسيين/ الاقتصاديين. على هذا النحو ، كان هدف المشروع هو بناء منصات للشباب بالاستجابة لأزمات حقوق الإنسان التي تحدث محلياً ووطنياً ودولياً. لقد تم تصميمه لخلق مساحة يمكن فيها تخيل ، ثم بناء مستقبل بديل يتميز بقدر أكبر من الحريات الثقافية والاقتصادية والسياسية. على هذا النحو ، يأمل المشروع أن يكون جزءًا من الجهود الجماعية لبناء مساحة عامة يكون لكل فرد فيها الحق والقدرة على المشاركة. في الواقع ، يشير مصطلح "Twiza" إلى الفعل الجماعي للأفراد الذين يتحدون لبناء هيكل مادي ، مثل حظيرة أو منزل ، لدعم أحد الجيران. يهدف هذا المصطلح إلى التحدث إلى العمل الجماعي للشباب الذين يعملون بنشاط لبناء مجتمعاتهم وبناء الهياكل المادية التي يمكن أن تدعم حقوق الإنسان الشاملة في مجتمعاتهم.

وُسِعت حواراتنا. سُئلنا ما الذي يجعل الفرد قائدا في المجتمع المدني؟ ما هو Twiza من خلال مشروع الأساس لهذا المجتمع المدني؟ من يمكن أن يكون قائدا؟ كيف أثرت وسائل التواصل الاجتماعي على الطريقة التي نتصرف بها كقادة داخل مجتمعاتنا؟ على الرغم من نشأتها في البلدان التي تفصل بينها عدة أميال إضافة إلى تاريخنا وثقافاتنا المتباينة ، بدأت فصولنا في إيجاد مفهوم مشترك للمجتمع المدني المثالي. تمكنت مجموعتينا من الاتفاق على أن العديد من قيم الديمقراطية التي كانت تعتبر مفاهيما مهمة لم تتحقق بالكامل في كلا بلدينا. ثم مع تقدمنا في الحوارات ، جماعياً ، بدأنا في مشاركة الحلول الممكنة. لاستخدام خبرتنا وتعليمنا لتصور مدى اختلاف الفصول الدراسية لدينا.

ومع ذلك ، لم نتفق طوال الوقت. قد لا تعمل الحلول المطروحة في سياقنا مع زملائنا في بلد مختلف. الأفكار لم تكن دائما تعبر الحدود بسهولة. في الواقع ، وجدنا في كثير من الأحيان أن اللغة المستخدمة ، والمصطلحات التي يفهم بها أحدنا العالم تواجه أيضًا مشكلات "ترجمة". ما اعتبره أحدنا مصطلحًا محايدًا ، مصطلحًا محببًا ، توددا ، يمكن اعتباره مهينًا عند عبور هذا المصطلح للحدود. والمصطلحات السياسية ، التي تكون دائمًا محفوفة بالمخاطر ، تحتاج إلى مناقشتها وتحديدها وإعادة صياغتها بحيث يمكن تطوير فهم مشترك. في فصل دراسي حول الكتابة، اكتشفنا عن كثب صعوبات صهر لغاتنا الخاصة وطرق التحدث لغرض مشترك.

من هذا المفهوم المشترك للتعليم الذي يحتاج إلى دعم المجتمع المدني ، بمعنى أن هذه القيمة المشتركة يجب أن تنفذ بشكل مختلف محليًا ، ظهر إحساسنا بمشروع الكتاب المحتمل. لقد بدأنا ندرك أنه قد تكون هناك حاجة ملحة إلى منشور يدعم هذه المحادثات. قد تكون هناك قيمة لأحد المنشورات التي حولت لدينا السخرية الأولية حول أهداف التعليم إلى رؤية إيجابية تحدثت عن تطلعات جيل. قد تكون لدينا الفرصة لمعرفة كيف يحاول الطلاب الآخرون ، في جامعات أخرى ، في بلدان أخرى بناء تعليم نشط وموجه نحو العامة. وقد نتعلم من جهودهم.

بالنسبة للطلاب في الولايات المتحدة الأمريكية ، كانت أهداف الفصل الدراسي مفاجئة بعض الشيء. لم نكن نحن (شحادة ، نابو ، أوينز) أو زملائنا في الدراسة ندرك أننا سنشارك في مثل هذه الحوارات. عند التسجيل في الفصل الدراسي، لم يتم عرض هذا المشروع علينا بدءا. معظمنا كان لا يزال يحاول استكشاف الحرم الجامعي كطالب جديد. وبينما استمعنا بحماس إلى أستاذنا (باركس ، وهو جديد أيضًا في جامعتنا) ، كنا أيضًا نتشارك قدرًا لا بأس به من الشك. ما الذي يعنيه أن نكون طرفا في حوارات مع الطلاب في الجزائر؟ هل ندعو أيضًا أفراد من حرمنا الجامعي وما وراءه للمشاركة؟ ما الذي سيؤدي إليه عملنا الجماعي؟ هل كنا نتحدث عن إنتاج كتاب؟

بالنسبة للطلاب في الجزائر ، جاء كل منهم إلى المشروع أكثر وعياً بالعمل الذي يتعين القيام به كونهم شاركوا سابقًا في مشروع ممائل مع أستاذهم الجزائري (حشلاف) وكذلك أستاذنا (باركس). ومع ذلك، فإن المستلزمات اللوجستية للمشروع التي اعتمدت على الإستعمال المستمر إلى الإنترنت ، والحوار المنسق عبر فروق المناطق الزمنية و العابر للحدود الوطنية ، بدت وكأنها تتجاوز حدود الإمكانيات. ومثل نظرائهم في الولايات المتحدة ، بدت فكرة إنتاج كتاب معقدة. ماذا سيكون محور الكتاب؟ من سيختار المحتوى؟ هل سيتمكن الطلاب الآخرون في الولايات المتحدة والجزائر من المشاركة؟ بعد القليل من المحادثات الأولية بين جميع الطلاب المشاركين ، بدا أنه لم يكن لدى أي منا خبرة كبيرة في هذا العمل.

ومع ذلك ، وكما يوضح الكتاب الموجود بين يديك الآن، فقد نجحنا في إنتاج مادة على شكل عمل جماعي. يحدونا الأمل في أنها تعكس فهمنا العابر للحدود لما يعنيه أن تكون منخرطا بشكل مدني وكيف ينبغي أن يمكّن التعليم الجامعي الطلاب من أن يصبحوا مشاركين فاعلين في مجتمعاتهم بعد التخرج. قبل قراءة هذا العمل، نريد أن نسرد لكم قصة كيف أدت مجموعة من الحوارات المقترحة إلى هذا الكتاب ، الإنصاف والعدالة: جيل منخرط، عالم مضطرب.

إنشاء حوارات عابرة للحدود

اتصلت فصولنا الدراسية في البداية من خلال مجموعة من الحوارات عبر الإنترنت. ربما يكون من الإنصاف القول إن هذه المحادثات الأولية كانت تتعلق بمشاركة الخبرات الشخصية أكثر من تقديم أي رؤى سياسية عميقة. إذا نظرنا إلى الوراء ، فإن أهمية بناء الثقة، وإثبات أننا جميعًا نشترك في بعض التجارب المشتركة في فصولنا الدراسية ومجتمعاتنا كانت ضرورية للغاية. جميعنا اجتاز المرحلة الثانوية، اتفقنا جميعا أن المحاضرات والاختبارات الموحدة لم تكن أبدا اكتسابا للمعرفة بالشكل الذي أردناه. كنا نطمح جميعًا إلى الحصول على تعليم يمكّننا من أن نصبح نشطين في مجتمعاتنا.لقد شعرنا جميعًا بالقلق من أن هذا الفصل بين أهدافنا التعليمية والمدنية قد يجعل من الصعب على جيلنا الاعتماد على نجاحات الأجيال التي سبقتنا. وبينما كنا نشارك في الحوارات ، بدأت محادثاتنا الخاصة تدمج نفسها الذي قدم الدعم للحوارات الأولية والمنشورات التي كنا أردنا إنجازها Twiza. في مشروع

كجهد تعاوني بين أعضاء هيئة التدريس في أمريكا الشمالية وشمال إفريقيا والشرق Twiza برز مشروع الأوسط. حيث يحاول المشروع التحدث عن الانقسامات الطائفية والتحيز، وغالبًا ما يقترن بالنقاش المستقطب ، والذي أدى إلى تطرف السياسة التي تقوم على ما يبدو على التعصب والكراهية. ويعتقد

المقدمة

مايكل شحادة ، أليكس جرانر ، أحمد عبد الحكيم حشلاف ، مادو نابا ، سامانثا أوينز ، ستيف باركس

اقتراحنا لحوار دولي

يبلغ طلاب الجامعة في سنتهم الأولى من العمر عادة تسعة عشر عامًا تقريبًا.

في هذه الفترة الزمنية القصيرة ، مرت حياة هؤلاء، بما يلي:

هجمات 11 سبتمبر 2001 على مركز التجارة العالمي

حرب أفغانستان

حرب العراق

انهيار الاقتصاد العالمي لعام 2008

حركة "إحتلوا وول ستريت"

الربيع العربي

لقد عبرت هذه الأحداث العالمية الحدود الدولية في تأثيرها ، تاركة ندوبا في الجيل الذي خاض هذه الحروب ، و آثارا بالغة في أولئك الذين ناضلوا من أجل السلام وحاولوا تحقيق العدالة. كانت هناك جهودا عالمية للعثور على اللغة والهياكل التي يمكنها من خلالها تعزيز الدروس المستفادة من هذه الأحداث لبناء مجتمع مدني يلبي احتياجات وتطلعات أولئك الذين نجوا.

واحدة من هذه المحاولات وقعت في شتاء عام 2019.

بدءًا من شهر يناير واستمرارًا حتى شهر مايو ، اجتمعنا كطلاب وأعضاء هيئة التدريس في الفصول الدراسية بجامعة فرجينيا بالولايات المتحدة والمدرسة العليا للأساتذة بالأغواط بالجزائر ، لدراسة المسارات الممكنة للمضي قدمًا في هذا المسعى. كان هدفنا هو الدخول في حوارات حول معنى حقوق الإنسان في اللحظة السياسية الحالية، وكذلك دور المشاركة المدنية الموجهة نحو الإنصاف والعدالة. كنا نأمل أن تنتج حواراتنا طريقة جديدة للتحدث والكتابة و فهم ذلك ، ليس لفائدتنا فحسب ، بل للآخرين أيضا خارج فصولنا الدراس.

إلى جميع المعلمين والطلاب ، الذين وبعيدا عن الأضواء ، ينحتون وجه المستقبل ويكافحون من أجل العدالة في كل مكان في هذا العالم. لم يكن هذا العمل ممكنًا لولا المجموعة المذهلة من الطلاب القادة على جانبي الأطلسي ، الذين عكسوا اتجاه التدريس وعلمونا معنى الكفاح المستمر على الرغم من اللحظة السياسية العاصفة.

أنا مدين للغاية لستيف باركس، إنسان رائع ذو قدرة مذهلة على إخراج أفضل ما لدى الناس وجعل الأمور ممكنة بشيء من السحر. كان قادرًا على تحويل قطع من الكتابة المبعثرة إلى كتاب متسق. أود أيضًا أن أشكر جميع المسؤولين الذين سمحوا بحدوث مشروع التويزة الفكري على الرغم من عدم منحنا الإذن الصريح بذلك.

أود أن أشكر بالتحديد آمنة بولفعة على مساعدتها في عملية التحرير و جميع التربويين الذين قدموا لنا التشجيع الذي احتجناه بشدة.

أحمد عبد الحكيم حشلاف
أخصائي التربية والمشاركة المدنية
المدرسة العليا للأساتذة - الأغواط - الجزائر

XI

شكر وعرفان

"لديك بالفعل كل ما تحتاجه لتحقيق ما تريد."
أستخدم هذه العبارة غالبًا في المساحات التنظيمية للمجتمع. إنها دعوة ليدرك المجتمع المهارات والرؤى والموارد الموجودة بالفعل داخله.

الإنصاف والعدالة: جيل منحرط، عالم مضطرب هو شهادة على حقيقة هذا البيان. بدأت هذا المشروع خلال أسبوعي الأول في جامعة فرجينيا ، حيث عملت مع الطلاب المسجلين في دورة مقياس الكتابة التمهيدية. معا ، كنا لا نزال نتعلم كيفية التنقل في الحرم الجامعي ، وتكوين صداقات / زملاء جدد ، واكتشاف أفضل الأماكن لتناول الطعام. لهذا السبب ، أريد للبدء بتقديم العرفان للطلاب الذين تولوا مهمة إنشاء حوارات مع طلاب في الجزائر ، يتخيلون كتابًا محتملاً ، وجمعوا أكثر من 200 مقال من مختلف أنحاء العالم، الولايات المتحدة والجزائر ، تم اختيارها وتحريرها ، وفي نهاية المطاف ،وقاموا بتصميم الكتاب الذي هو أمامكم الآن. تجدر الإشارة للمساهمات الخاصة لكل من أليكس جرانز ، سامانثا أوينز ، لوسيا شوف هيك ، مايكل شحادة ، الذين واصلوا العمل في هذا المشروع خلال فصل الصيف. بشكل جماعي ، أظهروا أن طلاب جامعة فرجينيا يمتلكون بالفعل ما هو مطلوب لاستخدام تعليمهم لإحداث تغيير إيجابي في العالم.

أي معلم يتولى مشروعًا يشرك طلابه محليًا أو دوليًا ينجح المشروع فقط من خلال دعم جامعتهم وكليتهم وقسمهم. بدون بصيرة وعمل الأفراد التاليين ، لم يكن المشروع ليرى النور: كيث ستيفنسون ، جيمس سيتز ، كيث درايفر ، ستيف أراتا ، كيفين سميث ، تيريز مونبرج ، ميكالا جونز ، كارولينا كامبوس ، وفاء صلاح ، فيكتور لوفتيج ، تراسي سويكي ، روميو جارسيا ، كاميلو سانشيز ،و ديفان أرد، . وأود أن أشكر بالتحديد سارة أرينجتون وستايسي ترايدر الذين وفروا لي الاستشارة القانونية في عدد لا يحصى من سياسات وممارسات جامعة فرجينيا. وقد فعلوا ذلك بكثير من الصبر والتفهم و اللطف الذي سأتذكره طويلا.

وأخيرا ، أود أن أعترف بالصداقة والبصيرة لأحمد عبد الحكيم حشلاف ، الذي برؤيته تم تفعيل مشروع وكذلك المساهمات القوية له وكذا طلابه في هذا الكتاب. أن طلابه واصلوا، (Twiza twizaproject.org) التركيز على تعليمهم ، وعملهم مع طلابي ، بينما يسيرون في الشوارع من أجل أن تصل الجزائر إلى أعلى التطلعات ، وكان ذلك مصدر إلهام. آمل أن تكون هذه القيم قد سُنت في الصفحات التالية.

ستيف باركس
برنامج الكتابة والبلاغة
قسم اللغة الإنجليزية
جامعة فرجينيا

الفصل الثالث: وسائل الإعلام الاجتماعية والنضال المجتمعي

خاطرة الافتتاح
73	صوفي بيكمان

الحوار: وسائل التواصل الاجتماعي والنضال المجتمعي
75	نشاط الطلاب الجزائريين والأمريكيين

بمشاركة كل من
82	آلي ماسترسون
83	إيزابيل إزراتي
85	مايكل شحادة
88	كارولين كامبوس
90	أميثاف ريدي
92	جوناثان براون
93	فريدريك بيهلر
94	أليكسيس مارتينز
97	أميناف ريدي
	سيمران كور
98	سليمة طالبي
99	هند بلكحل
100	أليكس مارنيتيز
	بشرى رحموني
102	محند شيبان
104	شيماء هاشمي
105	ديفين ويليس

أفكار ختامية
113	شيراز رتيمي
	جمانة هديل بوغازي

الفصل الثاني: المجتمع المدني والمظالم

خاطرة الافتتاح
47 محي الدين واڤي

الحوار: المجتمع المدني والمظالم
49 شيماء هاشمي
     سامانثا أوينز
     نجاة بوشريط
     علاوة هشام خليل
50 عيسى صديقي
     نجوى حرزي
51 عيسى صديقي
     ميريديث غالاغر

بمشاركة كل من
52 شيراز رتيمي
53 فيكتوريا هانتر
54 بيريس جونز
56 ايرين برانتلي ريدجواي
     مادلين بورتر
     كريستيان كافاندر
58 شالي هوست
60 سامانثا أوينز
62 ميريديث ديوليا
66 نور الهدى بلخضر
67 بشرى رحموني

أفكار ختامية
69 فؤاد بلفرد شريف
     علاوة هشام خليل

جدول المحتويات

XI	شكر وعرفان
1	المقدمة

الفصل الأول: التعليم والقيادة

خاطرة الافتتاح

15	أسباسيا تسامباس

الحوار: التعليم والقيادة

17	شيراز رتيمي
	سامانثا أوينز
18	بشرى رحموني
	ميريديث غالاغر

بمشاركة كل من

19	مونيكا ميلز
21	اليكس جرانر
22	ميليسا ميركادو وديفيا باريتي
24	هيرسي غابريال
25	جمانة هديل بوغازي
27	جوشوا فارس
31	كلير سونغ
34	تايلوربلاي
35	جايدن ويليامز
36	خديجة خليد
43	شيلي وايمنت
	هاشمي شيماء

أفكار ختامية

44	بشرى رحموني

مجموعة الكتاب المشاركين في مشروع Twiza

مديرا المشروع
أحمد عبد الحكيم حشلاف ، المدرسة العليا للأساتذة- الأغواط- الجزائر
ستيفن باركس ، جامعة فرجينيا- الولايات المتحدة الأمريكية

أعضاء المشروع
إيزابيل ألكساندر
هند بن لكحل
هديل جمانة بوغازي
نجوى حرزي
مايكل أنتوني شحادة
شيماء هاشمي
فؤاد شريف بلفرد
نجاة بوشريط
ميريديث نويل ديويا
أبيجيل دوجيرتي
جوناثان هارت إليس
إيزابيل إزراتي
ميريديث غالاغر
اليكس جرانر
أوماري جونز
هشام خليل علاوة
خديجة خليد
سليمة آية طالبي
مادهوميتا نابا
سامانثا روز أوينز
كاثلين ريجالادو
شيراز رتيمي
بشرى رحموني
ساكب رزقي
عيسى صديقي
لوسيا شاف-هيك

مع هذا الكتاب، نجح مشروع تويزة في التسبب في صدع في قلعة بنيت من قبل بعض الممارسات التعليمية التي عفا عليها الزمن، والتي تميل في أكثر لأحيان ، إلى الانبعاج من الداخل في شكل مجتمع ممارسة، حريص وجاهز لتطوير برامج التوعية التعاونية. هذه الأنشطة اللاصفية تطور المهارات اللينة والتي تواصل الجامعات تجاهلها. من خلال حوار مستمر عابر للحدود، سوف توسع تويزة بلا شك من الصدع، حتى يتسنى لجميع الأصوات أن تسمع، مانحة الفرصة لظهور مجتمع مدني حقيقي ، واع بدور المشاركة الفردية و الجماعية في ترسيخ حقوق الإنسان. النتيجة المتوخاة: مجتمع أكثر التزاما بالعدالة والإنصاف. هذا ليس حلما طوباويا، بل الحجم الهائل لإمكانات الشباب.

د. محمد ملياني
أخصائي تعليمية اللغة، ماجستير و دكتوراه تربية
جامعة وهران -الجزائر

مشروع طموح ومدرك تمامًا، يشرع حقًّا لصنع المعرفة العابرة للحدود، والمشاركة المدنية ، والحوارالثقافي، من خلال الكتابة. الأصوات في هذا الكتاب تدل على كل هذا، طلاب المرحلة الجامعية لديهم القدرة على سن عدالة اجتماعية لخلق عالم أفضل. أنها توفر أملا عميقا لمجتمع عالمي أحسن. هذا الكتاب مرجع لا بد منه للأساتذة الذين يسعون لإشراك طلابهم في الأمور الواقعية كما يجب أن يقرأه الطلاب الذين يبحثون عن رؤية لعالم مختلف.

د. ريبيكا دينغو
جامعة ماساتشوستس

الإنصاف والعدالة:
جيل منخرط ، عالم مضطرب

مايكل شحادة، أليكس غرانر، أحمد عبد الحكيم حشلاف، مادو نابا، سامانثا أوينز، ستيف باركس

The Twiza Project
New City Community Press
Working and Writing for Change, Parlor Press

www.ingramcontent.com/pod-product-compliance
Lightning Source LLC
Chambersburg PA
CBHW021851230426
43671CB00006B/350